CROSSING THE BOUNDARIES IN LINGUISTICS

SYNTHESE LANGUAGE LIBRARY

TEXTS AND STUDIES IN
LINGUISTICS AND PHILOSOPHY

VOLUME 13

CROSSING THE BOUNDARIES IN LINGUISTICS

Studies Presented to Manfred Bierwisch

Edited by

WOLFGANG KLEIN and WILLEM LEVELT

D. REIDEL PUBLISHING COMPANY

DORDRECHT : HOLLAND / BOSTON : U.S.A.

LONDON : ENGLAND

Library of Congress Cataloging in Publication Data

CIP

Main entry under title:

Crossing the boundaries in linguistics.

(Synthese language library ; v. 13)
Bibliography: p.
Includes indexes.
1. Linguistics—Addresses, essays, lectures. 2. Bierwisch, Manfred. I. Bierwisch, Manfred. II. Klein, Wolfgang, 1946– III. Levelt, W. J. M. (Willem J. M.), 1938– . IV. Series.
P26.B46C7 410 81–5157
ISBN 90–277–1259–X AACR2

Published by D. Reidel Publishing Company,
P.O. Box 17, 3300 AA Dordrecht, Holland.

Sold and distributed in the U.S.A. and Canada
by Kluwer Boston Inc.,
190 Old Derby Street, Hingham, MA 02043, U.S.A.

In all other countries, sold and distributed
by Kluwer Academic Publishers Group,
P.O. Box 322, 3300 AH Dordrecht, Holland.

D. Reidel Publishing Company is a member of the Kluwer Group.

Printed in The Netherlands

TABLE OF CONTENTS

MANFRED BIERWISCH

PREFACE

It was in the course of 1980 that it dawned upon several friends and colleagues of Manfred Bierwisch that a half century had passed since his birth in 1930. Manfred's youthful appearance had prevented a timely appreciation of this fact, and these friends and colleagues are, therefore, not at all embarrassed to be presenting him, almost a year late, with a Festschrift which will leave a trace of this noteworthy occasion in the archives of linguistics. It should be realized, however, that the delay would have easily extended to 1990 if all those who had wanted to contribute to this book had in fact written their chapters. Under the pressure of actuality, several colleagues who had genuinely hoped or even promised to contribute, just couldn't make it in time. Still, their greetings and best wishes are also, be it tacitly, expressed by this volume.

Especially important for the archives would be a record of the celebrated one's works and physical appearance. For the convenience of present and future generations this Festschrift contains a bibliography of Manfred Bierwisch's scientific publications, which forms a chapter in itself. The frontispiece photograph was taken unawares by one of our accomplices.

The title of this Festschrift may allow for free associations of various sorts. One interpretation, however, should not be missed: there is the existential presupposition that boundaries do exist in linguistics. One of the most characteristic aspects of Manfred's work is that these boundaries are recognized. Bierwisch will never confuse syntax, semantics and pragmatics, nor, under his hands, will linguistics fade into psychology. But at the same time the conscious crossing of these boundaries is an equally characteristic trait of his approach in the study of language: Manfred Bierwisch has published in almost all areas of linguistics, and has worked in many adjacent disciplines. The list includes syntax, semantics, phonology, pragmatics, historical linguistics, language variation, aphasiology, graphematics, psycholinguistics – especially language and memory, and language and music – to mention the most important ones. In performing these wide-ranging studies, Manfred Bierwisch shows a trait somewhat similar to what we know about Leibniz's way of work: it is all done in the solitary enclosure of the library, but at the same time in intensive interaction with the major intellectual currents of his era. Boundaries don't count here; Manfred quietly resides in the midst of his web, registering far away vibrations just as well as close-by turbulence.

Leibniz, the great founder of the Akademie der Wissenschaften, would doubtless appreciate the fact that, three centuries later, his spirit is still alive in this illustrious place.

Nijmegen, The Netherlands

W. K.
W. L.

MORRIS HALLE AND JEAN-ROGER VERGNAUD

HARMONY PROCESSES*

Harmony processes characteristically regulate the distribution of a given feature or feature complex in specific, not necessarily contiguous phonemes of a word. For example, in Finnish words the back-front contrast in rounded and in low vowels – but not in nonlow unrounded vowels – agrees with that of the stem, whereas in Navaho words, the contrast of anterior-nonanterior in coronal affricates and continuants – but not in other phonemes – is determined by the last coronal affricate or continuant in the word. Harmony processes fall into two distinct types depending on whether the harmonic features propagate in one direction only, or whether the propagation occurs in both directions. We shall term the former type, directional harmony, and the latter type, dominant harmony. We propose that the facts of dominant harmony are best described with the devices of autosegmental phonology, whereas those of directional harmony are best characterized by making use of the tree construction developed in recent work in metrical phonology.[1] We illustrate these proposals in sections 1 and 2 below; in section 3 we compare the descriptive effectiveness of the two mechanisms in dealing with different bodies of data.

1. DOMINANT HARMONY ILLUSTRATED

In languages with dominant harmony the vowels fall into two sets: a dominant set and a recessive set. As a first approximation one can say that the morphemes of the language are of two kinds. Dominant morphemes have vowels which belong to the dominant set and which never alternate with vowels in the recessive set. Recessive morphemes, on the other hand, appear in two different shapes: in words containing a dominant morpheme the vowels of recessive morphemes belong to the dominant set; in words without dominant morphemes, all vowels belong to the recessive set.

A typical example of dominant harmony is provided by the East African language (or language group) Kalenjin. As described by Beatrice Hall et al. (1974) Kalenjin has the two sets of vowels shown in (1a).

W. Klein and W. Levelt (eds.), Crossing the Boundaries in Linguistics, 1–22.

(1a)	i	u	I	U
	e	o	ɛ	ɔ
	ɑ̸		a	
	dominant: [+ATR]		recessive: [-ATR]	

Our authors report that "within a phonological word Dominant morphemes (those with [=ATR] vowels) cause contiguous Recessive morphemes (those with [-ATR] vowels) to shift harmonic series and become [+ATR] . . . If there is a [+ATR] vowel in the word whether in the root, or in the affix, then all Recessive vowels become [+ATR]." But if there is no [+ATR] vowel in the word, all vowels in the word remain [-ATR]. These facts are illustrated in (1b):

(1b) kI-a-gɛr "I shut it" kI-a-bar-In "I killed you (sg.)"
ki-ɑ̸-ge:r-in "I see you (sg.)" ki-ɑ̸-ger-e "I was shutting it"

Kalenjin has three morphemes that can be classed as neither dominant nor recessive. Following the Halls we shall term these morphemes *opaque*. To quote our source: "Opaque morphemes are those with [-ATR] vowels which do not shift harmonic class when contiguous to a dominant morpheme . . . The three opaque affixes which we have found . . . are the negative prefix *ma-*, the perfectivizer *ka-*, and the reflexive suffix *kɛ* . . . Opaque affixes . . . prevent harmony from applying to preceding (and/or following -MH/JRV) morphemes."

(1c) i. ki-a-un-gɛ: "I washed myself" ma-ti-un-gɛ: "don't wash youself"
ii. ka-ma-ɑ̸-ge:r-ɑ̸k "I didn't see you (pl.)" ka-ma-ga-go-ge:r-ɑ̸ "and he hadn't seem me"

In (1ci) the vowel of the reflexive suffix [gɛ:]~[kɛ:] and of the negative prefix [ma] remain [-ATR], although the stem [un] "wash" is dominant and induces [+ATR] harmony in all morphemes contiguous to it. In (lcii) the negative prefix[ma] not only is unaffected by the [+ATR] induced by the stem [gɛ:r]~[kɛ:r] "see", but also blocks the spread of the harmony to the morpheme on its left.

The framework that seems to us most appropriate for dealing with the facts just sketched is that of autosegmental phonology pioneered by John Goldsmith (1974) in his dissertation. One of the central innovations of autosegmental phonology was to represent certain features or feature complexes on distinct autosegmental tiers which are separate from one another as well as from the phonological core. We refer to the entities on the different autosegmental tiers as *autosegments*. While the entities in the central core will be referred to as *slots*. Particular autosegments can be linked only to particular slots. Thus, in many languages tones are linked only to vowels, but not to consonants; but there are languages where tones are linked to sonorant consonants as well as to vowels. Autosegmental representations must, therefore, be subject to the formal requirement (1d):

(1d) For each autosegmental tier it is necessary to stipulate the class of slots in the phonological core to which the autosegments may be linked.

It is obvious that in the Kalenjin examples sketched above, it is the feature [ATR] that will be represented on a separate autosegmental tier (in a fashion to be detailed directly) and that we must stipulate that the [ATR] autosegments can be linked only to vowel slots.

We assume that the fact that a particular feature or set of features is represented on a separate autosegmental tier does not necessarily preclude the same feature or features from being specified also in the phonological core. However, when a slot in the core is linked to an autosegment, the specification of the autosegment overrides the specification in the core. Moreover, a distinction will be made between autosegments that are linked to one or more slots in the core, and unlinked or floating autosegments; i.e., autosegments that are not linked to any slot in the core. All associations between slots and autosegments are subject to the constraint that linking lines must never cross.

A number of further conditions on the linking of autosegments and slots have been proposed in the literature. In particular, Goldsmith (1974) has proposed for tonal autosegments the conditions (1e):

(1e) i. Each vowel slot is linked to at least one tonal autosegment.
ii. Each tonal autosegment is linked to at least one vowel slot.
iii. Floating tonal autosegments are linked to (vowel) slots one-to-one from left to right. Slots and autosegments remaining unlinked at this point are linked to their nearest accessible counterpart.

According to (1e) two or more tonal autosegments may be linked to a given vowel slot; and this possibility is made considerable use of in treating a variety of tonal phenomena. It is amply motivated by the existence of contour tones and by the phenomenon of melody stability – i.e., by the important fact that when a vowel is deleted the tone associated with it frequently does not disappear, but shifts rather to an adjacent vowel. Since there are no analogous phenomena in harmony processes, somewhat different conditions will have to be imposed here. In particular, we propose that harmony processes are subject to the conditions in (1f) rather than those in (1e).

(1f) i. Each (vowel) slot is linked to at *most* one (harmony) autosegment.
ii. Floating autosegments are linked automatically to all accessible vowel slots.
iii. Unlinked autosegments are deleted at the end of the derivation.

In the light of these proposals we now examine the Kalenjin facts sketched above. We assume that in underlying representations all vowels are (redundantly) specified as [-ATR]. Dominant morphemes – and only they – are supplied in their lexical representation with a floating [+ATR] autosegment. The three opaque morphemes of Kalenjin are represented with a linked [-ATR] autosegment:

[–ATR]	[–ATR]	[–ATR]
|	|	|
ma	ka	kɛ

Typical underlying representations are shown in (1g):

(1g)		[+ATR]	[–ATR] [+ATR]
	kI-a-gɛr	kI-a-gɛr-ɛ	ka-ma-a-gɛ:r-ak
	"I shut it"	"I was shutting it"	"I didn't see you (pl.)"

The first example in (1g), consisting exclusively of recessive morphemes, is subject to no modifications and surfaces in its underlying form as far as [ATR] harmony is concerned, since all vowels are redundantly specified as [-ATR]. In the second example all vowels are [+ATR] because the floating [+ATR] autosegment will be linked to all vowels as required by (1fii). In the third example, the word-initial syllable cannot be linked to the floating autosegment since such a link would cross the line linking the opaque morpheme *ma* to its [-ATR] autosegment. The absence of linking does not result in a segment unspecified for [ATR] since as just noted all vowels are redundantly specified [-ATR]. The last three vowels are linked to the floating [+ATR] autosegment.

In his important paper on vowel harmony in Akan G. N. Clements (1980) provides excellent arguments showing that the facts of Akan vowel harmony are best dealt with by means of the autosegmental framework. We shall not review his discussion but only examine a few examples of vowel harmony in Akan as they shed light on the viability of condition (1f). Like Kalenjin, Akan is also subject to [ATR] harmony of the dominant-recessive type and it can be treated in the same general manner as Kalenjin requiring only a few minor modifications to account for certain differences between the two languages which we now list: a. Whereas in Kalenjin both stems and affixes may be either dominant or recessive; in Akan this option is available only to stems, suffixes are always recessive. (Cf. 2ai) b. Whereas Kalenjin has only three opaque morphemes, in Akan the low vowel /a/ is systematically opaque. This vowel does not participate in harmony processes and blocks the spread of the [+ATR] harmony to other syllables. (Cf. 2aii–iii) c. Unlike Kalenjin, Akan has a special class of morphemes which induce [+ATR] in affixes (=prefixes) but do not themselves contain any [+ATR] vowels. We illustrate these facts in (2a):

(2a) i. o-fiti-i "he pierced (it)" ɔ-cIrɛ-I "he showed (it)"
ii. o-bisa-I "he asked (it): ɔ-kari-i "he weighed it"
iii. pIrako "pig" fuɲanI "to search"
iv. o-ɲanI "he woke up" ɲanI "to awaken"

We obtain the correct results if we postulate the underlying representations in (2b):

```
             [+A]                        [+A] [–A]       [–A] [+A]
                                               |            |
(2b)    i. ɔ-fItI-I    ɔ-cIrɛ-I    ii.  ɔ-bIsa-I        ɔ-karI-I

          [–A] [+A]   [+A] [–A]       [+A] [–A]     [+A] [–A]
            |               |               |              |
        iii. pIrakɔ        fuɲanI      iv. ɔ-ɲanI          ɲanI
```

All but the examples in (2biv) are self-explanatory. The examples in (2biv) show that in Akan the floating [+ATR] autosegment may appear in morphological contexts where it will have no vowel slot to which it can be linked.

Recall that in the case of tonal processes an unlinked tonal autosegment would be linked to the nearest vowel. In the case of harmony, however, unlinked autosegments are deleted as required by (1fiii).

The most striking examples known to us that bear on the difference between the autosegmental treatment of tonal processes and various kinds of harmony are provided by the South American language Capanahua. Our disscussion here is based on an as yet unpublished study by K. Safir (1979) and on the monograph by Loos (1969), which also was utilized by Safir. Capanahua is subject to nasal harmony of a very interesting kind. In this language vowels and glides are nasalized in position before nasal consonants. This process affects not only the phoneme immediately preceding the nasal consonant, but also any number of preceding glides and vowels provided only that no [+cons] segments intervene. Nasal consonants are subject to deletion in position before glide and word finally. Concomitant with this deletion, nasality spreads rightward, again affecting the entire consecutive substring consisting exclusively of [-cons] segments. We illustrate this in (3a):

(3a) cipõ*n*ki "down river" bãna-wi "plant it" wirãn-ai "I pushed it"
h̃ãma-wi "step on it" h̃ãmã-?̃õna "coming stepping"[2]
wiran-wi > wirãw̃ĩ "push it over" wiran-yaṣ̌a?n-wi > wirã-ỹãṣ̌ã?̃-w̃ĩ
"push it over sometime"

What is crucial about the facts just cited from our point of view is that [+cons] slots block the spread of nasality. They act therefore like opaque slots in Kalenjin and Akan, and will be represented like these, i.e., with a linked [*α* nasal] autosegment. By contrast, vowels and glides, i.e., [-cons] slots, are not opaque and will therefore be represented without linked autosegments. To account for the spread of nasality we need two ordered rules. The first of these inserts a floating [+nas] autosegment to the left of a linked [+nas] autosegment. The second rule deletes a nasal consonant before glide and word finally. The conventions (1f) produce the correct outputs given the underlying representations shown in (3b):

```
(3b)  [–N] [+N]            [–N] [+N]     [–N]   [+N]
       |    |               |    |        |      |
       b  a n  a - w i   w  i r  a n - y  a ṣ̌ a ? n - w i
```

The Capanahua example is especially significant because it shows that the opaque autosegment only serves to block the dominant harmony, it does not initiate a harmony of its own. In the cases from Kalenjin and Akan discussed above this was not self evident; the same output would have been produced if the opaque segments had been allowed to initiate a "recessive" harmony of their own. In the Capanahua case this alternative is excluded, for if the opaque /n/ in *banawi* had been allowed to initiate its own harmony all but the initial stop of the word would have been nasalized in obvious contradiction of the facts of the language.

Our last example of dominant harmony is that of Finnish. Finnish has usually been treated as an example of directional harmony since the harmonic feature – backness – is always propagated from left to right. This fact, however, is not basic but rather a consequence of two other, more fundamental facts, namely, that in Finnish, like in Akan, only stems may be either dominant or recessive but affixes are always recessive, and secondly, that in Finnish there are no prefixes. As a result harmony can only spread rightward, from a stem to the suffixes.

Finnish vowels are traditionally classed into two sets: a harmonizing set consisting of vowels that are either [+round] or [+low], and a neutral set, consisting of the vowels [i,e] which are [-round, -low]. Only vowels of the former set participate in harmony; vowels of the latter set are never affected by harmony. To account for this fact, we shall assume that Finnish vowel harmony is subject to the stipulation that

(4a) autosegments on the tier for the feature [back] may be linked only with vowel slots which are either [+round] or [+low].

A second dichotomy that has long been recognized is that of harmonic and disharmonic stems. Harmonic stems occur in words where all vowels are either [-back] or [+back]. To capture this formally all vowels in the phonological core will be redundantly specified as [-back]; this applies both to stem- and suffix-vowels. Harmonic stems that trigger [+back] harmony are, moreover, supplied in their lexical representation with a floating [+back] autosegment. We illustrate this in (4b):

(4b)

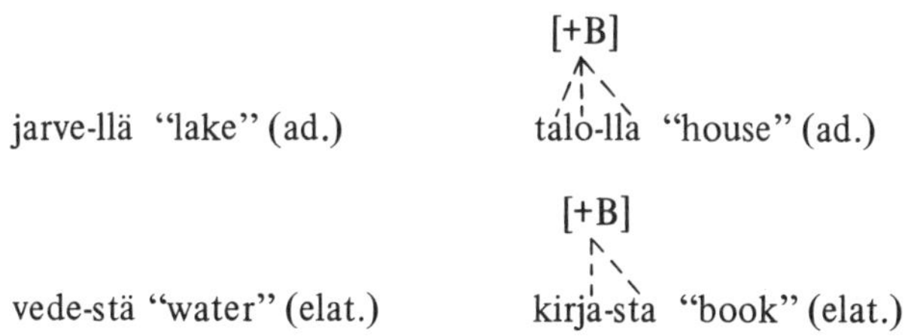

The essential difference between harmonic and disharmonic stems is that in the former all vowels agree in backness, whereas in the latter that is not the case. To capture this property of disharmonic stems we postulate that the last or only harmonizing vowel in a disharmonic stem is *linked* to an [αback] autosegment:

(4c)

[-B] | afääri "business"	[+B] | Pariisi "Paris"
[-B] | analyysi "analysis"	[+B] | olympialaiset "Olympic games"

Disharmonic stems with a linked [-back] autosegment may take either front or back suffixes. Thus, the elative of the first word in [4c] is

(4d) *afääristä* or *afäärista*

On the other hand, disharmonic stems with linked [+back] autosegment take always [+back] suffixes, never [-back]. Thus, we find no *olympialaisissähän* but only *olympialaisissahan*. We think that this state of affairs is due to the existence of two dialects: one of which is more conservative than the other. In the more conservative dialect there is a rule that places a floating [+back] autosegment to the right of a linked [+back] autosegment. In the less conservative dialect, the rule introduces a [+back] autosegment to the right of a linked autosegment regardless of whether it is [+back] or [-back]. The alternative pronunciations of suffiexes after disharmonic stems with a linked vowel that is [-back] must then be attributed to the fact that speakers switch from the more to the less conservative dialect and back.

2. DIRECTIONAL HARMONY ILLUSTRATED

Directional harmony differs from dominant harmony in several essential respects. First, directional harmony propagates in the same direction – left-to-right or right-to-left – in all words, whereas as we have seen above dominant harmony may spread in one direction in one word, in the opposite direction in another word, and in both directions simultaneously in a third word. As a consequence of the uni-directional character of directional harmony the location of the triggering element – sequence-initial or sequence-final – is determined automatically by the direction of propagation. Hence, directional harmony is triggered exclusively by elements that are terminal – i.e., initial or final – in the harmonizing sequence, whereas in dominant harmony the position of the triggering element in the sequence is of no moment. Finally, in dominant harmony a distinction is made between triggering and opaque elements. No such distinction is made in the case of directional harmony: all triggering elements are opaque, and each opaque element induces a harmony of its own. Moreover, the terminal element in a word – the initial element in the case of left-to-right harmony, and the final element in the case of right-to-left harmony –always triggers harmony of its own (see (5bii)).

A simple example of these properties is provided by the rounding harmony of modern Turkish[3]. As shown in (5ai), in Turkish a string of consecutive high vowels agrees in rounding either with an immediately preceding non-high vowel or, in the absence of a non-high vowel, with the word-initial vowel in the word:

(5a) i. gɨd-ɨyor-um "I am going" agɨr-las-ɨyor-mus "it was said to be getting heavy, serious"
gurur-un-uz "your pride" kɨz-ɨm-ɨz "our girl"

Another example of directional harmony is provided by Navaho. In this language the feature [anterior] in coronal affricates and continuants is determined by the right-most coronal affricate or continuant in the word: where the latter is [+anterior] (alveolar) so are all those to its left; when it is [-anterior] (palatal), the same is true of the other coronal affricates and continuants in the word. We illustrate this in (5aii) with the Navaho morphemes /ǰi/ "he (4.p.)" and the perfective morpheme /z/ (examples from Sapir and Hoijer (1967)

(5a)
ii. ǰi-di-baah "he (4.p.) starts off to war"
ji-siii "he (4.p.) steams it"
ji-z-ti "he (4.p.) is lying"
ǰi-ž-γiiš "he (4.p.) is stooped over"

It is, in principle, possible to characterize directional harmony processes with the same descriptive devices as those employed for the characterization of dominant harmony processes. However, the complications which this course of action frequently entails (for some examples see Sec. 3) are such as to raise questions about the validity of this approach: are these types of harmony phenomena in reality special instances of a single process, or are the similarities between the phenomena more superficial than might appear at first sight? Questions such as these have led us to explore the possibility that the two types of harmony processes are based on essentially different linguistic mechanisms, both of which are provided by universal grammar. Specifically, we propose that whereas for dominant harmony languages make use of the mechanism sketched above which is essentially an adaptation of the mechanism employed in various tonal processes; for directional harmony, languages make use of a mechanism, to be outlined below, which is an adaptation of the metrical structure mechanism that is otherwise employed in various stress and accent systems.

Fundamental to metrical phonology is the idea that two adjacent elements are gathered into a single unit by erecting a branching structure over them:

In the branching structures of interest here it will always be the case that one of the two branches (the left branch or the right branch) is superordinate or dominant over the other. A given process – e.g., stress distribution or rounding harmony in a particular language – employs branching structure of only a single type of superordination or dominance.

Conditions of various sorts may be imposed on the nodes A and B that are connected into a single binary branching structure. E.g., it may be required that A and B must dominate a [+syl] slot or that A and B may not dominate [-syl] slots (cf. 1f). In the former case, tree construction would be limited to the single binary branching structure illustrated above. If the latter condition were imposed instead, a greater variety of trees would be admitted, as shall be illustrated directly.

Among the conditions to be imposed on branching structures perhaps the most interesting for our purposes is (5b):

(5b) i. The subordinate or recessive branch of a binary structure may not dominate a node that is branching or that is specially marked by being linked to an autosegment on a separate tier.

ii. All elements in a string must be incorporated into branching structures.

Among the consequences of the above conditions the following are worthy of special note: All trees are uniquely left- (resp. right-) branching. Trees such as those in (5c) are ruled out as a violation of (5b), where the asterisk above a particular element indicates that the element in question is marked:

(5c)

As these properties of trees have been extensively discussed in the literature on metrical phonology, we will not dwell on them here further. Additional information about these matters can be found in the first volume of M.I.T. Working Papers in Linguistics (K. Safir, ed. (1979)) and in B. Hayes' (1980) dissertation. There is one respect in which stress trees differ from harmony trees, and that is with respect to the labelling of their nodes. In stress trees, such as those of English, only the designated terminal node is marked [+stress], all other nodes are labelled [-stress]. In harmony trees, by contrast, all terminal nodes are labelled the same as the designated terminal node. Following a suggestion of J. -R. Vergnaud (1975), we propose that the feature specification of the designated terminal node is copied by a rule on to the root of the tree and percolates downward from there to all terminal nodes of the tree. We illustrate this with examples from Navaho and Turkish in (5d):

(5d)

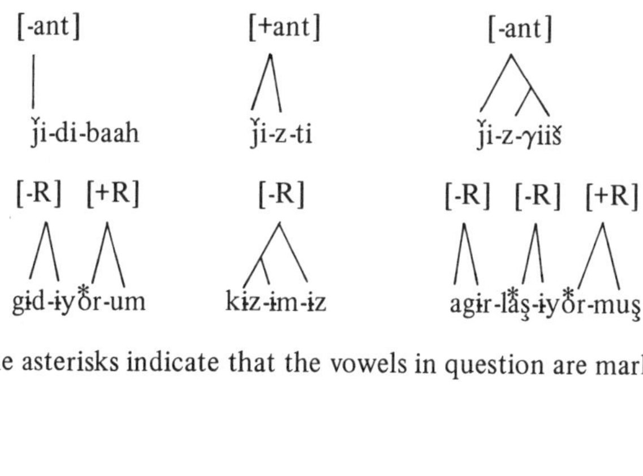

(The asterisks indicate that the vowels in question are marked.)

It is important to note that a root labelling rule of this kind must always *copy* feature specifications from a slot in the core; it cannot assign an arbitrary feature specification to the root. This is a significant limitation on the power of the directional harmony mechanism.

In addition to opaque elements like those above which block and trigger harmony, there appear to exist elements that only block, but do not trigger any harmony of their own. A particularly interesting example is provided by rounding harmony in Khalkha Mongolian, which has been studied in a recent paper by Steriade (1979). Like Turkish, Mongolian has both backness and rounding harmony, and as in the case of Turkish we shall restrict our discussion to rounding harmony alone. We summarize in (6a) the main facts of interest.

(6a) i. Non high vowels undergo and trigger RH:
ot-ox "to keep watch on"; org-ox "to raise"; avr-ax "to save"; hem-ex "to add".

ii. High vowels do not trigger RH:
düü-gees "from the younger brother"; gur-ba "three".

iii. High vowels do not undergo RH:
dag-uul "to cause to follow"; med-uul "to cause to know"; morin "horse".

iv. /i/ does not block RH:
oril-ox "to weep"; xorin-ood "by twenties"; morin-oor "horse" (inst. sg.).

v. Round high vowels block RH:
xoyor-dugaar "second"; yos-dugeer "ninth"; boodg-uul-ax "to hinder".

In order to account for these facts on the assumption that they are instances of directional harmony, we stipulate that [+high, +round] vowels are opaque, for they interrupt rounding harmony. In the case of directional trees this means that each opaque vowel will initiate a separate tree, as illustrated in (6b). Moreover, since harmony here propagates from left to right, the trees to be constructed must be left-dominant.

(6b)
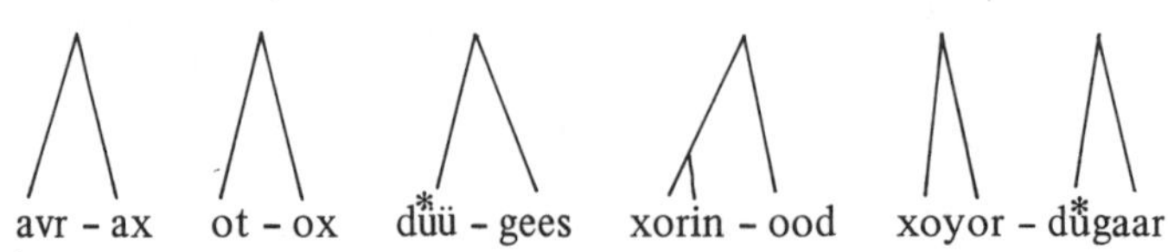

We propose that the algorithm for the construction of directional harmony trees admits a second step in which certain branches in the tree are pruned while leaving the remaining structures intact. In the cases of Mongolian, the nodes to be pruned are all [+high] vowels. This produces the trees in (6c):

(6c)

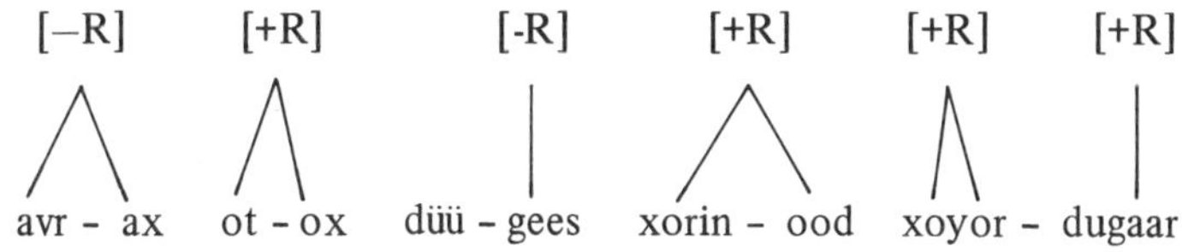

The feature specification of the trees is supplied by the root labelling rule which copies the rounding specification of the designated (i.e., left-most or only) node of the tree. This completes the derivation.

We complete the illustration of the directional harmony algorithm by a discussion of voicing assimilation in Russian. As will be seen below, this phenomenon, whose full complexity has been brought out clearly only in the last decade thanks to the pioneering studies of A. A. Reformatskij (1971) and of Roman Jakobson (1978), can readily be accounted for if treated as an instance of directional harmony with the devices sketched above.

Almost every grammar of Russian includes the information that in obstruent clusters voicing is governed by the last obstruent in the cluster. This distribution of voicing is illustrated in (7a) with the prepositions *ot* "from" and *bez* "without" which contrast in voicing before vowels but lose the contrast before obstruents:

(7a)	o[t]ozera "from a lake"	be[z]ozera "without a lake"
	o[t]strasti "from passion"	be[s]strasti "without passion"
	o[t]pragi "from Prague"	be[s]pragi "without Prague"
	o[t]ptic "from birds"	be[s]ptic "without birds"
	o[d]banka "from a bank"	be[z]banka "without a bank"
	o[d]grexa "from a sin"	be[z]grexa "without sin"
	o[d]bdenija "from a vigil"	be[z]bdenija "without a vigil"

A possible way of dealing with these facts would be by stipulating that this is an instance of directional harmony where the last obstruent in a cluster is opaque. We can then construct right dominant trees illustrated below:

In order to make this proposal work it is necessary to stipulate that the voicing autosegments can be linked only with obstruents and that obstruents are opaque unless followed by another obstruent. This rather complex stipulation, however, does not cover the facts completely. It will have to be supplemented by additional stipulations in order to account for the distribution of voicing in consonant clusters containing both obstruents and sonorants as illustrated in (7b):

(7b)	o[t]nravov "from morals"	be[z]nravov "without morals"
	o[t]Mcenska "from Mtsensk"	be[s]Mcenska "without Mtsensk"
	o[t]mstitel'nosti "from vindictiveness"	be[s]mstitel'nosti "without vindictiveness"
	o[d]mgly "from fog"	be[z]mgly "without fog"
	o[d]lguni "from the liar"	be[z]lguni "without the liar"

In these clusters not all presonorant obstruents are opaque. For example, in *o[d]mgly* and *be[z]mgly* the *g* preceding the *l* is opaque, whereas the obstruents preceding the sonorant *m* are not opaque as shown by the fact that they assimilate voicing from the *g*. Thus, at the very least we would have to amend our stipulation to state that obstruents are opaque when followed by a sequence of any number of sonorants terminating with a vowel or a word boundary. In addition to being unwieldy this revised formulation fails to do justice to the actual process. As noted by Jakobson (1978) what actually transpires is that in consonant clusters voicing propagates across sonorants; these sonorants are simply disregarded. Since the solution sketched above cannot readily express this state of affairs, there is reason to consider an alternative.

As an alternative we propose to follow the two step procedure in tree construction illustrated above with regard to rounding harmony in Mongolian. Specifically, we propose that in the first stage of tree construction all segments be taken into account and that vowels be regarded as opaque; the trees to be constructed on these sequences are right-dominant as illustrated below. Note that word final phonemes – consonants as well as vowels – are opaque by the convention requiring that every phoneme in the string be incorporated into a foot.

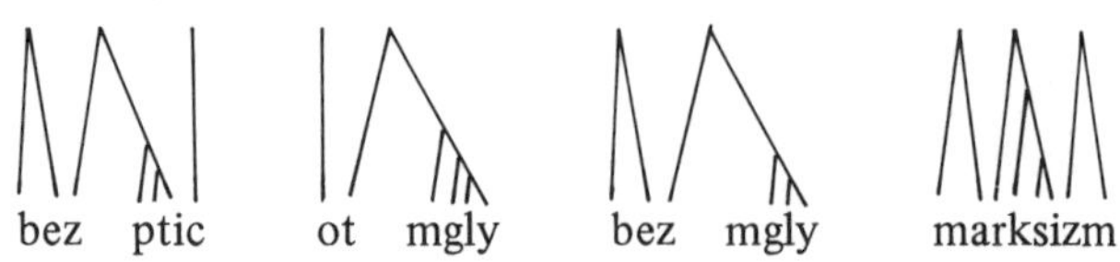

In the second stage of tree construction branches terminating in a sonorant are filtered out yielding the trees:

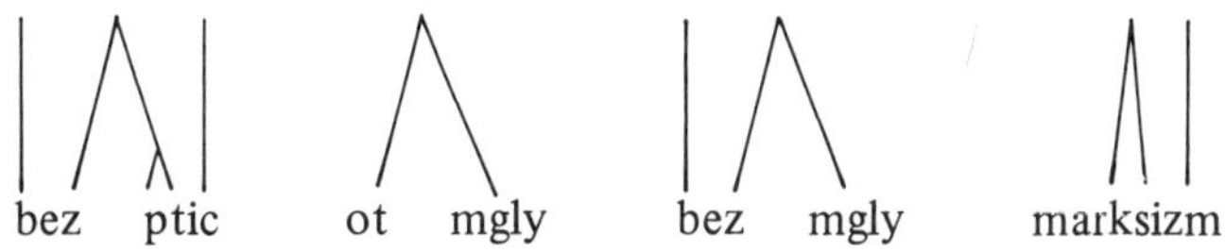

At this point we apply the rule copying on to the root of the tree the voicing feature of the designated (in this case, right-most) element of the tree, producing thereby the correct outputs as shown below:

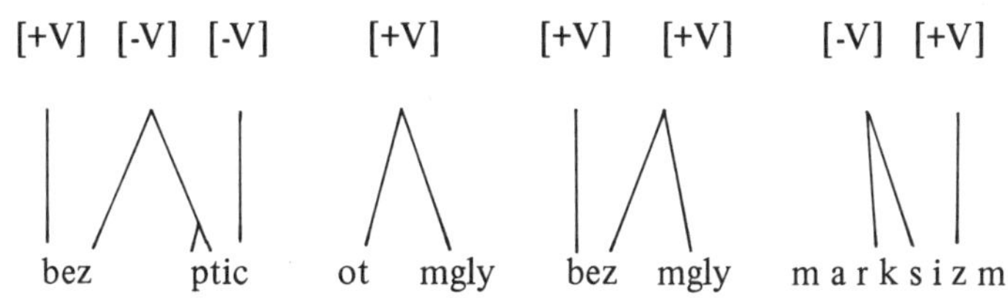

Consider next the treatment of voicing in position at the end of the word. We illustrate in (7c) the facts both in absolute final position and before enclitics.

(7c)	zve[zd]a "star"	tol[st]a "stout"	ži[zn']i "life"	my[sl']i "thought"
	zve[st]	tol[st]	ži[zn']	my[sl']
	zve[st]li	tol[st]li	ži[zn']li	my[sl']li
	zve[st]to	tol[st]to	ži[zn']to	my[sl']to
	zve[zd]že	tol[zd]že	ži[zn']že	my[sl']že

Like German, Russian devoices obstruents in word final position. The fact that an entire obstruent cluster devoices word finally, as shown by forms such as *zve*[*st*] from underlying zve[*zd*], indicates that the rule devoicing word final obstruents must be ordered before the rule that copies the voicing specification on to the root of the tree. Since only word final obstruents are devoiced, the [z] in *ži*[*zn'*] is unaffected by the devoicing rule.

The examples in the last two rows of (7c) show that enclitics affect the voicing in word final clusters if these are made up entirely of obstruents, but not if they include sonorants; cf., e.g., *tol*[*zd*]*že* with *my*[*sl'*]*že* or *ži*[*zn'*]*to*. Since word final phonemes are opaque the word final cluster is not in the same tree as the enclitic, as illustrated below:

This produces the correct results for words ending in sonorants, but it fails in the case of *tol*[*zd*]*že*. What is needed here is a special rule that incorporates two adjacent obstruents into a single tree. This rule affects

because in the latter the obstruents do not adjoin. If we assume that the rule of foot incorporation precedes the rule copying the voicing specification on to the root of the tree, the facts noted above are fully accounted for.

The behavior of word final sonorants sheds light on a very interesting phonetic observation made by A. A. Reformatskij. Reformatskij noticed that in his speech and in that of other speakers of the Moscow dialect, obstruents preserved voicing in word final position before underlying /v/, in spite of the fact that phonetically word final /v/ is devoiced.

(7d)	ja[zv]a "wound"	tre[zv]a "sober"	xoru[gv']i "banner"
	ja[zf]	tre[zf]	xoru[gf']

These voiced-voiceless obstruents clusters are otherwise totally unprecedented in Russian. They would, of course, be fully explained if the Russian /v/ were to be regarded as the underlying glide /w/. Being a sonorant, word final /w/ is pruned from the word final foot:

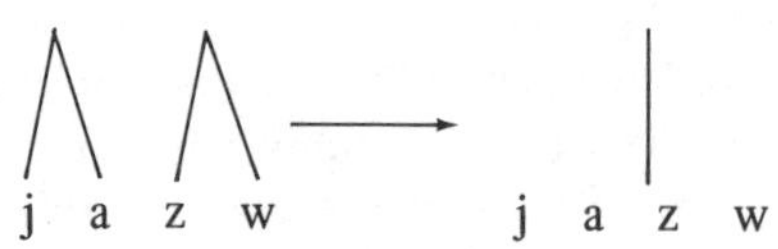

A subsequent rule turns /w/ into the obstruent /v/. If this rule is ordered before word final devoicing we obtain the correct output [jazf].

There are very good reasons for treating /v/ as an underlying glide. First, like glides /v/ deletes before consonants whereas obstruents are preserved:

(7e)	znaj-u	"I know"	nes-u	"I carry"	živ-u	"I live"
	zna-la	"I know" f.s.	nes-la	"carried"	ži-la	"lived"

Secondly, unlike obstruents /v/ does not trigger voicing harmony in preceding obstruents:

(7f)	tvoj "your"		o[t]vas	"from you"
	dva "two"		be[z]vas	"without you"

These facts fall out directly if /v/ is represented underlyingly as a glide, and is turned into an obstruent by a special rule that precedes word final devoicing and the labelling of roots of voicing harmony trees.

There is yet one final set of facts to be considered and that is that behavior of /v/ inside obstruent clusters. As observed by Jakobson (1956) such /v/ are transparent to voicing assimilation; they function in this respect precisely like sonorants; i.e., word medially they allow voicing harmony to affect the preceding obstruent; word-finally, on the other hand, they block voicing harmony.

(7g)	o[dvd]ovy "from a widow"	be[zvd]ovy "without a window"
	o[tft]oroj "from the second"	be[sft]oroj "without the second"
	tre[zft]o "sober, though"	tre[zvž]e "sober, indeed"

The rules developed to this point account for the spread of voicing to obstruents in clusters containing /v/, they do not account fully for the distribution of voicing in /v/ itself. In particular, we have not accounted for the distribution of voicing in such examples as *be[sft]oroj* and *tre[zvž]e*. Given the rules developed above and the order: foot incorporation

w → v

word final obstruent devoicing

copy feature on root

the forms just quoted would be expected to surface as

be[svt]oroj tre[zfž]e

The obvious move here is to add a rule affecting only /v/ and /f/ and having these assimilate from a following obstruent

$$[\text{-son, +lab, +cont}] \longrightarrow [\alpha\text{voiced}] / \_\_ \begin{bmatrix} \alpha\text{voiced} \\ \text{-son} \end{bmatrix}$$

3. THE TWO HARMONY PROCESSES COMPARED

The facts of the different harmony processes in the preceding sections do not force us to adopt the particular solution that was presented. It is, for example, not impossible to describe the consonant harmony in Navaho as an instance of dominant harmony, or the rounding harmony in Finnish as an instance of directional harmony. In this section we compare alternative treatments of some of the examples discussed above in order to make explicit the basis on which choices between alternatives are made.

Consider first the Navaho facts given in (5a). The solution advanced in section 2 was based on the assumption that these are instances of directional harmony. This solution required us to stipulate the facts in (8a-i):

(8a) i. Terminal nodes of tree: [+coronal] continuants and affricates
Direction of propagation: right to left
Harmony process: [αanterior] is copied by rule on to root of tree (from designated terminal element).

We compare this information with the information that would have to be stipulated if the Navaho facts were treated as instances of dominant harmony:

(8a) ii. Terminal nodes of tree: [+coronal] continuants and affricates
Harmony process: [αanterior] is copied by rule from right-most [+coronal] continuant or affricate in the word onto separate autosegmental tier.

In comparing these two solutions it is to be noted that given the mechanism for directional harmony developed above the stipulations in (8a-i) are the minimum necessary to construct a directional harmony tree. By contrast, the stipulations in (8a–ii) are not the minimum necessary to specify a dominant harmony process. In particular, a rule stipulating that the floating autosegment is always [+anterior] or [-anterior] is surely simpler than the stipulation in (8a–ii). Moreover, unlike the directional harmony mechanism the dominant harmony mechanism does not select the right-most unit in a string in preference to any other unit. Given the dominant harmony mechanism it would be equally simple to select the unit preceding a voiced coronal or following an affricate. In view of this it seems fair to conclude that the facts of Navaho are more correctly treated as instance of directional, rather than of dominant harmony.

The opposite conclusion emerges in the case of backness harmony in

Finnish (cf. (4b) and (4c)). It was assumed in section 1 above that Finnish backness harmony is an instance of dominant harmony, and this required us to stipulate the following information.

(8b) i. Terminal nodes: [+low] or [+round] vowels
Opaque: right-most [+low] or [+round] vowel in disharmonic stems
Harmony process: floating [+back] is supplied either lexically, or introduced by rule to the right of an opaque (linked) [+back] autosegment

Moreover, in the more conservative dialect the rule introducing the [+back] autosegment applies only if the opaque vowel of the disharmonic stem is also [+back], whereas in the less conservative dialect, it suffices that the stem is disharmonic for the floating [+back] autosegment to be introduced.

We compare the preceding with the information required if the Finnish facts were to be viewed as an instance of directional harmony:

(8b) ii. Terminal nodes: [+low] or [+round] vowels
Direction of propagation: left to right
Opaque: [+low] and [+back] vowels in disharmonic stems
Harmony process: [back] copied by rule on to root of trees

For the more conservative dialect where suffixes are [+back] only after disharmonic stems whose last harmonizing vowel is [+back], nothing further needs to be stipulated. For the less conservative dialect, however, where suffixes are [+back] after all disharmonic stems, a rule of considrable complexity is required. This rule will have to render opaque the first suffix with a harmonizing vowel by supplying it with a linked [+back] autosegment. The need for this kind of a rule is a direct consequence of the decision to treat the Finnish facts as instances of directional, rather than dominant harmony, and it suggests that it would be more correct to view the Finnish facts as instances of dominant harmony as was done in section 1 above.

Consider next the rounding harmony facts of Khalkha Mongolian quoted in (6a). The information that has to be stipulated for a description of these facts as a case of directional harmony is summarized in (8c-i):

(8c) i. Terminal nodes: all vowels in the word
Opaque: [+high, +round] vowels
Direction of propagation: left to right

Pruning rule: eliminate [+high] nodes from tree
Harmony process: [αround] is copied by rule on to root of tree

The preceding should be compared with a treatment of the same facts as instances of dominant harmony. The information that has to be supplied in such an account is given in (8c-ii):

(8c) ii. Terminal nodes: [-high] and [+high, +round] vowels
Opaque: [+high, +round] vowel
Harmony process: [+round] is introduced by rule as a floating autosegment if stem begins with a [+round, -high] vowel.

The two accounts differ primarily with regard to their characterization of the harmony process. In the "dominant" account the introduction of the floating [+round] autosegment requires special reference to the fact that the left-most vowel in the stem is [+round, -high]. In the "directional" account there is no need to focus special attention on the left-most vowel of the stem, since once the direction of propagation has been stipulated as left to right, the left-most vowel is the only one from which features can be copied on to the root of the tree. Thus, the extra information that must be included in the "dominant" account of Mongolian rounding harmony is not due to the complexity of the phenomenon, but rather to the (incorrect) decision to describe Mongolian rounding harmony as an instance of dominant harmony.

Our final and perhaps most telling example is the treatment of voicing assimilation in Russian. The facts of interest here were given in (7a) to (7g) above where also a "directional" treatment of the phenomena was presented. The information that must be stipulated for this treatment is summarized in (8d-i):

(8d) i. Terminal nodes: all slots in phonological core
Opaque: vowels
Direction of propagation: right to left
Pruning rule: eliminate [+sonorant] nodes from tree
Harmony process: [αvoiced] is copied by rule on to root of tree

We omit from consideration here the special treatment of obstruents in position before enclitics and the complications introduced by the behavior of /v/ because these do not provide evidence for choosing between the two solutions being compared. These facts apart, the Russian voicing assimilation can be treated as an instance of dominant harmony provided that the information in (8d-ii) is stipulated:

(8d) ii. Terminal nodes: obstruents
Opaque: obstruent followed by a sequence of sonorants ending with a vowel or a word boundary
Harmony process: a floating [αvoiced] is introduced to the left of an (opaque) [αvoiced] autosegment linked to an obstruent

It is self-evident that the information in (8d-ii) is significantly more complex than the information in (8d-i). The specification of the opaque elements in (8d-ii) is particularly unwieldy and unnatural. Further complexity is added by the rule describing the harmony process in (8d-ii). We conclude from this that Russian voicing assimilation is an instance of directional, rather than of dominant harmony.

NOTES

* The material presented in this study is to be included in a longer work on metrical phonology which has been in preparation for some time, see Vergnaud and Halle (1979) and Halle and Vergnaud (1980). We are grateful to G. N. Clements, L. Hyman, P. Kiparsky, W. Poser, D. Steriade and M. L. Zubizarreta for comments and criticisms. This work was supported in part by National Institutes of Mental Health Grant #5 PO 1 MH 13990–14.

1 In a paper now in preparation Paul Kiparsky develops an alternative treatment of the processes discussed here. Although Kiparsky's primary concerns are somewhat different from those that are central here, his work may lead to a revision of the proposals made below.

2 Loos (p. 175) quotes these forms without nasalization; his discussion, however, makes it all but certain that the forms are actualized with nasalization as indicated.

3 As is well known, Turkish has both rounding and backness harmony, and these two types of harmony are subject to different principles. The remarks here are limited to rounding harmony.

REFERENCES

Clements, G. N.: 1976, 'The autosegmental treatment of vowel harmony', *Phonologica* 1976, ed. by W. Dressler and O. Pfeiffer, Innsbruck.

Clements, G. N.: 1980, 'Akan vowel harmony: a nonlinear analysis', *Harvard Studies in Phonology* 2.

Goldsmith, J.: 1974, *Autosegmental Phonology*, New York: Garland Publishing, Inc. 1979.

Hall, B. et al.: 1974, 'Nilo-Saharan vowel-harmony from the vantage point of Kalenjin', *Afrika und Übersee* 57, 241–267.

Halle, M. and J.-R. Vergnaud: 1980, 'Three-dimensional phonology', *Journal of Linguistic Research* 1, 83–105.

Hayes, B.: 1980, *A Metrical Theory of Stress Rules*, unpublished PhD dissertation, MIT Department of Linguistics.

Jakobson, R.: 1956, 'Die Verteilung der stimmhaften und stimmlosen Geräuschlaute im Russischen', *Festschrift für Max Vassmer*, Berlin, 199–202.

Jakobson, R.: 1978, 'Metrical assimilations of Russian voiced and voiceless consonants', *Studia Linguistica* **32**, 107–110.

Loos, E.: 1969, *The Phonology of Capanahua and Its Grammatical Basis*, Norman, Oklahoma: Summer Institute of Linguistics.

Reformatskij, A. A.: 1971, '[zf] iz ⟨zv⟩', *Fonologičeskie ètjudy*, Moscow: Nauka, 129–133.

Safir, K.: 1979, 'Hierarchical structures in Capanahua: A case study in local phonology', unpublished paper, MIT Department of Linguistics.

Safir, K. (ed.): 1979, *Papers on Syllable Structure, Metrical Structure and Harmony Processes, MIT Working Papers in Linguistics* 1.

Sapir, E. and H. Hoijer: 1967, *The Phonology and Morphology of the Navaho Language*, Berkeley-Los Angeles: U. of California Press.

Steriade, D.: 1979, 'Vowel harmony in Khalkha Mongolian', *MIT Working Papers in Linguistics* 1, pp. 25–50.

Vergnaud, J. -R.: 1975, 'Formal theory of vowel harmony', *Occasional Papers in Linguistics* 5, University of Massachusetts.

Vergnaud, J. -R. and M. Halle: 1979, 'Metrical phonology – A fragment of a draft', unpublished paper, MIT Department of Linguistics.

NICOLAS RUWET

THE "EPISTEMIC DATIVE" CONSTRUCTION IN FRENCH AND ITS RELEVANCE TO SOME CURRENT PROBLEMS IN GENERATIVE GRAMMAR

1. The sentences in (1) are instances of a construction which, though little studied, is quite common in French[1]. For lack of a better term, I will call it the "epistemic dative" construction (EDC)[2]:

(1) (a) Je lui croyais une maîtresse dans chaque port. (I him_D believed a mistress in every port.)
(b) Je lui trouve beaucoup de charme. (I her_D find much charm.)
(c) Le médecin prévoit une issue fatale à cette maladie. (The doctor foresees a fatal end to that illness.)
(d) Leo Strauss a découvert une interprétation ésotérique au *Prince* de Machiavel. (Leo Strauss has discovered an esoteric interpretation to Machiavelli's *Prince*.)

These sentences seem to be paraphrases[3] of those in (2):

(2) (a) Je croyais qu'il avait une maîtresse dans chaque port. (I believed that he had a mistress in every port.)
(b) Je trouve qu'elle a beaucoup de charme. (I find that she has much charm.)
(c) Le médecin prévoit que cette maladie aura une issue fatale. (The doctor foresses that that illness will have a fatal end.)
(d) Leo Strauss a découvert que le *Prince* de Machiavel a une interprétation ésotérique. (Leo Strauss has discovered that Machiavelli's *Prince* has an esoteric interpretation.)

A by no means exhaustive list of verbs which may both enter the EDC of (1) and the sentential complement construction of (2) is given in (3):

(3) accorder (grant), assurer (assure), concevoir (conceive), croire (believe), découvrir (discover), décréter (decree), deviner (guess), imaginer (imagine), inventer (invent), postuler (postulate), prédire (predict), pressentir (to have a foreboding), prétendre (pretend), présumer (presume), prévoir (foresee), proclamer

W. Klein and W. Levelt (eds.), Crossing the Boundaries in Linguistics, 23–49.

(proclaim), promettre (promise), reconnaître (recognize, acknowledge), refuser (refuse), souhaiter (wish), soupçonner (suspect), subodorer (suspect), supposer (suppose), trouver (find), voir (see), vouloir (want), etc.

Several, but not all, of these verbs, can cooccur with both an indirect object and a full finite sentential complement; contrast (4)–(5) with (6)–(7):

(4) (a) Je promets qu'il aura des ennuis. (I promise that he will have troubles/that he will get into trouble.)
(b) Je lui promets des ennuis.
(c) Je te promets que tu auras des ennuis. (I promise you that you will get into trouble.)

(5) (a) J'ai prédit qu'il aurait un bel avenir. (I predicted that he would have a bright future.)
(b) Je lui ai prédit un bel avenir.
(c) Je lui ai prédit qu'il aurait un bel avenir.

(6) (a) J'imagine qu'il a de nobles qualités. (I imagine that he has noble qualities.)
(b) Je lui imagine de nobles qualités. (I him_D imagine noble qualities.)
(c) *Je lui imagine qu'il a de nobles qualités.

(7) (a) Je prévois qu'il aura un bel avenir. (I foresee that he will have a bright future.)
(b) Je lui prévois un bel avenir.
(c) *Je lui prévois qu'il aura un bel avenir.

It follows that, with some of these verbs, such as *promettre* or *prédire*, the double object construction will be ambiguous, the difference in meaning between the two readings being somewhat subtle. Thus, in (4) (b), *lui* can be understood as being, or not being, the receiver of the promise (compare *je te promets des ennuis, je te promets qu'il aura des ennuis*)[4].

In earlier times, one might have been tempted to derive the sentences in (1) from structures similar to those underlying the sentences in (2), by means of a rule deleting *avoir* plus a transformation raising the embedded subject to the main IO position (or, alternatively, deleting the embedded subject under identity with a base-generated IO)[5]. If, however, one adheres to (some version of) the lexicalist hypothesis, such a derivation seems highly unlikely, It would be rather easy to formulate about the EDC various arguments of the same type as those which have been classically adduced in favor of a lexical over a transformational analysis[6]. I will not insist on this, though some of the facts discussed below are relevant to the issue, and I will consider EDC sentences as being generated in essentially their surface form in the base. This does not mean of course that there does not exist some sort of systematic relation between the EDC and *avoir*-constructions, but I think that clarifying this issue must await a more general discussion of the relations between *avoir*, the dative in general, and, probably, possessive constructions; I am afraid that, as has too often happened in the past, piecemeal derivations of some of those constructions from other, apparently simpler, constructions would only help confuse the general issue.

Many of the verbs in (3), such as *croire, trouver, imaginer, voir, deviner, proclamer, prétendre, supposer*, etc., also occur in another, better-known, construction, the V – NP – Predicate construction known in French as the *construction à attribut de l'objet* (henceforward abbreviated in CAO)[7]; see (8)–(9), and compare (8) (a)–(b) with (1) (a)–(b):

(8) (a) Je le croyais polygame. (I him_{Acc} believed polygamous.)
(b) Je trouve cette fille trés charmante. (I find this girl very charming.)

(9) (a) Je croyais qu'il était polygame. (I believed that he was polygamous.)
(b) Je trouve que cette fille est trés charmante. (I find that this girl is very charming.)

The EDC and the CAO have much in common and should be carefully compared[8]. Actually, the semantic relation between the direct object and the indirect object in the EDC is very similar to the relation between the predicate and the direct object in the CAO[9]; in both cases some sort of intrinsic quality or property is predicated of the referent of an NP (the IO in the EDC, the DO in the CAO) – hence the similarity in meaning between (1) (a) and (8) (a), (1) (b) and (8) (b). This may help us explain why some *avoir*-constructions have no EDC correlates; compare (10) and (11):

(10) (a) Je crois qu'il a l'impression qu'il va pleuvoir. (I believe that he has the feeling that it's going to rain.)
(b) Je trouve qu'il a une femme insupportable. (I find that he has an unbearable wife.)

(11) (a) *Je lui crois l'impression qu'il va pleuvoir.
(b) *Je lui trouve une femme insupportable[10].

In the subordinate clauses of (10), *l'impression qu'il va pleuvoir* and *une femme insupportable* do not describe properties of the subject in the sense in which *beaucoup de charme* in (1) (b) or even *une maîtresse dans chaque port* in (1) (a) do. Rather, in (10) (a), *avoir l'impression* behaves, semantically as well as, partly at least, syntactically, like a simple verb ("think", "feel"), of which *qu'il va pleuvoir* is the object. In (10) (b), the main predication (within the subordinate clause) relates *insupportable* to *femme*[11]: (10) (b) is almost synonymous with *je trouve que sa femme est insupportable* or *je trouve sa femme insupportable*. This relates to the fact that, in the most natural interpretation of (1) (a), the object, *une maîtresse dans chaque port*, is non-specific, while in the most natural interpretation of (10) (b), *une femme insupportable* is specific[12].

Relevant to the question of the underlying structure of the EDC are various kinds of meaning differences between EDC sentences and the corresponding sentences involving sentential complements. These differences closely parallel those we find between the CAO and the *V que S* constructions (see Ruwet 1979, section 6). A first case in point shows up in the following:

(12) (a) Pierre croit qu'il est malade. (Pierre believes that he is ill.)
(b) Pierre croit qu'il a des ennemis partout. (Pierre believes that he has enemies everywhere.)

(13) (a) Pierre se croit malade. (Pierre believes himself (to be) ill.)
(b) Pierre se croit des ennemis partout. (Pierre himself$_D$ believes enemies everywhere.)

(14) (a) ?Je me crois malade. (I believe myself (to be) ill.)
(b) ?Je me crois des ennemis partout. (I myself$_D$ believe enemies everywhere.)

While the sentences in (12) simply report a belief of Pierre about himself, those in (13) suggest, in addition, that the belief in question is unfounded. Hence the strangeness of (14) – which disappears as soon as the sentences are put in the past tense, cf. *En ce temps-là, je me croyais des ennemis partout*[13].

Secondly, some verbs take on, in the EDC, an "active", even "performative" meaning which they lack in the sentential complement counterpart. Consider:

(15) (a) Le gouvernement a reconnu le droit de grêve à ces ouvriers. (The government acknowledged the right to strike to those workers.)

(b) Le gouvernement a reconnu que ces ouvriers ont/avaient le droit de grêve. (The government acknowledged that those workers have/had the right to strike.)

(15) (a) expresses an (official) act on the part of the government, and is almost synonymous with "the government gave the workers the right to strike"; this element of meaning is normally lacking in (15) (b), in which the right in question can be an already existing one. Accordingly, while (16) (b) is acceptable, (16) (a) is rather incongruous[14]:

(16) (a) ?Ma concierge a reconnu le droit de grêve à ces ouvriers. (My janitor acknowledged the right to strike to those workers.)
(b) Ma concierge a reconnu que ces ouvriers ont/avaient le droit de grêve.

Thirdly, notice that (18) is a natural continuation to (17) (a), but not to (17) (b):

(17) (a) J'ai découvert une seule solution à ce problème. (I have discovered only one solution to that problem.)
(b) J'ai découvert que ce problème a/avait une seule solution. (I have discovered that that problem has only one solution.)

(18) . . . , mais il en a peut-être d'autres. (. . . , but maybe it has others.)

The reason for this is that (17) (b) implies the truth of its complement sentence, while nothing of the sort holds for (17) (a). Similarly, (19) (a) is a paraphrase neither of (19) (b) nor of (19) (c), none of which makes much sense anyway:

(19) (a) Je lui trouve chaque jour de nouvelles qualités, à ce livre. (I it_D find each day new qualities, to that book.)
(b) ?Je trouve chaque jour qu'il a de nouvelles qualités, ce livre. (I find each day that it has new qualities, that book.)
(c) ?Je trouve qu'il a chaque jour de nouvelles qualités, ce livre. (I find that it has each day new qualities, that book.)

In (19) (a), the new qualities found in the book on day d_i are new with respect to those found on days d_{i-1}, d_{i-2}, etc., and they are new to *me* (they may have always been present in the book though I did not notice them on my earlier readings). This close connection between *chaque jour, nouvelles qualités*, and *je*, is lacking both in (19) (b) and (19) (c). (This "scope" relation in (19) (a) is similar to that between *une seule solution* and *je* in (17) (a).)[15]

From these semantic considerations, let us turn to another observation, which is relevant both for the question of the underlying structure of the EDC and for the discussion to follow. Verbs such as *donner* ("give"), *attribuer* ("attribute"), *prêter* ("lend"), etc., are typical double object verbs, which describe actions:

(20) (a) Pierre a donné/prêté ce livre à Paul. (Peter gave/lent that book to Paul.)
(b) Le jury a attribué le Prix Nobel à William Faulkner. (The jury attributed the Nobel Prize to W. F.)

These verbs, which never cooccur with sentential complements, frequently occur in sentences whose meanings are very similar to those of (1):

(21) (a) On lui attribue beaucoup de bonnes fortunes. (They him_D attribute many affairs with women.) (Cf. (1) (a))
(b) *On (lui) attribue qu'il a beaucoup de bonnes fortunes.

(22) (a) Les Alliés prêtaient à Napoléon l'intention de battre en retraite. (The Allies lent Napoléon the intention of retreating cf. The Allies believed that Napoléon intended to retreat.)[16]
(b) *Les Alliés prêtaient (à Napoléon) qu'il avait l'intention de battre en retraite.

(23) (a) Je lui donne quarante ans, pas plus. (I him_D give forty years (of age), not more.)
(b) *Je (lui) donne qu'il a quarante ans, pas plus.

(23) (a) is more or less a paraphrase of (24) (b), while (24) (a) is unacceptable (see Note 7):

(24) (a) *Je lui estime quarante ans, pas plus.
(b) J'estime qu'il a quarante ans, pas plus. (I estimate that he is forty years of age, not more.)

Obviously, one would not want to distinguish between two verbs *donner,* two verbs *attribuer*, etc., with different subcategorization frames in the base; the identity of the surface structures would then appear to be a mere coincidence. These facts thus seem to strongly support the hypothesis that the EDC is generated as such in the base.[17]

2. Chomsky (1980) has suggested that various restrictions on the distribution of reciprocal phrases, such as *each other* in English or, presumably, *l'un (P) l'autre* in French, should best be dealt with in the following way: (a) the lexicon of English or French states that *each other* (*l'un (P) l'autre*) is a reciprocal phrase[18]; (b) reciprocal phrases are freely generated (in the base or by means of the transformational rule "move α") in all possible NP (or PP) positions; (c) a rule of "construal", operating in Logical Form (LF), assigns a (plural) antecedent to *each other* (*l'un (P) l'autre*)[19]; (d) in LF, reciprocal phrases, as other anaphors, are treated as variables, and are subjected to the "conditions on binding"; one such condition is the "opacity condition" (OP, formerly the "specified subject condition"), which states that:

(25) (= Chomsky 1980, (27), p. 13) If α is [a variable] in the domain of the subject of β, β minimal, then α cannot be free in β, [where $\beta = \overline{S}$ or NP].

This allows Chomsky, among other things, to account for the ungrammaticality of (26) (= Chomsky's (36) (a)):

(26) *They expect [$_{\overline{S}}$ the books to be given to each other].

Given that "we find data suggestive of opacity conditions in structures lacking a syntactic subject at surface structure", such as:

(27) (a) *They regard me as very much like each other.
*I impress them as very much like each other.

and that "there seems to be no syntactic motivation for assigning anything beyond the obvious surface structure to such sentences", Chomsky (1980, 17–18) then suggests that such sentences should be assigned the representations (28) in LF, by means of a "structure-building rule":

(28) (a) They regard me$_i$ as [$_{\overline{S}}$ PRO$_i$ be very much like each other].
(b) I$_i$ impress them as [$_{\overline{S}}$ PRO$_i$ be very much like each other].

It is easy to see that in such structures *each other* is both free in $\bar{S}$ and in the domain of PRO (which is controlled by *me/I*); thus the Opacity Condition can apply, blocking (27) as required.

Given my non-transformational analysis of the CAO (see Ruwet 1979), I presume that Chomsky would deal in the same way with the following facts:

(29) (a) *Pierre et Paul croient Marie amoureuse l'un de l'autre. (Peter and Paul believe Mary (to be) in love with each other.)
(b) *Pierre et Paul ont rendu Marie amoureuse l'un de l'autre. (Peter and Paul caused Mary (to be) in love with each other.)

Now the EDC displays a distribution of reciprocal phrases which is very similar to that found in the above examples: in (31) (b), (33), the dative clitic *me* (or for that matter a corresponding full indirect object[20]) blocks the construal rule relating *l'un P l'autre* to the subject in the same way as *me* or *I* in (27) seem to block it:

(30) (a) Je crois qu'ils ont du respect l'un pour l'autre. (I believe that they have respect for each other.)
(b) Je leur crois du respect l'un pour l'autre.
(31) (a) *Ils croient que j'ai du respect l'un pour l'autre.
(b) *Ils me croient du respect l'un pour l'autre.
(32) Je leur prête de mauvaises intentions l'un envers l'autre. (I lend them bad intentions toward each other.)
(33) *Ils me prêtent de mauvaises intentions l'un envers l'autre.

In the spirit of Chomsky 1980, one could thus introduce another "structure-building" rule in LF, which would convert (31) (b) into (34) (a) and (33) into (34) (b), with the obvious results with respect to the Opacity Condition:

(34) (a) Ils me_i croient [$_{\bar{S}}$ PRO_i avoir du respect l'un pour l'autre].
(b) Ils me_i prêtent [$_{\bar{S}}$ PRO_i avoir de mauvaises intentions l'un envers l'autre].

At first sight, the behavior of sentences like (1) (a)–(b) under Passive seems to provide an additional piece of evidence in favor of this analysis. Sentences such as those of (35) are unacceptable:

(35) (a) *Une maîtresse dans chaque port lui était crue.

(b) *Beaucoup de charme lui est trouvé (par tout le monde). (Much charm is found her (by everyone).)

Given current assumptions of trace theory, the S-structure of, say, (35) (b) would be (36)[21]:

(36) Beaucoup de charme$_i$ lui$_j$ est trouvé t$_i$

The structure-building rule would convert (36) into (37) in LF:

(37) Beaucoup de charme$_i$ lui$_j$ est trouvé [$_{\bar{S}}$ PRO$_j$ avoir t$_i$]

It is easy to see that the trace of *beaucoup de charme* is now free in $\bar{S}$, while being in the domain of the subject of $\bar{S}$[22].

3. For a variety of reasons, however, such a solution cannot possibly work. Consider first the case of passive sentences. (35) may be unacceptable, but, in fact, most of the verbs of (3), as well as EDC *prêter, attribuer*, etc., can undergo Passive, while still blocking the reciprocal construal rule. See (38)–(41), and compare with (33) and the examples in Note 20:

(38) (a) Une issue fatale est prévue à cette maladie (par le médecin). (Cf. (1) (c)).
(b) Une interprétation ésotérique a été découverte au *Prince* de Machiavel (par Leo Strauss). (Cf. (1) (d).)

(39) (a) ?Une maîtresse dans chaque port lui est souvent imaginée. (Cf. (1) (a) as well as Notes 12 and 14.)
(b) Des aventures extravagantes lui ont été imaginées. (Extravagant adventures him$_D$ have been imagined.)
(c) Une tête à trois cornes lui a été imaginée par Jérôme Bosch. (Cf. Note 14.)

(40) (a) Le droit de grêve est reconnu à ces ouvriers par le gouvernement. (Cf. (15).)
(b) Un grand respect pour les institutions établies est reconnu à ce vieux monsieur. (A great respect for established institutions is recognized this old gentleman.)

(41) (a) Beaucoup de bonnes fortunes lui sont attribuées. (Cf. (21).)
(b) L'intention de battre en retraite est/était prêtée à Napoléon (par les Alliés). (Cf. (22).)

So the behavior of *croire* and *trouver* under Passive, rather than typical, is somewhat exceptional. Once again, the comparison between the EDC and the CAO is instructive. Under Chomsky's analysis, one would not expect Passive to be blocked in the case of the CAO and indeed, most of the time, CAO sentences have passive counterparts:

(42) (a) L'accusé a été jugé coupable (par le tribunal). (The defendant has been judged guilty (by the tribunal).)
(b) Le candidat a été déclaré incompétent (par tout le monde). (The candidate has been declared incompetent (by everyone).)

In the case of *croire* and *trouver* however passive CAO sentences need special conditions[23] to be acceptable; they are generally bad in the present tense:

(43) (a) *Ce vieux marin est cru polygame (par Paul/par tout le monde). (Cf. (8) (a).)
(b) *Cette fille est trouvée charmante (par Paul/par tout le monde). (Cf. (8) (b).)
(44) (a) Ce vieux marin a longtemps été cru polygame (par Paul/par tout le monde).
(b) Cette fille a été trouvée charmante (par Paul/par tout le monde).

Thus, and though the facts are not exactly the same in the EDC and the CAO, the main division between acceptable and unacceptable sentences cuts across the two constructions, while an analysis along Chomskyan lines would predict a sharp difference between them.

A similar distribution of acceptability and unacceptability is to be found within the so-called *Tough*-constructions (*facile* = "easy", *difficile* = "difficult"), though these are generally worse than their passive counterparts:

(45) (a) *Une maîtresse dans chaque port est difficile à lui croire.
(b) *Beaucoup de charme est facile à trouver à cette fille.
(46) ?D'extravagantes aventures sont faciles à lui imaginer.
(47) Une interprétation ésotérique serait difficile à découvrir aux oeuvres de Lakoff. (Cf. (1) (d).)
(48) (a) ?Les plus extravagantes bonnes fortunes ne sont pas difficiles à lui attribuer.
(b) ?L'intention de battre en retraite était facile à prêter à Napoléon.

Similarly with the CAO:

(49) (a) *Ce vieux marin est facile à croire polygame.
(b) *Cette fille est facile à trouver charmante.
(50) (a) ?L'accusé sera difficile à juger coupable.
(b) ?Le candidat a été facile à déclarer incompétent.

Once again, it is not clear how a Chomskyan analysis would account for this distribution of facts. In particular, the similarity between (35) and (45), (43) and (49), is hard to explain if one adopts Chomsky's analysis of *Tough*-constructions, given that the trace of WH-movement does not count as a variable with respect to the Opacity Condition (see Chomsky 1977b, to appear[24]).

4. Let us come back to reciprocals. We have seen that sentences involving verbs like *prêter*, etc., in their "epistemic" interpretation, are subject to the Opacity Condition, as shown in (32), repeated here as (51):

(51) (a) Je leur prête de mauvaises intentions l'un envers l'autre.
(b) *Ils me prêtent de mauvaises intentions l'un envers l'autre.

The problem is that, in sentences where they occur with their usual, causative meaning, verbs like *prêter*, etc., generally do not block the reciprocal construal rule. Contrast (51) with (52), and see also (53)–(56):

(52) (a) Je leur ai prêté des livres l'un pour l'autre. (I lent them books for each other.)
(b) Ils m'ont prêté des livres l'un pour l'autre. (They lent me books for each other.)[25]
(54) (a) Je leur attribue des aventures l'une avec l'autre. (I attribute them affairs with each other.)
(b) *Elles m'attribuent des aventures l'une avec l'autre.
(55) (a) ?Je leur ai attribué les cotes l'un de l'autre. (I attributed them each other's marks.)
(b) ?Ils m'ont attribué les cotes l'un de l'autre. (They attributed me each other's marks.)[26]
(56) (a) Je leur ai prêté/donné des portraits l'un de l'autre. (I lent/gave them pictures of each other.)
(b) Ils m'ont prêté/donné des portraits l'un de l'autre. (They lent/gave me pictures of each other.)

Thus, after all, one might have to distinguish two different verbs *prêter*, two different verbs *attribuer*, etc. One of them only would be subjected to the structure-building rule mentioned above (see (34)) – which seems to mean that we would have to have recourse to some sort of rule feature, an unwelcome result. Of course, one might try to make use of the difference between those verbs in terms of the causative feature. This would hardly be sufficient, however; in the case of *attribuer*, for instance, it is easy to build minimal pairs such as the following:

(57) (a) Les Français attribuent généralement à Grouchy la responsabilité de la défaite de Waterloo. (The French generally attribute to Grouchy the responsibility for the defeat of Waterloo.)

(b) Le 28 mai 1873, le tribunal a attribué à Bazaine la responsabilité de la défaite de 1870. (On May 28, 1873, the tribunal attributed to Bazaine the responsibility for the defeat of 1870.)

(58) (a) Les philologues s'accordent à attribuer à Platon vingt-huit des trente-cinq dialogues qui nous sont parvenus sous son nom. (Philologists agree to attribute to Plato twenty-eight of the thirty-five dialogues which have reached us under his name.)

(b) Dans un important article, en 1935, Friedländer a définitivement attribué la Septième Lettre à Platon[27]. (In an important article, in 1935, Friedländer conclusively attributed the Seventh Letter to Plato.)

Examples (a) seem to be clear cases of the EDC; (57) (a) for instance is more or less synonymous with "The French generally think that Grouchy is responsible for the defeat of Waterloo"[28]. On the other hand, examples (b) are in a sense closer to cases of the purely causative use of *attribuer* (cf. (20) (b)): (57) (a) describes an act on the part of the tribunal, and it would be incongruous to paraphrase (58) (b) by "In an important article, in 1935, Friedländer conclusively thought that Plato is the author of the Seventh Letter." I suppose we would prefer not to split the *attribuer* which occurs in those examples into two different verbs. What these examples suggest is rather that the subtle differences in meaning between the (a) and the (b) examples should be accounted for in terms of some global properties of the sentences: for instance, the (a) sentences are generic, while the (b) sentences involve a punctual moment in time.

On the other hand, the differences in meaning which separate examples (b) from examples (a) hardly seem to have any effect on the distribution of reciprocals. Examples using *attribuer* are a bit far-fetched, but still, consider the following:

(59) (a) Je leur attribue de mauvaises intentions l'un envers l'autre.
(b) *Ils m'attribuent de mauvaises intentions l'un envers l'autre. (Cf. (51).)

(60) (a) J'ai décidé de leur attribuer de grandes responsabilités l'un envers l'autre. (I decided to attribute them great responsabilities toward each other.)
(b) *Ils ont décidé de m'attribuer de grandes responsabilités l'un envers l'autre.)[29]

Examples with *reconnaître* are maybe clearer (recall that similar nuances show up in the case of *reconnaître*; compare (40) (a) and (40) (b), and recall the discussion about (15)). The following examples indicate that the causative/non-causative distinction has no effect:

(61) (a) Je leur reconnais une grande ressemblance l'un avec l'autre. (I them$_D$ recognize a great resemblance with each other.) (With *reconnaître* non-causative.)
(b) *Ils me reconnaissent une grande ressemblance l'un avec l'autre.

(62) (a) Je leur reconnais des droits l'un envers l'autre. (With *reconnaître* "causative".)[30]
(b) *Ils me reconnaissent des droits l'un envers l'autre.

Thus, in order to distinguish between (60), (62), and, say, (56), one would need something more than the presence vs absence of some causative feature.

The verb *promettre* ("promise") raises a different, though related, kind of problem (see (4) above). Consider first:

(63) (a) Je leur promets du respect l'un pour l'autre. (I promise them respect for each other.)
(b) Ils me promettent du respect l'un pour l'autre.

Recall that EDC sentences involving *promettre* are often ambiguous, due to the status of the IO (receiver or not of the promise). (63) (a) is acceptable if it means "I promise (them) that they will have respect for each other", not if it means "I promise (one of them) that I will have respect for the other and

I promise (the other one) that I will have respect for the first one". (63) (b) is acceptable if it means "They promise me that they will have respect for each other", not if it means "one of them promises (me) that I will have respect for the other one and the other one promises (me) that I will have respect for the first one". (Here, apparently, in (63) (b), *me* must be understood as the receiver of the promise.) This seems to mean that we will have to distinguish two verbs *promettre*, one of which (with the IO optionally interpreted as the receiver of the promise) is subjected to the structure-building rule mentioned above, the other verb being subjected to a different rule in which the inserted PRO is controlled by the subject (this reminds one of the usual subject-control verb *promettre*; notice that here the IO must be the receiver of the promise); alternatively one might mark *promettre* as subjected to a variant of the structure-building rule which leaves open the choice of the controller of PRO (depending in part on the way the IO is interpreted). This sounds fairly complicated, but consider now:

(64) (a) Je leur/vous promets des ennuis les uns avec les autres. (I promise them/you trouble with each other.)
(b) *Ils me promettent des ennuis les uns avec les autres.

(65) (a) *Il nous a promis des biographies les uns des autres. (He promised us biographies of each other.)
(b) Nous lui avons promis des biographies les uns des autres.

The asterisks represent the judgments which seem to be the most natural at first sight. (64) (a) is acceptable if it means "I promise (them/you) that they/you will run into trouble with each other", so that there is no difference in this respect with (63) (a). The problem is why (64) (b) does not seem to be acceptable with the reading "They promise me that they will have trouble with each other". Another problem is that, in the case of (65), the judgments are reversed. However, the differences in acceptability might be due to pragmatic factors, linked with the meanings of *ennuis* and *biographies*. The unacceptability of (64) (b) might be due to the strangeness of someone promising to get into trouble[31]. Similarly, (65) (b) is acceptable because the most natural way to interpret it is to imagine we (*nous*) as being writers promising our common publisher that each of us will write a biography of each of the others; (65) (a) sounds unacceptable because it seems to mean something like "He (a prominent writer of biographies) promises each of us that he will write biographies of the others" (cf. **He promised us to write biographies of each other*); in other words, in both cases, the main subject tends to be interpreted as the agent/subject of *biographies*. (65) (a) would probably be acceptable if it could simply be understood as meaning "He promised us that we will have biographies of each other" (compare (56)). So we might stick to (one or the other variant of) the solution just alluded to involving a structure-building rule, and leave the judgments expressed about (64)–(65) to be accounted for in terms of semantico-pragmatic factors.

Once we have reached this point however, we may be tempted to get rid altogether of the structure-building rule, at least in the case of *promettre*, and to try to account for the whole range of facts in semantico-pragmatic terms[32]. But (i) the fact remains that at least some of the facts mentioned are uncomfortably close to those which the Opacity Condition was supposed to deal with (the fact that only one of the two a priori possible meanings of (63) (a) and (63) (b) is possible, the "understood subject" of *biographies* in (65)); (ii) given the trouble we have gone into in the case of the other verbs, we may want to try to extend a semantico-pragmatic solution to the whole of the EDC, which may lead us to suspect that there is something wrong about the Opacity Condition in general[33].

5. My results up to now, at least at the explanatory level, have been mainly negative. Within the scope of this article, it is out of the question that I try to give a coherent, general, solution to the problems which we have run into. I will limit myself to one or two points.

First, a methodological remark. I disagree with most of the criticisms recently directed against generative grammar by Gross 1979; in general I find them unfair or irrelevant[34]. Gross has one point however. Most Chomskyans, especially Chomsky himself, have always tended to underestimate the complexity of the interrelation between syntax and the lexicon. The usual practice, while studying some rule or constraint, has been to take a few verbs (such as *believe/croire, seem/sembler, want*, etc.) as paradigmatic of a whole class, while relegating to footnotes casual remarks about "exceptional" verbs, whose idiosyncracies are supposed to be amenable to some kind of lexical treatment which is seldom specified. The least one could do, while proposing some rule or constraint, would be to have a look at a wider range of lexical items than is usually done: one might then discover, more often than is generally suspected, that "paradigmatic" verbs represent rather extreme cases – as, I think, I have shown in the case of *croire* within the EDC and the CAO.

Secondly. Simplifying a lot, we may say that we have distinguished three main groups among the verbs discussed: (a) verbs such as *croire, trouver*, etc., which allow neither passive (except under special conditions) nor reciprocals with a subject antecedent; (b) verbs such as *reconnaître*, EDC *prêter*, etc., which allow passive but do not allow reciprocals; (c) "ordinary" *prêter, attribuer, donner*, etc., which allow both passive and reciprocals. On the other hand, we have mentioned several semantic or pragmatic factors which seem to be related to this distribution of facts – such as the generic vs punctual aspect, the "active" or "causative" character of the main verb, etc.

To my mind, only a theory which takes those semantic or pragmatic factors into account can explain the facts. Such a theory cannot be constructed as long as we do not have careful descriptions of the semantico-pragmatic behavior of all or most of the verbs involved. (I have in mind descriptions of the kind of that which Ducrot 1975 has provided for the verb *trouver* (See Note 11), though for our purposes it would still be insufficient in many respects). I would like to add that I would prefer not to make a distinction between semantics and pragmatics[35], and to talk, in a deliberately loose way, of "meaning", or rather of representations – I mean the representations of the process(es) or state(s) of affairs which a sentence evokes in the mind. In other words, what we need first are "phenomenological" descriptions of those representations. I will only be able to make a few suggestions.

All the sentences discussed, whether they belong to the EDC, the CAO, the "ordinary" double object construction[36], or the full complement sentential construction, evoke rather complex representations – in the sense that the process(es) that they represent are (plenomenologically) more complex than, say, the processes represented by *It is raining, The stone fell*, or even *John killed Bill*[37]. The whole problem lies in this, that, given several factors (the meaning of the verb, the relative syntactic complexity of the construction, etc.) the various elements of the representation are connected in various, more or less direct, intimate, or fused ways. For instance, in the full complement sentential construction, the syntax clearly separates two parts of the representation (presence of the complementizer *que*, two independent occurrences of the tense), while in the EDC or the CAO, those two parts are more intimately connected[38].

Passive and the reciprocals seem to be sensitive in different ways to the nature and internal complexity of the representations. What seems to characterize reciprocals (as well as reflexives, so-called intrinsic possessives, etc.) is a relation to representations whose parts are in some way closely knit together. A general characterization of the notion "reciprocal" would have to take this into account (see Note 18)[39]. In all sentences involving verbs of groups (a) and (b) above, it is possible to distinguish two parts in the representation, (i) a mental state or mental act on the part of the subject, and (ii) some process which this mental state or act is about. This distinction seems to be sufficient to prevent reciprocals from relating to the subject[40], as if, to speak metaphorically, there is too much distance between those two parts within the representation. All sentences in the (c) group, on the other hand (see examples (20), (56)), represent situations which, though complex in a sense, are grasped as a single, concrete, unified whole, where all participants (those represented by the subject, the OD, the IO) simultaneously participate in one process[41].

Passive, on the other hand, seems to be sensitive mainly to the relatively static or active character of the mental process represented by the verb: *croire*, which expresses an opinion, can be thought to represent a mental state, while *reconnaître, découvrir*, EDC *prêter*, sometimes *imaginer*[42], rather represent mental acts. We might try to relate this connection between passive and the relatively active character of the process represented by the verb with the often made observation that, in a variety of cases, passive sentences are acceptable only if the referent of the passive subject can be conceived as being "affected" in some way by the process represented by the sentence[43].

It may seem strange that we characterize EDC *prêter* or *attribuer* as involving a mental act rather than a mental state, given the way we have paraphrased, for instance, (22) (a), repeated here as (66):

(66) Les Alliés prêtaient à Napoléon l'intention de battre en retraite. (The Allied lent Napoléon the intention of retreating; cf. The Allied believed that Napoléon intended to retreat.)

However, a more careful paraphrase of (66) would be something like "The Allied made/were making the hypothesis, which they might have been ready to discard, that Napoléon intended to retreat." In other words, a connection (which is, admittedly, metaphorical) is felt between EDC *prêter* and "ordinary" *prêter*[44].

I am well aware that all of this is still terribly vague. But let me repeat that my point was not to try to give a full-fledged explanation of the facts discussed, but rather to suggest that some of the problems that a theory of autonomous syntax faces might profitably be viewed from a very different point of view.

Generally, I have no quarrel with Chomsky's view of grammar as a system of autonomous though interrelated subcomponents, each of which is subject to its own laws and is amenable to a precise, general and systematic treatment. The problem is that, while Chomsky has made very precise proposals concerning some of these subsystems (those constituting syntax in general), he has been extremely reticent to say anything beyond a few casual remarks about some of the others, especially those which have to do with semantics and pragmatics. This often results – as was the case in the now defunct theory of generative semantics – in the temptation to deal in purely syntactic terms[45] with facts whose nature would require a very different treatment. There certainly is a basis to the notion of autonomous syntax, but it runs the risk of remaining shaky if we continue to neglect those other aspects of language.

We can, in a way, understand Chomsky's wariness about semantics and pragmatics. Semantics and pragmatics pose a problem which noone, to my knowledge, has stated as clearly as Kuroda (1974, 198–199):

> (In syntax and phonoloy) the primary data to be accounted for by a formal model can be said, to be sure with some abstraction, to be given in a form of combinatorial representation of a sort. The primary phonological given of a sentence is basically in the form of a series of phones; the primary syntactic given of a sentence is in the form of a series of words (. . .) The abstract underlying syntactic and phonological representations are ultimately grounded on such primary formal representations. Nothing of the sort exists for the formal theory of semantics (. . .) at no level of abstraction are meanings given to us in a form of formal entity (. . .) A difficulty with the notion of semantic representation resides in the fact that nothing which the semantic representation is supposed to represent or account for is given as a primary datum in a form of combinatorial character.

This means that we may have to approach semantic problems in a very different way from those with which generative grammar has made us familiar; on the other hand, we cannot leave those problems aside, given the import they have for facts which at first sight might seem to be syntactic in nature (such as the distribution of passives and reciprocals). This may also mean, as Kuroda has suggested elsewhere[46], that, in order to deal with those problems, we will have to go beyond some of the philosophical assumptions which are in the background of generative grammar in general – I mean the assumptions of analytical philosophy – and start again to look at the problem of meaning in the light of traditional continental linguistics from Plato to Hegel and Husserl. But this, of course, is another story[47].

NOTES

[1] To my knowledge, only Gaatone 1975 has a brief discussion of this construction, which, more recently, is also mentioned in Morin 1980, 209–210 (see Note 9 below), and in Kayne (to appear).

[2] This label is purely menmonic; I choose it because many of the verbs involved, such as

croire, are "epistemic" verbs. The translations of the examples are only meant to help the reader understand them; I have made no systematic attempt at translating them literally or in good English. Subscript D means "Dative clitic"; DO means "direct object", IO "indirect object"; I will call the construction involving an IO and a non-sentential DO the "double object construction".

The EDC is sometimes more natural with a dative clitic than with a full indirect object. but this is by no means true in general, as shown by (1) (c)–(d); *je trouve beaucoup de charme à cette femme/à cette musique* is as good as (1) (b); *je croyais une maîtresse dans chaque port à ce vieux marin* ("that old sailor") is only slightly less acceptable than (1) (a). The CAO (see below) is also sometimes better with an object clitic.

[3] But see below, p. 26ff.

[4] In (4) (a), as well as in both readings of (4) (b), it is not necessarily understood that *je* will be the cause of the trouble that *il/lui* will get into. *Promettre* thus can take on a meaning rather close to that of *prédire* in (5).

[5] Combining these two approaches would have allowed one to account for the ambiguity of (4) (b), (5) (b).

[6] In Ruwet 1978, 191ff., I argued against deriving the *avec NP PP* "absolute" construction by means of an *avoir*-deletion rule; several of the arguments mentioned there carry over to the case of the EDC. Compare for instance: *je crois qu'elle a raison/de bonnes raisons pour faire cela* ("I believe that she is right/that she has good reasons to do that"), *je suppose qu'il a peur/une peur terrible des femmes* ("I suppose that he is (terribly) afraid of women"), and *je lui crois *raison/de bonnes raisons pour faire cela, je lui suppose *peur/une peur terrible des femmes.*

Various idiosyncracies are also relevant. For instance, the verb *connaître* cannot (except with a strong archaic flavor) cooccur with a sentential complement: **je connais qu'il a beaucoup d'ennemis* ("I know that he has many enemies"); but *je lui connais beaucoup d'ennemis* is acceptable. These facts follow if we base-generate the EDC and subcategorize *connaître* in terms of an object NP (see *je connais Pierre/l'oeuvre de Platon/cette ville*, "I know Pierre/Plato's work/that city").

[7] See Ruwet 1979 and the references cited therein. Some verbs occur naturally in the EDC but not in the CAO, and vice versa; compare: *je le juge coupable* ("I judge him guilty")/*?*je lui juge un mauvais caractère* ("I him$_D$ judge a bad temper"), *je l'estime très intelligent* ("I estimate him (to be) very intelligent")/*??je lui estime beaucoup d'intelligence* ("I him$_D$ estimate much intelligence"), and *je lui soupçonne des aventures extra-maritales* ("I him$_D$ suspect extramarital affairs")/**je le soupçonne menteur* (OK: *je le soupçonne d'être menteur*, "I suspect him of being a liar"); compare also (4) (b) in the text and *?*je le promets malade* ("I him$_{Acc}$ promise ill", "I promise that he will be ill"). As is usual in such matters, I would expect some dialectal or idiolectal variation here.

[8] For instance I pointed out (Ruwet 1979, section 3) that, within the CAO, *croire* and *trouver* differ with respect to the possibility of questioning the predicate by means of *comment* ("how"; this can be a predicate in simple copulative sentences, cf. *Comment est-il? – Très intelligent.*). Thus we have (i) (a) but not (i) (b):

(i)(a) Comment le trouves-tu? – Très intelligent.
(How do you find him? – Very intelligent.)
(b) *Comment le crois-tu? – Très intelligent.

Similarly, the direct object can be questioned in (ii) (a), but not in (ii) (b):

(ii)(a) Qu'est-ce que tu lui trouves? – (Elle a) du sex-appeal.
(What do you her_D find? – (She has) sex appeal.)
(b) *Qu'est-ce que tu lui crois? – (Elle a) du sex-appeal.

[9] This has also been noticed by Morin 1980. Morin takes for granted that, within the EDC, the relation between the OD and the IO is the same as that between a predicate (*attribut*) and a subject. However, his sweeping generalization – "Lorsque l'attribut est un *SADj* (AP), l'objet est accusatif; lorsque l'attribut est un *SN* (NP), l'objet est datif" (p. 210) – is obviously false, cf. *je le/*lui crois mon meilleur ami* ("I believe him_{Acc} (to be) my best friend").

[10] (11) (b) has another, irrelevant meaning, cf. *I found an unbearable woman/wife for him.*

[11] In other words, in the terms of Ducrot 1975, p. 79, the *predication originelle* induced by *je trouve* . . . in (10) (b) does not bear on the whole subordinate VP, but only on the relation between *(sa) femme* and *insupportable.*

[12] Correspondingly, (i) *je lui croyais sa maîtresse à Paris* tends to be less natural than (1) (a), given that, under the most natural interpretation, *sa maîtresse* is referential. On the other hand, given the meaning of *imaginer, je lui imagine une femme insupportable/des maîtresses extravagantes* ("I him_D imagine an unbearable wife/extravagant mistresses") is quite natural.

When *sa maîtresse* in (i) is conceived as non-referential, (i) becomes acceptable; in that case, the DO can be cliticized: *je la lui croyais à Paris, sa maîtresse* (this might raise problems for Chomsky's Opacity Condition – see below). Compare also: ??*Je lui croyais son fils Pierre étudiant à MIT* ("I him_D believed his son Peter a student at MIT" – cf. *Il a son fils Pierre étudiant à MIT*), where it is hard not to take *son fils Pierre* as referential.

[13] The difference in meaning is more general than the examples in the text, which limit themselves to cases of reflexive objects, might suggest. Put in the present tense, (1) (a) sounds a bit awkward (*je lui crois une maîtresse dans chaque port*); compare also:

(i)(a) Pierre croit la fenêtre ouverte. (Peter believes the window (to be) open.)
(b) Pierre croit Dieu tout-puissant. (Pierre believes God (to be) omnipotent.)
(ii)(a) ?Je crois (OK: Je croyais) la fenêtre ouverte.
(b) ?Je crois (OK: Je croyais alors) Dieu tout-puissant.

[14] The behavior of *reconnaître* here is strictly parallel to that of *déclarer* ("declare") within the CAO. See Ruwet 1979, pp. 265–266; see also Borkin, 1973, 1974. There exists a similar, though more subtle, difference between (1) (d) and (2) (d). Compare also *Jérôme Bosch a imaginé que ce démon avait une tête à trois cornes* ("Hieronymus Bosch imagined that that devil had a three-horned head")/*Jérôme Bosch lui a imaginé une tête à trois cornes, à ce démon* ("Hieronymus Bosch him_D imagined a three-horned head, to that devil")/*Jérôme Bosch lui a dessiné une tête à trois cornes, à ce démon* ("H. B. drawed him a three-horned head . . ."); the meaning of the second sentence is in a way closer to that of the third rather than to that of the first.

[15] These facts are reminiscent, not only of the CAO, but also of other differences of meaning involving pairs of related constructions, one of which is simpler or more compact in structure than the other – such as the simplex vs complex causative constructions (see Ruwet 1972, ch. 4, and the references cited therein), the two indirect object constructions in English (see Oehrle 1976), etc. In all those cases, the more compact construction seems to involve some sort of more direct or intimate connection between its elements than is the case in the more complex construction. I am convinced that all these facts need to be treated together, and that in any case the semantic differences should be directly related to the differences in structure, rather than to various stages in derivations from some common source (as seems to be suggested, for instance, in Borkin 1974 and Postal 1974).

One more instance of meaning differences between the EDC and the full sentential complement construction; compare:

(i) Je ne lui connais que des amis, à Brejnev.
(I him_D know only friends, to Brezhnev.)
(ii) Je sais qu'il n'a que des amis, Brejnev.
(I know that he has nothing but friends, Brezhnev.)

(i) seems to imply that I am more or less personally acquainted with Brezhnev, while (ii) carries no such implication; in (ii), but not in (i), my knowledge can be based on hearsay for instance.

[16] On the precise meaning of (22) (a), see below, p. 39.

[17] I have left aside other facts which are possibly relevant here: besides EDC sentences, involving IOs, one finds sentences such as the following, which involve different (locative) prepositional complements:

(i) Je trouve beaucoup de charme dans ce livre.
(I find much charm in this book.)
(ii) J'imagine beaucoup de qualités chez cet homme.
(I imagine many qualities in this man.)

See also *Jérôme Bosch a imaginé ce démon avec une tête à trois cornes* ("Hieronymus Bosch imagined that devil with a three-horned head"), and compare with the examples in Note 14. See also Ruwet 1978, on the relations between *avoir* ("have") and *avec* ("with"). The possibility of having, or not having, the clitic *y* instead of *lui* should also be considered; see *j'y trouve beaucoup de charme, à/dans ce livre*, ??*le médecin y prévoit une issue fatale, à cette maladie* (OK: *lui prévoit . . .*) (see (1) (c)).

[18] Though Chomsky (1980, 9) "assum(es) that the notion "reciprocal" falls into its natural place within universal grammar," he has never attempted to give a characterization of that notion, beyond casual observations about the alleged synonymy between sentences such as *the men saw each other* and *each of the men saw the others* (see for instance Chomsky 1977a, 71). Also, the only reciprocal expression Chomsky ever mentions is *each other*; he never takes into account the whole range of reciprocal or related expressions. However, adverbs like *tour à tour* ("in turn"), *alternativement* ("alternately"), *séparément* ("separately"), etc., seem to obey something like the Opacity Condition; compare for instance *ils portaient la valise alternativement* ("they were carrying

the bag alternatively"), *ils faisaient* [*porter la valise à Paul*] *alternativement* ("they had Paul carry the bag alternatively"), and **ils faisaient porter la valise alternativement à Paul* ("they had Paul alternatively carry the bag") (OK: *ils faisaient porter la valise alternativement à Paul et à Jean*, "they had Paul and John alternatively carry the bag").

[19] This rule will have to distinguish between ordinary (semantic) plurals and *pluralia tanta*, cf. *the swords broke each other* vs **the scissors broke each other*. (See also *Les Etats-Unis se sont détruits* (*eux-mêmes/*les uns les autres*) "The United States destroyed itself/*each other").

[20] Cf. *Je croyais à Napoléon et* (*à*) *Wellington du respect l'un pour l'autre, on prête de mauvaises intentions l'un envers l'autre à ces deux tyrans*. Some other examples where the OC seems to apply: **Ils me trouvent* (*découvrent, reconnaissent*) *une grande ressemblance l'un avec l'autre* ("They me_D find (discover, recognize) a great resemblance with each other"), **Elles m'imaginent des désirs l'une envers l'autre* ("They me_D imagine desires for each other").

[21] To simplify, I have left aside the trace left by clitic-placement of *lui*; it does not seem to play any relevant role here.

[22] This analysis would parallel that by means of which Chomsky (1980, 35, Note 40) accounts for (i) **I was struck* (*by John*) *as pompous*. I have always had doubts about that explanation, for two reasons. First, Chomsky's solution does not naturally carry over to French. In the corresponding (active) construction, French has a PP instead of the English *as AP* constituent: (ii) *Pierre m'impressionne par son intelligence*; the passive form is unacceptable: (iii) **Je suis impressionné par Pierre par son intelligence* (OK: *je suis impressionné par son intelligence*, which is the passive of *son intelligence m'impressionne*). But notice that control is not involved in (ii)–(iii): instead of PRO we have a true pronoun (*son* in *par son intelligence*); this pronoun can be deeply embedded within the PP, cf. *Pierre m'a impressionné par la remarquable maîtrise que nous LUI avons vu déployer dans ces circonstances*, "Peter impressed me by the remarkable mastery that we saw *him* display in those circumstances"). Obviously, one would want the same explanation to work for both French and English.

Secondly, as Chomsky himself notes (*id., ibid.*), there are exceptions to the principle that verbs of subject control do not undergo passivization. Chomsky mentions double passives like *John was promised to be allowed to leave*, but he adds that "it seems that some syntactic property is involved, since substitution of a near synonym for the embedded passive changes the grammatical status to the expected *: e.g. **John was promised to get permission to leave*." Besides the fact that I know of at least one (British) native speaker of English who accepts sentences such as the latter (see Jones 1979, 292–293, Note 29), Chomsky ignores the facts about the French verb *menacer* ("threaten"), whose behavior, which seems to be very similar to that of *promise*, strongly suggests that semantic and even pragmatic factors play a crucial role in the question of control (see Ruwet 1972, 77–78, note, and especially Fauconnier 1976), and that there is not much hope that one will be able to deal with control in the purely structural way which Chomsky still advocates (Chomsky 1980, 33). On *promettre*, see also below, p. 35ff.

[23] This seems also to be true of *imaginer*; contrast (i) *je l'imagine intelligent* ("I imagine him intelligent") and (ii) ?**il est imaginé intelligent* (*par Paul/par tout le monde*); if we modify the tense and/or give a more active or causative meaning to the verb, passive sentences become more acceptable, cf. (iii) *Cette cité est/a été imaginée parfaite par Platon* ("That city is/has been imagined perfect by Plato"); see also (39).

24 I am aware that in Chomsky (to appear) the "On binding" framework has undergone considerable modifications. As far as I can tell, these changes have no bearing on the points at issue; I will thus keep to the more familiar framework.

25 In (52) (a), if *leur* refers to Pierre and Paul, the sentence means "I lent Pierre books for (him to give to) Paul and I lent Paul books for (him to give to) Pierre"; (52) (b) would mean "Pierre lent me books for (me to give to) Paul and Paul lent me books for (me to give to) Pierre."

One might wonder whether different constituent structures are involved, for instance, in (51) $[_{NP}$*de mauvaises intentions l'un envers l'autre*$]$, vs, in (52), $[_{NP}$*des livres*$]$ $[_{PP}$*l'un pour l'autre*$]$. If we look at the corresponding cleft sentences however, both possibilities seem to be realized in both cases: *C'est des livres pour Paul que j'ai prêtés à Pierre, c'est des livres que j'ai prêtés à Pierre pour Paul*, as well as *c'est de mauvaises intentions envers Paul que je prête à Pierre, c'est de mauvaises intentions que je prête à Pierre envers Paul*. In any case, in both (55) and (56), *les cotes l'un de l'autre* and *des portraits l'un de l'autre* seem to be NPs.

26 In order to understand (55) (a), one must imagine that I (*je*) am the examiner for some exam and that I have mixed up the copies of the candidates; in (55) (b), the candidates (of whom I am one) examine each other. If (55) is slightly less acceptable than (56) it is probably due both to the definite article in *les cotes* and to the complexity of the situation depicted.

27 The strangeness of *Platon a la Septième Lettre*, as compared with *Platon est l'auteur de la Septième Lettre* or *La Septième Lettre est de Platon* ("Plato has the Seventh Letter", "Plato is the author of the Seventh Letter", "The Seventh Letter is by Plato") is one more little bit of evidence against deriving EDC sentences from a complex sentence with a complement sentence whose main verb is *avoir* ("have"), maybe also against a restructuring rule in LF (on this however see Kayne, to appear).

28 On this alleged synonymy, see p. 39 below, however.

29 To make the examples sound convincing, one must imagine, for instance, that in (60) (a) I (*je*) am some high official, *leur* referring to two of my subordinates; in (60) (b) I am some subordinate official taking orders from two different higher ones. See also below, Note 44.

30 Once again, to make the examples convincing, one must imagine, for instance, that *je/me* and *leur/ils* refer to three heads of state negociating some treaty.

31 Similarly, it seems to me very hard to understand (4) (b) as meaning "I promise him that I will run into trouble"; compare *Je vous promets beaucoup de respect* (*pour vous*), which sounds fine to me ("I promise (you) that I will have much respect (for you)").

32 Along the lines of Fauconnier 1976 for instance. Notice that for Chomsky 1977a, p. 14, Note 13, control is irrelevant in sentences such as *Bill was promised a job*; but, if control is irrelevant, how are we going to account for the difference between *We promised him pictures of each other*, on the one hand, and, on the other, **I promise them respect for each other*, which, I have been told, is unacceptable? (In English, it seems, there is nothing corresponding to the *promettre* of example (4) (b)).

33 In a stimulating article, Williams has criticized Chomsky's use of structure-building rules (see Williams 1980, 235–236). One might try to inquire whether Williams's theory of predication can account for the facts we have been dealing with. I will limit myself to a few remarks. Williams would have to treat the DO in the EDC as a Predicate; this has some intuitive appeal, as we have seen, but the question is whether Williams would be

able to distinguish, in those terms and in a non-*ad hoc* way, the objects of the two *prêter*, the two *attribuer*, etc.; generally, he would have to distinguish DOs which are Predicates from DOs which are not. Similarly, he would have to say that *par son intelligence* in *Pierre m'impressionne par son intelligence* (see Note 22) is a Predicate. Moreover, as far as I can tell, his theory is not more successful than Chomsky's when it comes to the problems raised by *promise* in the Passive (see same footnote); he treats the subject of *promise* as a theme, which seems counterintuitive (Williams 1980, 210–211). More important maybe are counterexamples to his claim that the NP with which a Predicate is coindexed must c-command it. For me, sentences such as *L'arrivée de Pierre malade/en mauvaise forme m'a surpris* ("The arrival of Peter sick/in bad shape surprised me") are fine; but maybe *Pierre malade, Pierre en mauvaise forme*, are constituents here (see Kayne 1981). In the EDC the "antecedent" of the Predicate is either a Dative clitic (which might derive from a bare NP) or a full indirect object preceded by the preposition *à*: we would have to say that *à* does not count for c-command. In any case, I accept sentences such as *Je compte sur Pierre comme parrain de mon fils* ("I count on Peter as godfather of my son"), in which *sur Pierre comme parrain de mon fils* is not a constituent, as shown by *C'est sur Pierre que je compte comme parrain de mon fils* ("It is on Peter that I count as godfather of my son"), *C'est comme parrain de mon fils que je compte sur Pierre* ("It is as godfather of my son that I count on Peter"); similarly for sentences such as *Je tiens à Pierre comme parrain de mon fils* ("I value Peter as godfather of my son"). Generally, I have the feeling that most of the problems which the EDC raises for a Chomskyan approach are still problems within Williams's framework.

On the other hand, I have not yet had time to figure out how the EDC would fit into the theory recently proposed by Kayne (to appear); at first sight this theory has at least one advantadge: it gives a unified account in LF of sentences like *John gave Mary a book, John believes Mary a genius*, as well as, presumably, *Je lui croyais une maîtresse dans chaque port*. On the other hand, thia theory does not solve the problem raised by the distribution of reciprocals; rather it complicates it (it does not account for the acceptability of *They gave me pictures of each other*); moreover, I do not see clearly how Kayne would give a unified account of both the clitic and the full IO cases of the EDC.

[34] For a fair and critical appraisal of Gross's work, see Dominicy's (1979) review of Gross 1975.

[35] I certainly share Chomsky's and Jackendoff's doubts about the possibility of constructing a semantic theory "which is free of information derived from pragmatics and speaker's belief systems" (Jackendoff, to appear).

[36] For expository purposes, I have throughout distinguished the EDC and the "ordinary" double object construction. Of course, I would like to say that they are the same syntactic construction, at least as far as their base structure is concerned.

[37] For instance, *It is raining* represents the occurrence of some process without much internal structure, while *John gave a book to Mary* represents an action involving three different participants. I am not of course interested in the relative complexity of those processes in terms of the "real world" – which is no more "real" from our point of view than the phenomenological world.

[38] Recall the discussion above of examples (12) to (19).

[39] All generative treatments, whether in the Standard Theory, in Generative Semantics, or in Chomsky's recent proposals, try to capture this in terms which amount to having

the notion "simple proposition" play a crucial role. The problem is that we know very little about what would count as a proposition at some abstract level of representation of a sentence, whether it be the underlying structure of Generative Semantics or Chomsky's Logical Form.

Kayne (1975, section 4.8.) has an interesting discussion of counterexamples to the Specified Subject Condition within French causative sentences (such as *Ils se sont fait tomber des pierres les uns sur les autres*). It is significant that, though the facts have been known for quite a time and though Kayne 1975 has been widely discussed in the recent literature, noone, to my knowledge, has tried to account for those facts (they are still problems, for instance, for Rouveret and Vergnaud's (1980) recent proposals about the French causative construction). Moreover, even from a purely observational point of view, Kayne's discussion is not the last word on the subject; for instance, neither the causative (*laisser, faire*) vs perceptual (*voir, regarder*, etc.) character of the main verb, nor the agentive vs non-agentive character of the embedded subject suffice to account for the facts: see, for instance, (OK) *Napoléon et Wellington ont fait tirer leurs artilleries l'un sur l'autre* ("Napoléon and Wellington had their artilleries shoot at each other", where *each other* refers to Napoléon and Wellington), (OK) *Ils(se) sentaient des sanglots monter à la gorge l'un de l'autre* ("They felt sobs coming up to each other's throats", which is acceptable given suitable pragmatic assumptions, if, for instance, we think of two lovers closely embracing each other).

40 On the other hand, I am well aware that what I am suggesting would not account for the acceptability of sentences such as *They expected each other to win*, etc. But notice that Chomsky still needs some special provision to account for those facts, such as the $\bar{S}$ deletion rule of Chomsky (to appear). What I would like to suggest is that the behavior of embedded subjects (or of the DO in the CAO, the IO in the EDC), rather than reducing to the "normal" case, is what needs explaining.

41 Once again, neither the notion of "simple proposition" nor that of "causative" verbs are enough. There are cases of simple sentences, whose verb is clearly causative, which strongly tend to prevent reciprocals within a prepositional phrase from relating to the subject; see for instance *Les Spartiates ont dressé les Athéniens les uns contre les autres* ("The Spartans aroused the Athenians against each other"); while informants readily accept such a sentence if *les uns contre les autres* relates to *les Athéniens*, they reject it if the reciprocal phrase is meant to relate to *les Spartiates* (though, to me at least, *Pierre et Jean ont dressé Luc l'un contre l'autre* sounds acceptable, but much less so than *Pierre a dressé Luc et Jean l'un contre l'autre*). These judgments should be related, I think, to the fact that this sentence implies *Les Athéniens se sont dressés contre X* ("The Athenians raised against X"), in which *les Athéniens* is clearly an agent. Compare with Note 39, bottom.

42 Compare examples (39) (a) and (39) (b)–(c). See also Note 23. The role played by differences in the choice of the Tense should also be related to this.

43 See the literature on prepositional passives in English, for instance Cureton 1979. Facts very similar to those which in English have been discussed mainly in connection with prepositional passives also exist in French, where prepositions cannot be stranded. Compare ??*Paris a été quitté par Pierre*/*Paris a été quitté par Napoléon* ("Paris has been left by Peter/by Napoléon"), ??*Paris est habité par Pierre*/*Paris est habité par plus de deux millions de gens* ("Paris is inhabited by Peter/by more than two million people"). Even a simple sentence like *Ce tableau a été vu par Pierre* ("This picture has been seen by

Peter") sounds a bit strange to me, unless I know that *Pierre* is the name of a famous art expert for instance – this relates to the static quality of *voir* in its normal use.

44 Maybe the meaning of EDC *prêter* is clearer in the following: *Pour une fois . . . la rime aurait pu jouer le rôle qu'on lui prête* (from a recent article by Benoît de Cornulier: "For once . . . rhyme might have played the role which one lends it"). Notice that, given that there is no clear demarcation between the two *prêter*, the two *attribuer*, etc., one might expect cases of fuzzy acceptability even in sentences involving reciprocals; for instance (compare (54), (58)–(60)) I have the feeling that the following sentences are not completely unacceptable (one must imagine them spoken by Plato in his old age): *Aristote et Speusippe viennent de décider de m'attribuer des oeuvres l'un de l'autre* ("Aristotle and Speusippus have just decided to attribute me works of each other"), *Aristote et Speusippe ont la manie de m'attribuer des oeuvres l'un de l'autre* ("Aristotle and Speusippus are in the habit of attributing me works of each other"). See also: *ils se prêtent les rôles l'un de l'autre*, which, though hardly perfect, is not quite unacceptable. Recall the discussion about *promettre* above, as well as that about *dresser* in Note 41.

45 Though Chomsky used to make a distinction between "formal syntax" and Logical Form (see Chomsky 1977a), it is now obvious that he is interested only in the syntax of LF, and that LF is just the name for another subcomponent of "formal syntax". Talk about rules of interpretation in LF are confusing in this respect.

I also have the feeling that, maybe like Williams's use of the label Predicate, the increasingly frequent references in recent generative literature to notions like "thematic roles" are just another attempt at making one believe that very complex semantic notions are in principle amenable to a kind of formal treatment similar to that which is adequate, for instance, for category symbols.

46 See for instance Kuroda 1977, 1978.

47 I would like to thank for their comments and criticisms the participants in the seminar I gave in the Fall of 1980 at the University of Ottawa, Department of Linguistics, especially Paul Hirschbühler and Michael Szamosi; thanks are also due to Thelma Sowley, who helped me improve the style of this paper. I hope that this paper will not be too unfitting an homage to Manfred Bierwisch who, among his other outstanding qualities, has always been distinguished by an openmindedness exceptional in our profession.

REFERENCES

Borkin, Ann: 1973, '*To be* and not *to be*', in C. Corum *et al.* (eds.), *Papers from the Ninth Regional Meeting of the Chicago Linguistic Society*, Chicago, Ill., 44–56.

Borkin, Ann: 1974, *Raising to Object Position: A Study in the Syntax and Semantics of Clause Merging*, Unpublished Doctoral Dissertation, University of Michigan.

Chomsky, Noam: 1977a, *Essays on Form and Interpretation*, New York: Elsevier-North Holland.

Chomsky, Noam: 1977b, 'On WH-Movement', in P. W. Culicover, T. Wasow, A. Akmajian (eds.), *Formal Syntax*, New York, Academic Press, 71–132.

Chomsky, Noam: 1980, 'On binding', *Linguistic Inquiry* **11**, 1–46.

Chomsky, Noam: to appear, *Lectures on Government and Binding*, Dordrecht: Foris Publications.

Cureton, Richard D.: 1979, 'The exceptions to Passive in English: a pragmatic hypothesis', *Studies in the Linguistic Sciences* 9, 39–53.

Dominicy, Marc: 1979, Review of Gross 1975, *Revue romane*, 293–318.

Ducrot, Oswald: 1975, 'Je trouve que', *Semantikos* **1**, 63–88. Reprinted in Ducrot *et al.*, *Les Mots du discours*, Paris, Editions de Minuit, 1980, 57–92.

Fauconnier, Gilles: 1976, 'Complement subject deletion and the analysis of *menacer*', in M. Luján and F. Hensey (eds.), *Current Studies in Romance Linguistics*, Washington, D.C., Georgetown University Press.

Gaatone, David: 1975, 'Réflexions sur les verbes pronominaux réfléchis et réciproques', *Folia Linguistica* 8, 199–222.

Gross, Maurice: 1975, *Méthodes en syntaxe*, Paris: Hermann.

Gross, Maurice: 1979, 'On the failure of generative grammar', *Language* **55**, 859–885.

Jackendoff, Ray: to appear, 'On Katz's autonomous semantics', to appear in *Language.*

Jones, Michael A.: 1979, *La Sémantique des Constructions à Contrôle et à Montée en Français*, unpublished "Thése de troisième cycle", Université de Paris VIII.

Kayne, Richard S.: 1975, *French Syntax*, Cambridge, Mass.: The MIT Press.

Kayne, Richard S.: 1981, 'Binding, quantifiers, clitics and control', in F. Heny (ed.), *Binding and Filtering*, London: Croomhelm.

Kayne, Richard S.: to appear, 'Unambiguous paths', in *Levels of Syntactic Representation*, Dordrecht: Foris Publications.

Kuroda, S. -Y.: 1974, 'Geach and Katz on presuppositions', *Foundations of Language* **12**, 177–200. Reprinted in French in Kuroda, *Aux quatre coins de la linguistique*, Paris, Editions du Seuil, 1979.

Kuroda, S. -Y.: 1977, 'Description of presuppositional phenomena – from a non-presuppositionalist point of view', *Lingvisticae Investigationes* **1**, 63–161.

Kuroda, S. -Y.: 1978, 'On Japanese passives', *Festschrift for Professor Kazuko Inoue*, Tokyo.

Morin, Chales-Yves: 1980, 'Les bases syntaxiques des règles de projection sémantique: l'interprétation des constructions en *faire*', *Lingvisticae Investigationes* **4**, 203–212.

Oehrle, Richard: 1976, *The Grammatical Status of the English Dative Alternation*, unpublished Doctoral Dissertation, Cambridge, Mass., MIT.

Postal, Paul: 1974, *On Raising*, Cambridge, Mass.: The MIT Press.

Rouveret, Alain, and Jean-Roger Vergnaud: 1980, 'Specifying reference to the subject: French causatives and conditions on representations', *Linguistic Inquiry* **11**, 97–202.

Ruwet, Nicolas: 1972, *Théorie syntaxique et syntaxe du français*, Paris: Editions du Seuil.

Ruwet, Nicolas: 1978, 'Une construction absolue en français', *Lingvisticae Investigationes* **2**, 165–210.

Ruwet, Nicolas: 1979, 'On a verbless predicate construction in French', *Papers in Japanese Linguistics, vol. 6, Memorial Volume S. I. Harada*, 255–285.

Williams, Edwin: 1980, 'Predication', *Linguistic Inquiry* **11**, 203–238.

WOLFGANG KLEIN

SOME RULES OF REGULAR ELLIPSIS IN GERMAN

1. INTRODUCTION

The rules of German, as stated in the best available grammars, do not admit sentences like (a) "Karl der Mutter", (b) "Er gehen", or (c) "Arnim eine". But they are perfectly appropriate in certain contexts – for example as the second conjunct in (a) "Otto half dem Vater, – ", (b) "Sie wird kommen, – ", (c) "Wolfgang aß zwei Haxen, – ", or after questions like (a) "Wer half wem?", (b) "Wird sie kommen oder er gehen?", (c) "Wer aß wieviele Haxen?" Constructions like (a)–(c) are usually called elliptic. They follow rules. In particular, they are characterized by two properties: first, they require a specific context in order to be appropriate, and second, their total meaning is not merely a function of the meaning of their components, but partially derives from the context. The phenomenon of regular ellipsis is well known, of course, but not too much is known about the rules which govern it. There is indeed a relatively extensive literature about some special cases like "gapping" and "coordination reduction" (for a recent survey, see Neijt 1979), but it is highly restricted both in perspective and range of phenomena covered. This paper is an attempt to approach the field from a somewhat broader point of view. In section 2, I will discuss in more detail what is understood by "regular ellipsis" and what kind of conditions characterize it. In section 3, five very general rules for regular ellipsis in German are presented and extensively discussed. These rules go far beyond what, to my knowledge, has been said about ellipsis so far, but they suffer from several shortcomings. One of them is connected with intonation; the importance of intonational conditions is demonstrated in section 4. I don't know what the precise nature of these conditions is. It appears that intonation is the key device to integrate contextual information, on the one hand, and information given in the utterance itself, on the other. But until we know more about this central process of human language in general, it seems premature to formulate specific rules for the intonational structure of ellipsis. So, only some of the problems will be outlined, but no attempt is made to solve them.

W. Klein and W. Levelt (eds.), Crossing the Boundaries in Linguistics, 51–78.

2. REGULAR ELLIPSIS

All natural languages have specific means for integrating contextual information. Ellipsis is one of them; others are deixis and anaphora.

By regular ellipsis, I refer to the phenomenon that, under certain complex conditions, the meaning of an utterance is systematically completed by the meaning of expressions which are not uttered but whose meaning is derived from the context. This contextual information may be taken from preceding or following utterances, from the perceivable situation – as in the utterance "not very impressive" said in front of the Niagara Falls – or else from factual knowledge; a typical case of this type is when a surgeon in an operation room says: "scalpel"; this utterance is regularly interpreted as "give me the scalpel", not as "this is a scalpel" or "buy a scalpel", although nothing in the utterance says the one or the other: it is the nurse's factual knowledge that leads her to the correct interpretation in the given context. The regularities of the last two types of ellipsis seem much less stable and much more difficult to grasp than those of verbal context, although there appears to be no principled difference between them.

In any event, it seems most sensible to begin with the clearest and most straightforward cases: that is, context information given by immediately preceding or following utterances. In this paper, we will only be concerned with cases of this sort. It should be noted, however, that this is a methodologically rather than theoretically motivated restriction. Most typical examples of verbal context are so-called adjacency pairs. The utterance "John" is regularly interpreted as "John is my best friend" after the question "Who is your best friend", but as "He called John" after the question "Whom did he call?" The utterance "No, I am" is regularly interpreted as "No, I am the greatest fighter of the world" after the statement "Dempsey is the greatest fighter in the world", but as "No, I am writing this paper" after the statement "Arnim is writing this paper". The best-known cases are probably coordinate structures, such as "John loves Mary and Peter (loves) Kate", where the second occurrence of "loves" may be omitted, or "John loves (his mother) and Peter hates his mother", where the first occurrence of "his mother" may remain unexpressed. The last example differs from all others mentioned before, since what has to be understood at this place is not yet available in the context – it is introduced only at the end of the second conjunct. These cases of "backward ellipsis" considerably differ from those in which the meaning of the items omitted is already available; but they fulfill the general definition of regular ellipsis given above, and so they are not excluded here.

All these types of ellipsis follow certain conditions of various kinds. There is a first class of conditions which may be stated in syntactic terms; for example, there might be rules such as

– in coordinations, an identical verb may be left unexpressed at the second (possible) occurrence, but not at the first,

– in coordinations, an identical object may be left out at the first occurrence, but not at the second,

– a "who"-question may be answered by an NP, but not by a VP (if after "Who is your best friend", the subject in the answer is omitted, the copula has to be left out, too; it is possible to answer "My best friend is John", or "John", but not "is John").

Other conditions must be stated in semantic terms. There is a very general condition, which says that the *meaning* of the elements that are left unexpressed has to be derivable from the context; that means that in the case of verbal context, it has to be derived from the preceding or following utterances. It should be clear that ellipsis, as understood here, is not a *deletion of identical expressions*, although at least some cases of ellipsis may be described that way. Let us illustrate this by some examples. In

(1) A man saw John and _ called the police[1]

the first conjunct introduces a particular man – that man, who saw John – and this man is now available in the context. It should be clear that this particular man is not introduced by the expression "a man", but by the whole first conjunct. There are devices to refer to the same individual in the second conjunct, for example the expressions "this man", "the man who saw John", or simply "he"; but in general, it is not possible to use the expression "a man" to this end, since this expression, when used in the position marked by "_" in (1), does not specifically refer to the man introduced in the first conjunct; roughly speaking, it refers to some arbitrary man which can, but need not be identical to the individual which is given in the context. If we say that the second conjunct is elliptical at a certain position, this means that the meaning of "called a man" is regularly completed by a meaning given in the context, and in (1), this contextually given meaning would not be identical to the meaning of "a man". In

(2) Peter saw John and _ called the police

the unit introduced in the subject position of the first conjunct, the individual Peter, could be referred to by the expression "Peter" in the second conjunct again, and we could imagine (2) as being derived by a deletion from

(3) Peter saw John and Peter called the police.

But from (1) it should be clear that this is just a special, though not unusual case. Later on, we will sometimes speak of "identical strings", for example identical noun phrases as in (3); this always means that the corresponding strings *mean the same*, not that they are necessarily *identical in form*.

There is an obvious question at this point: what does "to mean the same" mean? I don't know. With many others, I assume that any speaker has an intuitive concept of "sameness of meaning", and without intuitive judgments based on this concept (or related concepts, like hyponomy), semantic analyses of languages seem hardly possible. But any attempt to give a satisfactory reconstruction of this intuitive concept in terms of a precise semantic theory, say model-theoretic semantics, soon faces numerous empirical problems, of which the specific problems in connection with ellipsis are only a particular facet. No such attempt can be made here; I will just illustrate the complexity of the phenomenon by discussing some examples which, incidentally, are still relatively straightforward when compared to the cases of ellipsis discussed in later sections of this paper.

In (1) and (2), the element introduced by the first conjunct and kept in the second conjunct was an individual. This need not be the case in elliptical constructions. In (4), no individual is introduced, but some rather abstract meaning entity; but it still can be "maintained" in the second conjunct:

(4) A Chinese tends to esteem old age and _ will always respect his parents.

The unit introduced here is something like the typical Chinese or the "generic" Chinese, and if we want to go on speaking about the generic Chinese in the second conjunct, he need not be referred to explicitly. If, on the other hand, we want to speak about a specific Chinese in the second conjunct, he could be introduced by the expression "a Chinese", too. But no ellipsis would be possible in this case:

(5) A Chinese tends to esteem old age, and (a Chinese) once taught me why.

Strictly speaking, it is not correct to say that the specific Chinese in the second conjunct is introduced by "a Chinese" in the first; rather, it is introduced and available henceforth by the whole conjunct: "the Chinese person who first taught me why a Chinese tends to esteem old age". Individuals and generic units are two possible types of meaning that can be introduced into the context and function as "elliptical items". There are others; in

(6) The witness has to wait until he is called and _ will obtain $ 5 per hour waiting time

no specific and no generic witness is introduced. In the following German example (English behaves slightly differently in this kind of ellipsis)

(7) Zwei wertvolle Bücher fehlten und ein weiteres kostbares _ war zerfetzt

it is something like the concept of book which, after being introduced in the first conjunct by "Bücher", is understood, but left unexpressed at the place marked by "_" in the second conjunct. – In

(8) Arnim was sitting in the sun and Wolfgang (was sitting) in the kitchen

the meaning introduced in the context and used in the second conjunct is that of "was sitting", that is "to sit + past + continuous action" etc. In

(9) Arnim was sitting in the sun and Wolfgang (was) writing in the kitchen

it is only something like the idea of "past" which is introduced and maintained.

These examples may suffice to illustrate the point. As said already, I shall make no systematic attempt to clarify what possible types of meaning can be introduced and how this is done. In what follows, I shall say that some meaning unit which has already been introduced in the context such that it might function as a possible object of ellipsis is *thematic*. This term, then, is restricted to cases in which the contextually given unit is already available at the place where it is left unexpressed; it does not cover cases of "backward ellipsis" like

(10) John loves _ and Peter hates his parents.

Here, I shall speak of *contextually expectable* meaning units. By and large, the same kinds of meaning units may be thematic and (contextually) expectable, but first, this is an empirical question, and second, their function in language processing is probably different. In the present context, thematic units are always introduced by preceding utterances, and expectable units by following utterances. It may be that this distinction cannot be sustained if, for example, units given by perceptual context are taken into account too, for they might be fully simultaneous (e.g., in pointing while speaking). But this need not concern us here.

So much for semantic conditions. There is a third class which may vaguely be labelled "pragmatic", that is, conditions like elegance of style, economy – which traditionally is viewed as the main source of ellipsis – or the tendency to avoid ambiguity. Pragmatic conditions of this sort doubtless play an important role in the use of elliptic constructions, but nothing will be said about them in this paper.

And finally, there are intonational conditions; we will come to this problem in section 4. There is one point, however, which should be mentioned here. I don't think that intonational conditions should be treated as an independent fourth class. They are closely tied to syntactic and semantic conditions. The central semantic condition, for example, requires that the unit which is left unexpressed is either thematic or (contextually) expectable. Now, in German there seems to be a simple intonational device which characterizes a unit as thematic: to mark a unit as a thematic unit by verbal means, the expression which introduces it must have rising ptich. The precise position of the rise depends on the kind of unit to be introduced; if, as in (7), it is just a lexical concept expressable by a lexical item, it has to be in the stressed syllable of this item; if the unit to be introduced as thematic is expressed by a whole phrase, it has to be at the end of that phrase; it can also be at the end of a determiner, for example, if the noun following this determiner is *already* thematic. Let me give two German examples.

If Franz is not thematic, i.e. not given in the preceding context in a certain way, and we want to say about him that he is asleep, the pitch contour will be

(11) Franz schläft

The meaning expressed by "Franz" will be available, then, for ellipsis. Note that it is "thematic" exactly before "schläft" begins, that is, it is thematic already for "schläft". It is important to keep in mind that the "thematic score" of on-going discourse is not stable; thus, Franz is not thematic when the utterance "Franz schläft" begins, but he is thematic when "schläft" begins; hence, it would be more accurate to say "thematic at point *i* and to use subscripts to indicate this changing thematicity; for the present discussion, we just stick to "thematic" without further qualification. Another *caveat* might be in order here. Thematic (and contextually expectable) elements are *meaning units*, that is, for example, the person who is denoted by the expression "Franz", not this expression itself. If there is no misunderstanding possible, we shall sometimes label expressions (in a given utterance) as being thematic; it should be clear that this is only a loose (but less clumsy) way of speaking. Let us conclude this by a somewhat more complex example.

If the concept of "parcel" (Paket) has already been introduced as a thematic unit, and we want to speak about a large one, than this large one has to be introduced as thematic, and the resulting pitch contour looks like this:

(12) ein großes Paket

- - ¯ (¯ ¯)

What has been said so far, is somewhat simplified[2], but it gives a first idea of how semantic concepts and intonation structure are linked.

3. RULES OF REGULAR ELLIPSIS IN GERMAN

The general semantic condition has already been mentioned:

A: *A meaning need not be expressed if it is derivable from the context, that is, if it is either thematic or contextually expectable.*

Not every contextually derivable unit may be left unexpressed, of course. There are a number of additional syntactic restrictions. The following rules try to cover most of them. The following abbreviations are used: NC ("nominal complex") refers to noun phrases with a lexical noun (N); they also comprise constructions with a preposition, like "in der Kirche", "dort neben der Tür"; pronouns and clauses functioning as noun phrases are not included. By VC, I mean a finite verb, auxiliary or modal (F) with the very many nonfinite parts (IF) it may have in German; for example, "geht" is a VC which just consists of a finite part; "ist gekommen" consists of a finite part ("ist") and a nonfinite part ("gekommen"); "verprügelt worden müssen sein soll" has a long IF ("verprügelt worden müssen sein") and the modal "soll" as its F; the distinction between F and IF plays an important role in German syntax, and it is crucial, too, for ellipsis. The notion "F-environment" refers to F and its immediately adjacent elements. Similarly "N-environment" means N and adjacent parts; for example, in "ein junges Mädchen mit blonden Haaren", there are, among others, the following N-environments: "Mädchen", "junges Mädchen", "Mädchen mit", "junges Mädchen mit", etc. Let us turn now to the rules. Basically, there are three[3]:

E 1: *Identical final string may be left unexpressed at the first occurrence in coordinations.*

E 2: *Identical initial string may be left unexpressed at the second occurrence in coordinations.*

E 3: *Thematic F-environment and thematic N-environment may be left unexpressed.*

These are the central rules. There are some clear and some doubtful extensions of E 3:

E 4: *With F, any further constituent may be left unexpressed.*

E 5: *With F expressed, there is a tendency of possible omissions:*

a) *IF (non-finite part) of V rather than NC*

b) *pronoun rather than full NC*

c) *the earlier the easier*

d) *subject rather than direct object rather than indirect object rather than prepositional object.*

Furthermore, there is a very general restriction on E 2 – E 5:

B: *For E 2 – E 5 to apply, the syntactic relations of the remnant to the remaining part of the sentence must be clear, and they are not allowed to cross subordinate conjunctions.*

Admittedly, this formulation is not very clear. We shall discuss some of the problems it raises in the following sections.

In addition, there are several restrictions on what may be thematic.

As a rule, it can be said that syncategorematic units as such never introduce thematic meanings, that is, the function of, e.g., a preposition, a quantifier, a determiner cannot be maintained. This, too, will be discussed in the following paragraphs.

In the remainder of this section, we will consider these rules and some restrictions in more detail.

3.1 Rule E 1: *Identical final string may be left unexpressed at first occurrence in coordinations.*

This rule is the only one which concerns contextually expectable rather than thematic units. It is extremely general: the only restriction seems to be that the contextually derivable unit has to be introduced in a coordination. It is open, however, which units are coordinated – clauses, verbal complexes, nominal complexes, or what else.

Secondly, it is not required that the unexpressed element correspond to a constituent nor, that the remnants be a constituent:

(13) Fritz soll seiner (Mutter helfen) und Gabriele soll ihrer Mutter helfen.

Obviously, neither "Fritz soll seiner" nor "Mutter helfen" is a constituent.

Third, the two last non-identical units – "seiner" und "ihrer" in (13) – have a special function; as a rule, there is an opposition between them which is expressed by intonation; they are often described as being "stressed"; what happens is that the first item – "seiner" in the example above – is relatively high in pitch, whereas its counterpart is relatively low.

Fourth, ellipsis in accord with E 1 does not have pronominalization as an alternative. This is trivially true in cases like (13), since there is no anaphoric device for strings like "Mutter helfen". But even when just a single NC is omitted, it cannot be substituted for by a pronoun:

(14a) Fritz haßt _ und Irma liebt das Leben.
(14b) Fritz haßt es und Irma liebt das Leben.

This does not mean, of course, that pronominalization is impossible in this position, but then, the corresponding item has to be introduced earlier, for example in the preceding sentence.

Fifth, it should be noted that not all omissions of a final segment in a first conjunct are instances of E1. They may be a case of E 3, if the item in question has been introduced before, that is, if it is a thematic item. After a question like "How many books did they buy", it could be alternatively said:

(15) Fritz kaufte zwei Bücher und Karl kaufte drei Bücher.
(16) Fritz kaufte zwei _ und Karl kaufte drei Bücher.
(17) Fritz kaufte zwei Bücher und Karl kaufte drei _ .
(18) Fritz kaufte zwei _ und Karl kaufte drei _ .

The second of these possible answers formally corresponds to an E 1-ellipsis, at least in its written form; intonation in these different cases would vary, however.

Sixth, the fact that in E 1-ellipsis, the contextually derivable element (or elements) is not thematic, but contextually expectable, does not mean that the expectable and eventually introduced element cannot be *made* thematic at the point where it comes in, just as in example (11) above ("Franz schläft") "Franz" is not yet thematic, but is made thematic by a specific intonation. Since this is not the place to discuss the interplay of such intonational devices and notions like "thematic" in more detail, I will just illustrate this point by a single example; in

(19) Zuerst kochte (Franz zwei Eier) und dann aß Franz zwei Eier

the NC "zwei Eier" may have thematic intonation – with eventual terminal fall, however; in this case, "aß" must be low; or else, "zwei Eier" has a fall in the stressed syllable; in this case, "aß" must be high.

Seventh, E 1 raises a special problem, if, in the first conjunct, only one constituent is left behind; if this constituent happens to be an NC, it is immediately followed by the first constituent of the second conjunct. The result looks like a simple coordinate NC. In this case, the verb has to be pluralized, if it was not already, and so do other items relating to these adjacent NCs such as possessive pronouns. This may be illustrated by the following series of examples:

(20) Fritz schenkte seiner Mutter drei _ und Karl versprach seinem Vater zwei Bücher.
(21) Fritz schenkte seiner Mutter _ _ und Karl versprach seinem Vater zwei Bücher.
(22) Fritz schenkte _ _ _ _ und Karl versprach seinem Vater zwei Bücher.
(23) Fritz _ _ _ _ _ und Karl versprachen seinem Vater zwei Bücher.

Obviously, there is a break between (22) and (23). This a simple consequence of what has been mentioned under point 3 above – that there has to be a certain opposition between the two last nonidentical units; this makes no sense in (23) because what is said about Fritz and about Karl is absolutely identical. If a conjunction is used which allows for such an opposition, for example "oder" in its exclusive reading, E 1 can be applied "radically" – that is, omitting anything but one constituent in the first conjunct.

(24) Fritz oder Karl versprach seinem Vater ein Buch.
(25) Fritz oder Karl hat gewonnen.

If "oder" does not have this exclusive reading and hence there is no opposition between the two NCs, E 1 cannot be applied; verb and possessive pronoun have to be pluralized:

(26) Fritz oder Karl versprachen ihrem Vater ein Buch.

There are cases, however, in which the idea of lacking contrastivity seems not to work and in which E 1 applies up to the first constituent in the first conjunct. For example

(27) Gestern und heute besuchte mich Franz

does not – on the most plausible interpretation – mean that Franz came to see me sometime in the period defined by "gestern und heute", but rather that he came twice: one time yesterday and one time today; that is, it means the same as

(28) Gestern besuchte mich Franz und heute besuchte mich Franz.

This is not restricted to adverbials. Sentence

(29) Mir und Otto hat man ein Buch geschenkt

can mean, that the group consisting of the two of us got a book, or it can mean what is unambiguously expressed by

(30) Mir (hat man ein Buch geschenkt) und Otto hat man ein Buch geschenkt.

Hence, (29) could be seen as being produced by a "radical" application of E 1. So, it does not seem plausible to restrict E 1 in such a way, that it is not allowed to reach the first constituent, though there are some cases in which this "radical" application appears to be inappropriate. We shall take up this issue in later sections.

Finally, E 1 indeed seems to require formal and not only semantic identity. It is possible to say

(31) Franz bestellte zwei _ und der Kellner brachte vier Eier

but it seems impossible to say

(32) Franz bestellte zwei _ und der Kellner brachte ein Ei

although the concept of "egg" is contextually given in both cases. (Note that (32) is possible, of course, if "Ei" was thematical already, but then, it would be an E 3-ellipsis.) If this is true, E 1 *could* be treated as a real case of "deletion". It should be observed, however, that formal identity again includes intonational characteristics. E 1 must not override "contrastively marked" items. This may be illustrated by two possible coordinations of NCs (the "contrastive" items are marked by accents):

(33) vór diesem Tisch und hínter diesem Tisch
(34) vor díesem Tisch und hinter díesem Tisch

In (34) only "Tisch" may be left unexpressed, whereas in (33), the whole NC may be omitted at the first occurrence. This does not mean, however, that only "unstressed" elements may be left out; it is possible to say "vor und nach díeser Schlacht", and this could be even synonymous to "vor díeser Schlacht und nach díeser Schlacht", if "díeser Schlacht" has the same pitch pattern in both cases – for example in opposition to something mentioned earlier. Hence, this does not violate the principle that E 1 requires identity in form (but not only identity in form, of course).

3.2 Rule E 2: *Identical initial string may be left unexpressed at the second occurrence in coordinations.*

This rule accounts for cases of ellipsis like:

(35) Wird der Held den Drachen bezwingen und (wird der Held) die schöne Jungfrau heimführen?
(36) . . . weil der Held den Drachen bezwang und (der Held) die schöne Jungfrau heimführte
(37) Der Held hat die schöne Jungfrau bezwungen und (der Held hat) den Drachen heimgeführt.

Thus, it seems to be the exact counterpart of E 1, and in early discussions of "coordination reduction", E 2 has often been treated on a par with E 3. This is misleading, however. First, ellipsis according to E 2 may be replaced by pronouns (if the thematic item allows for pronominalization at all), whereas ellipsis according to E 1 does not:

(38) Fritz klopfte mir auf die Schulter und er/Fritz/ ∅ lachte dabei.

Note, however, that the use of pronouns underlies certain additional restrictions; for example, it often seems impossible to use a pronoun in this position, if it replaces a (direct or indirect) object:

(39a) Dieses Buch schätze ich sehr und (dieses Buch) habe ich schon mehrfach verschenkt
(39b) Dieses Buch schätze ich sehr und es habe ich schon mehrfach verschenkt.

But this is rather a general problem of pronouns, since it is always strange to use a pronoun like "es" in object function in this position. There is no doubt that, in principle, NC-ellipsis according to E 2 has pronominalization as a true alternative.

A second and more salient difference is, that E 2 very often does not permit deletion of formally identical expressions. This was already discussed in section 2 (examples (1)–(3)); so, the sentence "A man saw John and _ called the police" is not an elliptic version of "A man saw John and a man called the police", since the semantic condition A is not fulfilled.

Thirdly, E 2 cannot "intrude" as easily into the second conjunct as E 1 does intrude into the first one. It is not possible to omit "mit seiner" in the second conjunct of:

(40) Mit seiner Schwester verstand sich Fritz gut und (mit seiner) Mutter unterhielt er sich häufig.

This is a simple consequence of the restriction expressed by condition B: the whole syntactic characterization of the NC is destroyed, and its relation to "unterhielt er sich häufig" is no longer transparent. There seems to be an additional reason. The meaning unit which is left unexpressed has to be thematic; the semantic function of elements like determiners or quantifiers (in brief, "binders") cannot be thematic, however (as opposed to the meaning of quantified or determined NCs, of course).

In brief, E 1 and E 2 are not just versions of a single rule, that differ only in their direction of application: identical final string to the left, identical initial string to the right. Their difference is essentially linked to the different ways in which the contextually derivable meaning units are given: in E 1, they are contextually expectable, in E 2, they are thematic.

Despite its more restricted application as compared to E 1, E 2 is still relatively unbounded. Thus, it is not restricted to specific constituents, so long as B is obeyed. In the following examples, the meaning left unexpressed corresponds to an NC, an IF and an F, respectively:

(41) Der Suppe fehlt das Salz und (der Suppe) täte weniger Wasser gut.

(42) Heiraten wollte der Vater Maria und (heiraten) mußte er meine Mutter.

(43) Wollte Fritz Maria heiraten und (wollte) Irma sich mit ihm verloben?

Moreover, neither the unexpressed part nor the remnant need to be a constituent at all; "Irma sich mit ihm verloben" and "mußte er meine Mutter" are definitely not constituents, nor is "wird der Held" in (35) or "der Held hat" in (37) a constituent.

Incidentally, these examples also show that some recently advanced restrictions on forward deletion, such as the "major constituent constraint" advanced by Hankamer (1973) and by Neijt (1979) or the "head constraint" by Fiengo (1974) are simply wrong for German.

Just as for E 1, E 2 may lead to some problems when applied "radically" – that is, when everything but one constituent is left out. It then becomes difficult to distinguish between immediate coordination of the two adjacent constituents and far-going application of E 2. This may again be illustrated by a series of expanding identical initial strings (for illustrative purposes they are identical in form, but it should be kept in mind that this is not the crucial point):

(44) weil Fritz seiner Mutter ein Buch versprach und _
seinem Vater eine Brieftasche schenkte
(45) weil Fritz seiner Muter ein Buch versprach und _ _
eine Brieftasche schenkte
(46) weil Fritz seiner Muter ein Buch versprach und _ _ _ _
schenkte

In (46), "versprach und schenkte" could be treated as a "compound verb", but there appears to be no clear criterion to decide between this description and the ellipsis-analysis. There are cases in which the "compound"-analysis – often labelled "phrasal conjunction" – seems preferable, for example, if the immediately adjacent constituents are in subject position, as in

(47) Einen Porsche fährt/fahren Maria und Günter.

Even in this case, it is not fully clear to me whether the plural "fahren" is obligatory – which would clearly indicate the compound-NC-analysis – or whether "fährt" is also possible.

In should be noted that the really clear cases of phrasal conjunction have a completely different intonation pattern. In all cases of E 2, the two corresponding items can be marked by a high-low-opposition, as in (45) "ein Buch" (high) vs. "eine Brieftasche" (low), or in (46) "versprach" vs. "schenkte" (low). It seems less possible to use this pattern in cases like

(48) Männer und Frauen füllten die Kirche zur Hälfte.
(49) Der Vater und die Mutter lieben sich.
(50) Fritz säuft und frißt abwechselnd.

Applying the contrastive pattern to "Männer und Frauen" in (48) – and similarly to the phrasal conjunctions in (48) and (49) – even seems to indicate that each group filled half of the church. This probably demonstrates that there are E 2-applications up to the last constituent.

E 1 and E 2 are both restricted to coordinations, though to coordinations of various constituents. But their function in these coordinations is quite different from a processing point of view. What happens in E 1 is that processing – both production and comprehension – is interrupted at a certain point by "und", a second parallel segment is built up until the corresponding point has been reached, and then, the still missing but expectable part is completed for both parallel segments. There is no such interruption and eventual completion in E 2, but something that is already contextually available ("thematic") is taken over, it remains valid in a certain function, and only what is new is added: after the first conjunct has been completely built up, another one which is partly identical in meaning is added, and so long as it is identical, everything is "silently" maintained. New elements are expressed right from the point where the second conjunct starts being different.

The contextual information supplied within coordination is always given in the immediate neighbourhood. This allows for relatively unlimited application of ellipsis, since the unexpressed, but thematic or contextually expectable meaning is under close control. There is the possibility, too, to omit elements whose meaning is less immediately given: those of E 3, to which we will turn now.

3.3 Rule E 3: *Thematic F-environment and thematic N-environment may be left unexpressed*

This rule could be seen as an extension of the classical "gapping" – rule (Ross 1970, Neijt 1979). As stated above, it is much more general, however. In particular, it goes far beyond the "deletion" of identical verbs, and it also includes NC-ellipsis and VC-ellipsis (in what follows, we shall consider almost no cases of VC-ellipsis, since they are relatively uninteresting; cf. Klein (1979), ch. 9). E 3 concerns thematic elements, like E 2, but as opposed to E 2, its application is not restricted to coordination. The most typical examples outside coordination are partially thematic NCs and question-answer-sequences (or adjacency pairs in general).

Typical cases of NC-ellipsis are

(51) . . . eine Wohnung in Stuttgart und eine (Wohnung) in München

(52) . . . besaß zwei neue Häuser in Stuttgart; es stimmt aber nicht, daß er auch einige (neue Häuser) in München hatte.

(53) . . . nur eine Frau mit roten Haaren gesehen; gesucht hatte er eine (Frau) mit schwarzen (Haaren).

(54) Ich hätte gern ein frisches (Handtuch) [raising a dirty towel].

The last example goes beyond verbal context; it shows that E 3 needs no verbal introduction of the contextually given item. This seems less plausible for ellipsis of F-environments, however, though it is not fully impossible. In the following example, both F ("hast") and an adjacent NC can be omitted:

(55) (Hast du/haben Sie) gut geschlafen?

Coming back to cases of verbal context, it may be noted first that in (52), the elliptical NC "einige in München" could also mean "einige Häuser in München" rather than "einige neue Häuser in München". E 3 only says that an N-environment may be left unexpressed, if it is thematic; in (52), both "neue Häuser" and "Häuser" are contextually given, and there is no requirement that the omitted part should be maximal, that is, should correspond to the largest possible thematic element. The way in which "einige in München" is interpreted depends on pragmatic criteria. But it could not mean "einige neue Häuser in München", if the preceding sequence has not introduced "neue Häuser", but "Häuser" only.

NCs with a missing N-environment should still be syntactically viable NCs, that is, they should be able to function as subject, object, or whatever, to a verb, etc. It might be helpful at this moment, to have a somewhat closer look to NCs in general. Roughly speaking, an NC consists of four types of elements:

(a) A *binder* (quantifier or determiner), which indicates a specific way of selecting something from something. Typical possibilities of binding may be paraphrased as
- an arbitrary and not further specified element of _ ("a");
- an arbitrary and not further specified amount of _ (partitive, often not morphologically marked);
- the obvious selection from _ ("the").

(b) A filling of the slot left open by the binder. There are several possibilities:
- by expressions of *concepts*, for example nouns, nouns with attributes, etc.; "a girl" means, "from among the girls a not further specified element"; "the girl" means "from among the

girls that one which is obvious, for example, known already or identifiable when you hear this", etc.

– by gestures; "that one" (with gesture) means "among all visually identifiable elements in this situation that one I am pointing to";

– by other contextually available units, in particular by thematic concepts; this is the starting point for NC-ellipsis.

(c) Elements which determine the syntactic functions of the NC, for example case markers, prepositions, etc.

(d) Suppletive parts, for example appositions, non-restrictive relative clauses and other elements, which may be added to the bound and syntactically marked concept.

Suppletive parts can never be thematic, nor can binders or syntactic markers as such be thematic. One should distinguish, however, between the function of a binder within an NC and the function of an NC, if this NC has no explicit concept element; this is often the case in elliptic NCs. The binder – or more generally, the remnant – then represents the whole NC. This is clearly marked by strong morphological inflection:

(56) Fritz suchte ein Mädchen; schließlich fand er ein*es*, das ihm gefiel.

What is meant is that he found a girl, not a somewhat; but since the indefinite article represents the whole NC, it is strongly inflected: "eines", rather than "ein".

Rule E 3, as formulated above, does not exclude that the binder belong to the N-environment and hence is also left unexpressed, if this N-environment is thematic. This may lead to a violation of B; in the following example, only a preposition would be left to represent a full NC in relation to subject and verb, and this leads to an unacceptable sentence:

(57) Vor dem Haus war ein kleiner Garten und hinter _ _ lag ein Acker.

Leaving "dem Haus" unexpressed is impossible here, but this is not because E 3 would not allow it in principle; if no syntactic relation to the remainder of the sentence exists, a preposition like "hinter" may indeed be used as a remnant of E 3. After uttering the following question

(58) Lag der Acker vor dem Haus oder lag der Acker hinter dem Haus?

a number of items are made thematic, in particular a house, a field, and that this field was located somewhere. There are various possible answers, if it was behind, for example

(59)	Der Acker lag hinter dem Haus	(no ellipsis)
(60)	hinter dem Haus	(F-environment)
(61)	hinter	(F-environment and N-environment).

This was one example of the second important group of cases where E 3 goes beyond E 2. To illustrate this point further, it seems best to give some examples of F-environment omission, with or without simultaneous N-environment omission. First, consider question contexts:

(62) Wer ist gekommen? Fritz (ist gekommen).
(63) Wer hat wen geheiratet? Franz (hat) Maria (geheiratet). (E 3 + E 4)
(64) Was hat Karl gemacht? (Karl hat) geschrieben.
(65) Ist Franz gekommen oder Karl gegangen? Karl (ist) gegangen.

A second group are rejections and corrections:

(66) Karl ist gekommen. Nein, Franz (ist gekommen).
(67) Karl hat Irma geheiratet. Nein, Franz (hat) Maria (geheiratet). (E 3 + E 4)
(68) Karl hat angerufen. Nein, (Karl hat) geschrieben.
(69) Franz ist gekommen. Nein, aber Karl (ist) gegangen.

E 3 also applies to coordinations, of course:

(70) Karl ist gekommen und Fritz (ist gekommen).
(71) Karl hat Irene geheiratet und Franz (hat) Maria (geheiratet).
(72) Karl hat angerufen und (Karl hat) geschrieben.
(73) Franz ist gekommen und Karl (ist) gegangen.

There is a slight overlapping between E 2 and E 3 in this last case, if the F-environment happens to be the initial string of the second conjunct – as in (72). But it is not possible to integrate E 2 into E 3, since in non-coordination contexts it is not possible, as a rule, to omit the initial string, if F remains. Compare

(74) Karl wollte zuerst etwas essen und (Karl/er) mußte deshalb etwas warten.

(75) Weshalb kam Karl nicht? (Karl/er) mußte etwas warten, weil er zuerst etwas essen wollte.
(76) Karl kommt sofort. Nein, (Karl/er) muß zuerst etwas essen.

Only in (74), ellipsis is possible; in (75) and (76), the individual Karl introduced in the preceding utterance has to be referred to again in the second utterance, either by repeating the name or by a pronoun. Thus, there are cases in which E 2 is applicable within coordination, but no corresponding ellipsis is allowed in other contexts. On the other hand, E 3 would not cover all possible cases within coordinations; in (77) ellipsis is possible, but E 3 would not allow it:

(77) Weil der Vater der Mutter seine Rückkehr ankündigte und (der Vater) (der Mutter) einen Ausflug versprach.

Hence, it seems necessary to keep E 2 and E 3 apart. It should be noted that many elliptical utterances produced by E 3 look very peculiar, at first glance. At first glance, most people would deny that

(78) Er das Hemd

is a syntactically well-formed utterance but it is a perfect answer to "Hat er das Hemd gekauft oder sie die Hose?". On the other hand, there are indeed some problematic outcomes, two of which we will consider now. E 3 does not say that the F-environment left unexpressed must be *maximal*, that is, if two constituents are thematic, one of them F, it is not required that both are really left out. This leads to impossible utterances, however, at least in some cases:

(79) Hat Fritz geschlafen? Nein, Fritz (hat) gearbeitet.
(80) Wer hat das Spiel gewonnen? Bayern München (hat) (das Spiel) gewonnen.
(81) Was kaufte er denn? Er (kaufte) das Hemd.

In all of these examples, the other omissable elements "gearbeitet", "gewonnen" or "er" must be left unexpressed, too. This would be easily accounted for by stipulating that in E 3, the F-environment has to be maximal. I am not very much in favor of this – possibly inevitable – solution, for three reasons. First, I would like to consider ellipsis in general as an optional device, whose application is left to the speaker and to pragmatic factors. Second, it is still possible to be *fully* explicit: it is perfectly appropriate to express everything in (79)–(82). And third, maximality is not required by the other ellipsis rules, in particular not for the N-environment. So, I would rather leave this matter for further research. But it should be clear that there is a quick way to remedy inappropriate output of E 3, as in (79)–(82).

The second problem seems somewhat related. Among the possible answers to "Lag der Acker vor oder hinter dem Haus?" (see (59)–(62) above), we did not mention one which is allowed by E 3 but which is completely inappropriate:

(82) (Der Acker lag) hinter dem (Haus)

"Haus", of course, is an N-environment, so (82) should be possible. But it is not. Note, first, that "hinter dem" is allowed, of course, if "dem" is "stressed", for example in

(83) Lag das Haus hinter dêm Haus? Nein, hinter dêm.

or

(84) Hinter welchem Haus lag der Acker? Hinter dém.

The easiest solution again would be to stipulate maximality, in this case maximality of N-environment. This is wrong, however. It is not necessary, though stylistically better, to omit "blauen" in

(85) Willst du díesen blauen Pullover? Nein, díesen blauen will ich.

Note, too, that it is not odd to repeat an (unstressed) indefinite article:

(86) vór einem Baum und hínter einem _
vór einem Baum? Nein, hínter einem _

Hence, this difference must somehow be attributed to the different functions of the determiner. Seemingly, a definite article, if not specifically "stressed", cannot represent a full NC, whereas an indefinite one can. In (86) and (87), the indefinite article has its usual function: to select an arbitrary element from the class defined by the concept, in this case the concept of "tree". Since "tree" is thematic already, it need not be repeated, and "einem" represents the whole NC. But this does not answer the question *why* "dem" (in (82)) cannot have this representative function. Obviously, nothing new is selected by repeating "dem", as opposed to "einem", and thus, it is superfluous. But saying "hínter dem Baum" rather than "hínter dem" is even more superfluous, and it is perfectly possible. Hence, it cannot be a purely pragmatic reason, either, such as a principle like "avoid redundancy". This is also clearly shown by the fact that a definite article may be kept in E 1 – ellipsis:

(80) vór dem _ und hínter dem Baum

There might be a completely different answer still, though it is a somewhat speculative one. For E 3 to apply, the meaning units in question must be thematic, that is, they have to be marked as thematic in the preceding context. It may well be, that an NC with "einem" can introduce two items as thematic, namely the meaning of "ein N" – that is, some unspecified element of N – , and the meaning of N – that is, the concept expressed by N; hence, both of them are accessible to ellipsis, but if the meaning of N is chosen, a full NC must be freshly marked as thematic, and this is done by "ein". On the other hand, an NC with a definite article can only mark or leave as thematic its content as a whole. Thus, after "der Baum", there is no concept as such available for ellipsis, and that is why "hinter dem" is impossible in this context. This seems to be confirmed by several observations.

First, "hínter dem" (not "hinter dém", which is possible anyhow) is not excluded if the ellipsis is not thematic but is ellipsis of contextually expectable elements; in (88), the concept is contextually expectable, and hence, ellipsis is possible.

Second, "hínter dem" is appropriate, too, if the preceding context is such that not only an NC-content, but a concept, too, is thematic:

(89) Zu meinem Erstaunen kam zuerst ein Chinese. Erst hínter dem sah man . . .

In (89) "dem" is even obligatory: it is impossible to use simply "hinter"; that is, (89) is the exact counterpart to (82), where it is excluded.

Third, this line of explication fits well the general idea of how a definite article is often used: it takes up the content of an NC which is already available in the given context.

3.4 Rule 4: *With F, any further constituent may be left unexpressed*

This rule confirms and even extends the crucial role of the finite element: any constituent may be left out, if it is thematic and if F is left out, too. Just as in the case of E 3, some outcomes are not fully convincing. Let us consider some examples first:

(90) Karl schenkte seiner Mutter ein Buch und
(a) Otto _ seiner Tante _ _.
(b) Otto schenkte seiner Tante _ _.
(c) Otto lieh seiner Tante _ _.

(91) Karl hat seiner Mutter ein Buch geschenkt und
(a) Otto _ seiner Tante _ _ _.
(b) Otto hat seiner Tante _ _ _.
(c) Otto hat seiner Tante einen Ring _.

(92) Fritz liebt Wagneropern und
(a) Otto _ _.
(b) Otto liebt _.
(c) Otto haßt _.

(93) Hat Otto seiner Mutter ein Buch geschenkt?
(a) Nein, Karl _ seiner Tante _ _ _.
(b) Nein, Karl hat seiner Tante _ _ _.

(94) weil der Vater seiner Freundin einen Ring schenkte und
(a) der Onkel _ _ einen Diamanten _.
(b) der Onkel _ _ einen Diamanten schenkte.
(c) der Onkel _ _ einen Diamanten versprach.

In all of these cases, only version (a) is possible, that is, the version without F. Two observations are particularly striking:

– It does not matter whether F is a lexical verb, as in (90) or (92), or an auxiliary; it may also be a modal verb, a case not represented in the examples above. Hence, the special role of F has nothing to do with the lexical content of a verb, but with "tensedness".

– The position of F does not matter, either; it may be in final position, as in (94), or in second position, as in (90)–(93); it may also be sentence-initial, a case not illustrated here. Hence it is not the specific function of F to mark subordinate, main and question clauses which gives it its key role for ellipsis.

As the examples in (93) show, the preceding utterance need not be coordinated with the (possibly) elliptic utterance, nor spoken by the same speaker.

The key role of F as an entrance gate to ellipsis is obvious; both the application of E 3 and E 4 crucially depend on whether F is gone or not. But it is hard to understand this specific predominance of F.

One of the most vexing points is the fact that this restriction holds independent of whether F is thematic or not. This is best exemplified in (92b) and (92c). Obviously, in (92b), both "liebt" and "Wagneropern" are thematic; but it is not possible to omit "Wagneropern" alone, just as it is problematic to omit "liebt" alone (this corresponds to the possible requirement that the F-environment has to be maximal). In (92c), only "Wagneropern" is thematic, but it cannot be left unexpressed, either. Finally, it should be noted that all of these kinds of ellipsis presuppose a rather characteristic intonation pattern. The last element left behind must have a "contrastive" counterpart in the preceding utterance: "seine Tante" is contrasted to "seiner Mutter" in (90), "Fritz" is contrasted to "Otto" in (92), etc. This is not a sufficient condition, however, as (92c) demonstrates.

3.5 Rule E 5: *With F expressed, there is a tendency of possible omissions*:
(a) *IF (non-finite part) of V rather than NC*
(b) *pronoun rather than full NC*
(c) *the earlier the easier*
(d) *subject rather than direct object rather than indirect object rather than prepositional object.*

This rule differs from the others, since it reflects only a tendency. Essentially, it is an exception to E 4. In some cases, the presence of E does not hamper the omission of other constituents, and this possibility is gradual: there are several scales, like position, syntactic function, etc. Since E 5 seems weakly founded, I shall only give some examples of the most clear cases where it holds. These are omissions of IF (i.e. the non-finite part of VC) with F in second position and nothing left behind F:

(95) Karl wollte kommen und Otto mußte _.
(96) Wollte oder mußte Karl heiraten? – Er mußte _.
(97) Ist oder war er in München? _ Er war _ _.
(98) Karl war in München _ Nein, er ist _ _.

In the last example, it is not an IF that is omitted, but an adverbial with predicative function. In general, application of E 5 is favored if the F left behind is an auxiliary or a modal verb rather than a lexical verb. However, I have no idea whether these tendencies are nothing but an artificial product of my (and some other speakers') idiosyncratic judgments, or whether they reflect some deeper grammatical principles. In what follows, no particular use is made of this rule, except in some clear cases, as in the examples quoted above (for a more detailed discussion, see Klein (1979), ch. 3, 4 and 9).

4. PROBLEMS

The rules discussed in the preceding sections are very simple and extremely general. They cover most cases of ellipsis in German. This seems to be a desirable result. But the rules, as they are, are unsatisfactory on at least three grounds:

1. There are a number of cases in which they lead to wrong or at least doubtful results; some examples have been given above, such as (79)–(82); it is not difficult to find others.

2. In many cases, the application of an ellipsis rule depends on a specific intonation pattern which, in turn, reflects particular syntactic or semantic functions of various elements in the utterance. I have pointed out some of these cases, and we will come back to this problem in a moment.

3. The rules, as they are currently formulated, give no clear and consistent picture. Why is leftward ellipsis so strikingly different from the other cases? Why does coordination differ – as in E 2 – from other possibilities for establishing a context by introducing thematic elements? How should one explain the extraordinary role of the inflected part of the verb? For a description to be an explanation, it has to make us happy; this one does not.

There is a final point which needs clarification – the interaction of the five rules, in particular E 1 (the only backward gapping rule) with the other ones. In some cases, simultaneous application is quite natural, for example E 1 and E 2:

(99) Karl lieh seiner Mutter (1000 Mark) und (Karl) schenkte seiner Freundin 1000 Mark.

But there are numerous cases in which simultaneous application of E 1 and, for example E 3 seems questionable or simply impossible:

(100) obwohl er ein altes Auto (besaß) und ein neues (Auto) besaß
(101) Karl lieh seiner Mutter (1000 Mark) und Otto (lieh) seiner Freundin 1000 Mark.
(102) Karl lieh (seiner Freundin) (1000 Mark) und der Onkel (lieh) seiner Freundin (1000 Mark).

The first two cases sound somewhat strange, but not fully unacceptable, whereas (102) is very peculiar and, to my judgment, impossible.

All of the insufficiencies mentioned above require further investigation. In the remainder of this paper, I shall discuss one of them in more detail: intonational conditions. The aim of this discussion is modest: we shall briefly consider three elementary cases of ellipsis, all of them known from section 3, which strikingly highlights the role of intonation. I cannot offer any answer to the problems raised there, and I don't see how the best available analyses of intonation – like Bierwisch (1966) for German – could be extended such as to account for them.

Let us consider a first case. A simple sentence like

(103) Arnim kochte und Wolfgang aß ein passables Abendessen.

can be interpreted in two ways, depending on whether "ein passables Abendessen" is taken to be the object of "kochte", too, or whether "kochte" is used as an intransitive verb. In the first case, it is an instance of E 1-ellipsis:

(104) Arnim kochte (ein passables Abendessen) und Wolfgang aß ein passables Abendessen.

In the second case, it is essentially synonymous to a conjunction of the two elementary sentences:

(105) Arnim kochte. Wolfgang aß ein passables Abendessen.

These two interpretations of (103) are clearly discriminated by different intonation patterns. It is not obvious, however, how they should be described in terms of traditional intonation analysis. In the non-elliptic reading, "kochte" seems to have a sort of "terminal intonation"; this would mean in von Essen's classical description (von Essen, 1956), that the first syllable of "kochte" is deep and/or has falling pitch. In the elliptic reading, on the opposite, it must be indicated that the first conjunct is not yet terminated, that it has to be completed by some contextually expectable unit; this means that, on the traditional analysis, pitch is not allowed to go down; and this amounts to what is traditionally called "progredient intonation". Moreover, it seems that, in the elliptic reading, the first verb "kochte" and the second verb "aß" must somehow stand in a certain opposition, and this, too, is expressed by intonation, probably by what is most often called "contrastive stress". In the non-elliptic reading, there exists some contrastivity, too. It seems to hold between the two full verb phrases "kochte" and "aß ein passables Abendessen" rather than between the verbs; this corresponds to the often noted fact that a coordination in general needs both parallelity and contrastivity (cf. Lang, 1977). The intonation contrast between the two readings, then, is described by an opposition between "terminal" and "progredient" intonation of the last element in the first conjunct, and by a different position of the contrastive stress in the second conjunct. This description, though covering some facts, is unclear, misleading and wrong. It is unclear, because the central notions "terminal intonation", "progredient intonation" and "contrastive stress" are either undefined or ill-defined, as I have shown elsewhere (Klein, 1980).

It is misleading because even in the elliptic reading, there may be different types of opposition between the two verbs; it is perfectly possible to have "Abendessen" *stressed*, and then, there is still a certain contrast between the two verbs; but it is of a different type which I find hard to describe. In any event, the intonational opposition changes, too, in this case (we already noted this fact in section 3.1). And it is wrong because even in the non-elliptic reading, the verb has no terminal intonation, at least not in the sense in which it is usually described. Quite to the contrary, the last syllable is rising, and this indicates progredient intonation. Hence, there is an obvious difference between the two readings, but it seems difficult to deal with it in terms of the established intonation analysis of German.

Let us turn now to another example. A question like

(106) War Blut auf oder unter dem Bett, Dr. Watson?

may be understood and answered in two ways. First in the sense of

(107) War Blut áuf (dem Bett) oder (war Blut) únter dem Bett?

An appropriate answer, in this case, would be "unter", if there was some blood under the bed. The second interpretation is non-elliptic, it corresponds to a coordination of the prepositions, something like

(108) War Blut (auf oder unter) dem Bett?

Actually, there are some other possibilities, but it may be sufficient to consider just these two readings, of which the second one can be answered by "yes, there was" or "no, there wasn't". The first reading reflects a simultaneous application of E 1 – concerning "dem Bett" and E 2 – concerning "war Blut". Both readings are again discriminated by different intonation patterns. In the elliptic reading, both "auf" and "unter" have to carry some special stress, probably contrastive stress, whatever precisely this may be. The other reading allows for various contours, depending on whether (108) is the first question, whether there was a preceding question for something else on or under the bed before, or whether there was a preceding question concerning the existence of blood in some other place. In any of these cases, the intonation pattern is different from the one for the elliptic reading. I will not make any attempt to describe all of these various patterns in terms of traditional German intonation analysis.

As a third and last example, consider the sentence

(109) Mozart bewunderte Haydn und Beethoven.

Historically, this sentence seems wrong: Mozart did not admire Beethoven, he even did not know him; that is, we interpret this sentence in the sense of

(110) Mozart bewunderte Haydn und (Mozart bewunderte) Beethoven.

of which the second conjunct, reduced by an application of E 2 – or E 3, which amounts to the same in this case – is wrong. But (109) could also be the result of a different kind of ellipsis of E 3:

(111) Mozart bewunderte Haydn und Beethoven (bewunderte Haydn)

Taken in this sense, it is historically true. In fact, this interpretation and this kind of ellipsis is possible only with a very marked intonation pattern; both "Mozart" and "Haydn" must carry some "heavy stress" and "bewunderte Haydn" has to be something like "destressed", whatever this may be; (111) would be possible after a question like "Can you tell me two composers who admired Haydn?", that is, if "bewunderte Haydn" is thematic right from the beginning. Note that this question could also be answered by

(112) Mozart (bewunderte Haydn) und Beethoven bewunderte(n) Haydn.

that is, by applying an E 1-ellipsis, but then, we are faced with the problem of plural, again (cf. section 3.1 above). If we neglect this problem for the moment, the question is raised what the relation between (111) and (112) is and whether it is reflected in intonation, too.

These three examples suffice to demonstrate two points:

– Intonational structure plays a crucial role for the application of ellipsis rules. It discriminates between elliptic and non-elliptic readings of utterances as well as between different kinds of ellipsis, and it often determines whether an ellipsis rule is applicable at all.

– These intonational patterns are very complex, and a relatively detailed and reliable descriptive technique is necessary to grasp them.

Thus, more refined analyses of sentence intonation are a necessary prerequisite for a better understanding of how ellipsis works.

5. CONCLUSION

As has been pointed out already at the beginning of section 4, the rules for regular ellipsis presented here are unsatisfactory in several respects. They can't be more than very first attempts to express the linguistically significant regularities of this relatively unexplored domain. "Wenn wir alle aufgestellten Regeln in diesem Sinne für hypothetisch halten, so erscheint uns zugleich wesentlich, daß damit grammatische Einsichten formal handhabbar, überprüfbar und in einem präzisen Sinne verbesserbar gemacht werden." (Bierwisch 1966)[4].

NOTES

1 Throughout this paper, places where an element is understood but not expressed are usually marked by "_"; if it seems to help understanding, several of these dashes are used, e.g., "_ _ _" for three words left out.

2 For example, the pitch of "Paket" could be lower; the example is taken from a larger utterance "ein großes Paket und ein kleines Paket", where there is an opposition between the two parcels.

3 The following rules are based on a rather detailed analysis of clauses, VCs and NCs; adverbs and various particles have not been considered. For details, see Klein (1979).

4 I wish to thank Simon Garrod, Robert Jarvella, Willem Levelt, and William Marslen-Wilson for helpful criticism.

REFERENCES

Bierwisch, M.: 1963, 'Grammatik des deutschen Verbs', *Studia Grammatica* **2**, Berlin: Akademie-Verlag.

Bierwisch, M.: 1966, 'Regeln für die Intonation deutscher Sätze', in Studia Grammatica 7, 99–201, Berlin: Akademie-Verlag.

von Essen, D.: 1956, *Grundzüge der hochdeutschen Satzintonation*, Ratingen: Henn.

Fiengo, R. W.: 1974, 'Semantic conditions on surface structure', M.I.T. – Dissertation.

Hankamer, J.: 1973, 'Unacceptable ambiguity', in *Linguistic Inquiry* **4**, 17–68.

Klein, W.: 1979, 'Reguläre Ellipsen im Deutschen', unpublished Ms., MPI für Psycholinguistik, Nijmegen.

Klein, W.: 1980, 'Der Stand der Forschung zur deutschen Satzintonation', in *Linguistische Berichte* **68**, 3–33.

Lang, E.: 1977, 'Semantik der koordinativen Verknüpfung', *Studia Grammatica* **14**, Berlin: Akademie-Verlag.

Neijt, A.: 1979, *Gapping*, Dordrecht: Foris Publications.

Ross, J. R.: 1970, 'Gapping and the order of constituents', in M. Bierwisch, K. E. Heidolph (eds.), *Progress in Linguistics*, Den Haag: Mouton, pp. 249–259.

DANIÈLE CLÉMENT AND WOLF THÜMMEL

SOME REMARKS ON SCOPE PHENOMENA

> Um den Zuhörer und Leser zu nöthigen, mit seiner Aufmerksamkeit immer zu dem, was folget, fortzueilen, hat sich der Grieche und Lateiner dieses zum Gesetze gemacht: alles das, was von andern regiert wird, vor= und das, wovon es regieret wird, nachzusetzen.

0. The principle quoted from Meiner (1781: 355) expresses an idea that – *in nuce* – frequently recurs in the long tradition of efforts to describe the architecture of natural language expressions. Of course, there is great variation in terminology as well as in the conceptual realization of the basic idea. We do not want to maintain that these attempts are all equivalent or refer to exactly the same phenomena. The only thing that is important for our exposition is that – despite all the differences in detail – a distinction should be made between something that

(a) depends on, is governed by, is head with regard to, is nucleus of, is determined by, is the scope of

some other thing which

(b) refers to, governs, is modifier with regard to, is satellite to, determines, operates on (is operator, functor, relator in respect to)

the first. The things in question are, as a rule, parts of expressions which belong to a certain natural language, as e.g. to English, Chinese or Bavarian. But there are also cases where one is dealing with formal languages in this context.

Our aim in this paper is to discuss some conceptions which seem to show similarities to that expressed in the Meiner quotation, and to attempt a reconstruction of the underlying idea within the framework of context-free syntaxes. To unify terminology we shall call the phenomena we find in the sense of (a) and (b) 'scope phenomena'.

1. In this section we shall give a sort of documentation in order to illustrate what we have in mind.

W. Klein and W. Levelt (eds.), Crossing the Boundaries in Linguistics, 79–93.

It is of no interest here whether the hypothesis quoted from Meiner is right or not. What is important here is his conception of the structure of what he, following the tradition, calls periods. Taking into account his comments on a series of examples from Greek and Latin, this structure can be represented schematically by (1), where the arrow ↑⎿⏌ means that in each case the right section governs the left one:

(1)

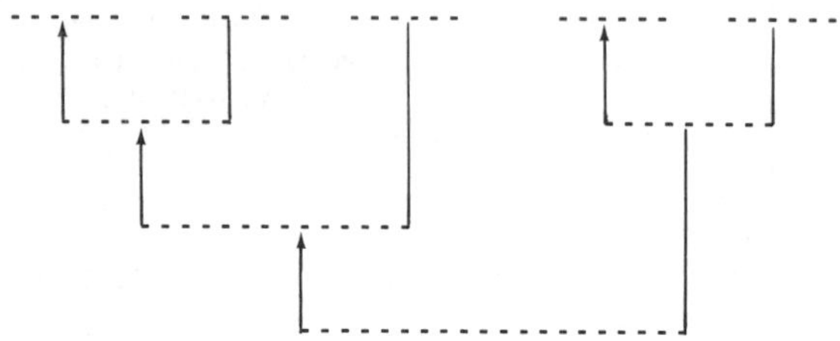

Quite a similar conception has been formulated by von der Gabelentz (1875: 137); he argues "dass jedes folgende Glied die vorhergehenden näher bestimmt, mit anderen Worten, das [psychologische] Prädikat zu diesem bildet, während dieses zu jenen sich als [psychologisches] Subjekt verhält". According to von der Gabelentz (1887: 104) this principle should hold not only for German, but "mit hoher Wahrscheinlichkeit [. . .] für die Sprachen überhaupt": "jedes Satzglied verhält sich zu der Gesamtheit der vorhergehenden als psychologisches Prädikat zum psychologischen Subjekte; die Grenze zwischen beiden ist also eine sich ruckweise verschiebende".

The difference between Meiner and von der Gabelentz is primarily a terminological one: (i) "a determines b" instead of Meiner's "a governs b", and (ii) "psychological subject" and "psychological predicate" introduced by von der Gabelentz. It is evident that von der Gabelentz's assumptions have a considerable affinity with the dichotomy of 'theme' vs. 'rheme' proposed by Czech linguists (above all by Mathesius, e.g. (1941)).

A somewhat different approach has been taken by the Danish linguist Aage Hansen (1933: 105), who proposes a structure like (3) for (2):

(2) Han udmærkede sig ganske særligt ved en naiv mangel på kendskab til alle praktiske ting

(3)

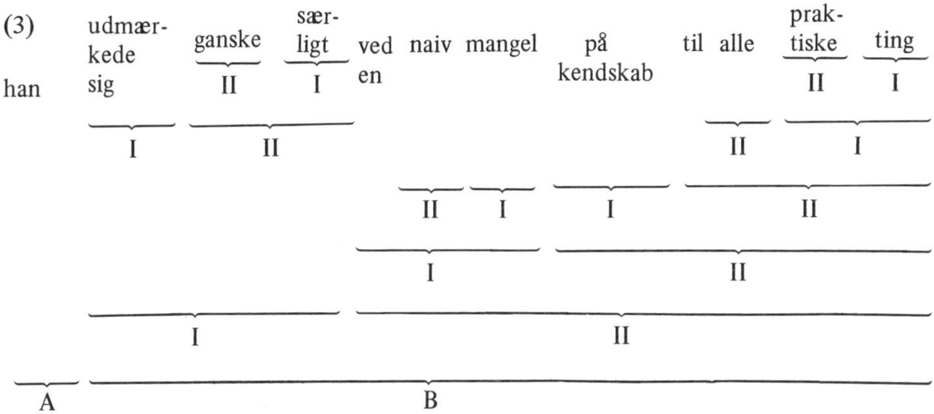

I and II in (3) are to be understood as 'II is determined by I, is qualified by I, is modified by I' and 'I determines II, qualifies II, modifies II' respectively (Hansen 1933: 89).

It is a widespread custom to speak of determination in this connexion. Thus, Bally (1944/65: 102) assumes, that every syntagm is divided into two parts: the déterminant and the déterminé:

> On retrouve ce genre de rapport dans tous les types de syntagmes: pas de sujet sans prédicat et vice versa; pas de copule sans un terme qu'elle rattache au déterminé (par exemple: pas de verbe transitif sans un complément d'objet; inversement, pas de complément d'objet sans un verbe transitif, etc.).

It is within this linguistic tradition that Martinet (1969/75: 114) characterises one way of making explicit the relation between a linguistic unit in the chain and the rest of the chain, i.e. between a "head" and some other unit which is "tagged to the head": "We shall call the type of linguistic relationship existing between the head and the second element one of *determination,* the element added to the head being the *determinant*".

As well as the terminology quoted in section 0, there is another widespread manner of referring to the phenomena, one that is known from school grammar: instead of saying that some element A determines some other element B when referring to scope phenomena, one says that A belongs to B. We shall take an example from Bierwisch (1963: 35), where he – as Meiner does in the passage quoted – links scope phenomena with order phenomena: "Läßt man die vorhin erwähnten Probleme der Artikelform und der Pronomina beiseite, so gilt im allgemeinen, daß im Satz ohne kontrastive Hervorhebung die Satzglieder um so näher am Satzende stehen, je enger sie zum Verb gehören".

2. In all the examples considered in section 1 the major distinction which is made between parts of one and the same expression is a binary one, though we do not mean to suggest that each of the two parts should not be open to subsequent analysis. Thus, within a categorial syntax, a functor may be complex and its scope (i.e. its set of arguments) may also have more than one member. Further, if a categorial syntax is to describe a natural language (NL) in such a way that an expression e_{FL} (of the formal language, FL, defined by that categorial syntax) divided into a functor and the corresponding scope is associated with an expression e_{NL} of the natural language being described, then there is no reason to presume that either the part e_{NL_f} corresponding to the functor of e_{FL} nor the part e_{NL_s} corresponding to the scope of the whole expression e_{FL} be simple. Likewise it is by no means intended by the respective authors that a dêterminant or a dêterminé in the sense of Bally and others should not consist of more than one element. It might be objected that the distinction made by Bally between 'déterminé' and 'déterminant' is not necessarily a binary one, since he also speaks of double determination in cases as e.g. French *plus – e*, which determines *fort* in *plus forte* (Bally 1965: 298, § 487). Nevertheless, *plus* and *-e* could easily be taken as two separated components of one discontinuous dêterminant.

Such cases of discontinuity of the two parts which are to be distinguished within one expression are also found in quite different theoretical and methodological frameworks. Elementary transformations of the type introduced by Harris (1964/1970: 487f.) appear to be a good example in this respect. So, e.g., *be--ing* and *have--en* are two operators on V (verb) and, evidently, they are discontinuous.

An example of discontinuous scope is given by E. Lang (1979: 205), who proposes for the German expressions (4) through (6) one common scope-structure (7):

(4) Hans schläft leider wahrscheinlich hier.
(5) Hans schläft wahrscheinlich leider hier.
(6) Wahrscheinlich schläft Hans leider hier.
(7) LEIDER [WAHRSCHEINLICH [p]]

[WAHRSCHEINLICH]p]] in (7) represents the scope of *leider*, which is evidently discontinuous in (4) through (6).

In this regard difficulties may arise if a description of scope phenomena is attempted by means of a categorial syntax. Taking (8) through (10) into account, which are similar to (4) through (6), Lehrberger (1974: 37) suggests:

Presumably *unfortunately* is a sentence operator (with index s/s in the first example [8]), but it may appear to the left, to the right or be inserted within its operand.

(8) Unfortunately, the crowd was angry.
(9) The crowd, unfortunately, was angry.
(10) The crowd was angry, unfortunately.

3. On the basis of the picture we have drawn in the previous sections it may be stated that there is, on the one hand, a tendency within the tradition of linguistics to cut up expressions of a natural language into two – not necessarily continuous – parts and that there is, on the other hand, a tradition of doing the same when constructing complex expressions of a formal language. Indeed, expressions of a formal language are built up by defined rules. This is not so in the case of the expressions of a natural language, though there might be theoreticians who would claim that the differences between the two kinds of language could – in principle – be overcome.

We start from the much less strong assumption that the linguistically observable differences between formal and natural languages are great enough to raise the question of how to handle them with regard to the problems discussed here, i.e. those of scope phenomena. Consequently we shall distinguish between scope as applied to formal languages and scope as applied to natural ones.

In this section we shall discuss briefly the question of whether scope has to do with syntax or with semantics, or with both.

It might be argued that scope phenomena are, on principle, purely semantical ones. Such a view is suggested by several formulations found in linguistic literature.

As far as formal languages are concerned at least, there should not be any doubt about the fact that one can speak of scope without any reference to semantics, i.e. of scope in a purely syntactical sense. We shall take an example from Cresswell (1973: 13). Let the ordered pair $\langle \Delta, S \rangle$ be a propositional language

where $\Delta = \langle \Delta_0, \ldots, \Delta_k \rangle$ is a finite sequence of pairwise disjoint, possibly empty, finite sets, and S [. . .] the smallest set such that:

1.1 $\Delta_0 \subseteq S$.
1.2 If $\delta \in \Delta_n (1 \leqslant n \leqslant k)$ and $\alpha_1, \ldots, \alpha_n \in S$ then $\langle \delta, \alpha_1, \ldots, \alpha_n \rangle \in S$.

Given the syntax (1.1 & 1.2), one can safely say – as Cresswell (1973: 5; 269), though only incidentally, does – that any sequence $\alpha_1, \ldots, \alpha_n$ is the scope of the corresponding functor δ. The same is valid ceteris paribus for categorial languages (Cresswell 1973: 78f.).

As an illustration suitable for our purposes we shall choose negation. Let $\sim \in \Delta_1$ and $\sim p \in S$. If $\alpha_{n=1} = p$, then p is the scope of $\sim$. Further, if $\alpha_1 = \sim p \in S$, then $\sim p$ is the scope of $\sim$ in $\sim(\sim p)$, the scope being set between brackets.

It goes without saying that negation also can be treated semantically. An illustration in the classical style is given by Cresswell (1973: 18): the value assignment V to $\sim \in \Delta_1$ "might be $\{\langle 1, 0\rangle, \langle 0, 1\rangle\}$, i.e. $V(\sim)$ associates 0 with 1 and 1 with 0, i.e. in functional notation $(V(\sim))(0) = 1$ and $(V(\sim))(1) = 0$".

In natural languages we are confronted with quite a different situation, because there is no syntax and no semantics inherent in them or in the expressions belonging to them. Indeed one might say that utterances of NL-expressions show certain regularities which are accessible to syntactical and even to semantical treatment, but that this treatment has to be carried out by the linguist. A terminological difficulty arises in so far as 'semantics' could mean at least two different things. Firstly, given a description d by means of a (formal) syntax, then 'semantics' could refer to the NL-expressions which are described by d (these problems are briefly discussed by Moreau 1975: 35f. and by Volkhard Scholten, forthcoming; cf. also Cresswell 1973: 210ff.). Secondly, 'semantics' could mean that a certain NL-expression could have one or more meanings, that we can use it (in the form of an utterance) when communicating in a meaningful manner, that one can paraphrase it, that one can extract presuppositions from it, and so on.

Unfortunately the distinctions we are proposing for consideration are not always recognized by those linguists who discuss scope phenomena. E. Lang (1979: 205) correctly points out that 'scope' and especially 'scope of an operator' are loans from symbolic logic. Of course one finds this terminology only sporadically in texts on symbolic logic. Within his approach to linguistic semantics E. Lang (1979: 204f.) confines 'scopus' (or 'Geltungsbereich') to semantics. This is simply permissible, although not necessary, terminological convention. The syntactical pendent to Lang's 'scope' is termed 'Bezugskonstituente' (i.e. 'constituent of reference').

For our part, however, we hesitate to decide whether the distinction drawn between one scope part and one non-scope part of a NL-expression should be called a syntactical distinction or a semantical one. Throughout the following discussion we shall leave this question open. The main point here is the fact that one can distinguish between scope and non-scope at all, and this on certain grounds, whatever these might be. We do not want to exclude the possibility that intuitive judgements on scope phenomena might be closely bound to different degrees of cohesion between the parts of a given expression. Cohesion intuitions are mentioned in Chomsky (1965: 101), and discussed in more detail by Levelt (1973–III: 25ff.), nevertheless they are far from being sufficiently investigated.

It is the primary aim of the following sections to consider some ways of constructing a syntax in such a way that it not only matches the division into scope and non-scope parts of NL-expressions, but also provides some criteria which allows us to decide which of the two parts should be taken as scope.

It should be added that it is not at all obligatory to associate functors, operators, relators, and the like which happen to occur in FL-expressions with any parts of NL-expressions. Thus, the connexions in the system of Grunig (1978) which correspond in certain respects to operators (or to functors, as Cresswell would say) are left uninterpreted in such a way.

4. For the discussion in this section we shall take context-free (CF) syntaxes as a basis. The reason for this choice is firstly that CF-syntaxes are very current in linguistic tradition, and secondly that for every categorial syntax K a CF-syntax Σ can be constructed in an effective way such that $L(\Sigma) = L(K)$ (cf. e.g. theorem 4.1 and its proof in Gladkij 1970: 123). Last but not least, we ourselves have tried to describe some properties of natural languages by means of CF-syntaxes (e.g. Clément & Thümmel 1976), and we are convinced that natural languages show many more regularities describable by CF-syntaxes than is commonly supposed.

As the division into one scope-part and one non-scope part within a NL-expression is a binary one, it is convenient to take that proper subset of CF-syntaxes for which, given $\varphi \rightarrow \psi$ as the general form of the rules, the length of ψ is $0 < \lg(\psi) \leqslant 2$. In order to gain as many criteria as possible for our purposes we also allow the length of ψ to be 1. Clearly, the case of $\lg(\psi) = 1$ involves certain undesired properties of the syntaxes in question. Therefore special conditions should be formulated such that these properties cannot appear. We shall assume that appropriate conditions have been specified.

Since structural descriptions obtained from CF-syntaxes can be given in the form of labelled trees, we shall make use of this kind of representation.

Let us now take a structure like (11), based on a given CF-syntax Σ_{11}:

(11)

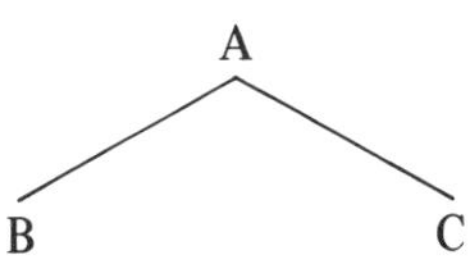

A corresponding structure based on a categorial syntax K_{12} (in a customary notation) could be (12):

(12)

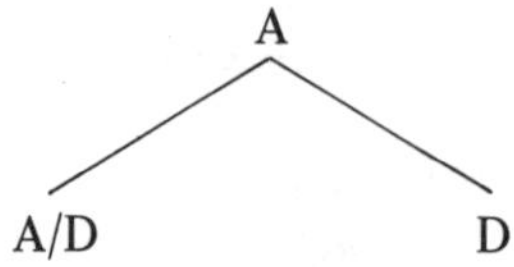

But, depending on the choice of those symbols which represent the basic categories of the categorial syntax, it is also possible to consider (13) an analogue to (11) on the basis of a categorial syntax K_{13}:

(13)

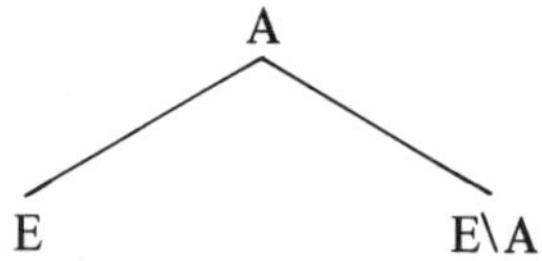

The difference between (11) on the one hand and (12) and (13) on the other is evident: for (12) and (13) it is clear which of the two nodes dominated by the A labelled node is to be understood as functor and which is not. This is determined by the previous setting up of the basic and non-basic categories of K_{12} and K_{13}, respectively. With regard to (11), and thus to Σ_{11}, there is no such procedure.

Methodologically, it is a very important but sometimes neglected point that there is for every categorial syntax K_i with more than one basic category a different categorial syntax K_j such that $L(K_i) = L(K_j)$, and certain (but not all) basic categories of K_i appear to be non-basic in K_j. An illustrative example is given by Kratzer, Pause and von Stechow (1973–I: 204f.) for (14), which might be described by (15) as well as by (16):

(14) gott schuf den affen

(15)

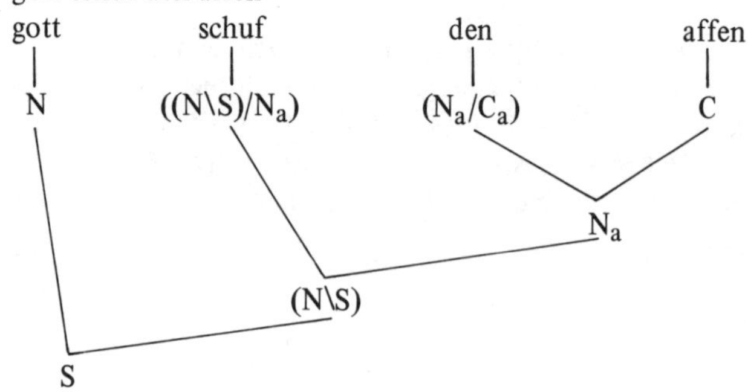

(16)

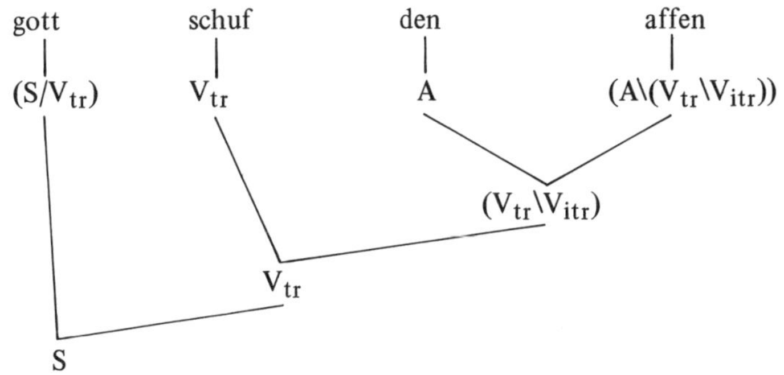

If we want to equip a CF-syntax of the defined subtype in a comparable way with that property characteristic of categorial syntaxes, we have to look for formal features that allow us to designate for each pair of nodes (α, β) both directly dominated by the same node γ either α or β to be associated with the scope part of the NL-expression described by the labelled pair (α, β). Our aim is to do this in a non-arbitrary manner, i.e. we shall try to use a device which avoids – as far as possible – such alternatives as shown by (15) vs. (16).

5. Before we are able to formulate some remarks on this point, a variety of concepts must be defined:

DEFINITION 1: 'initial node a_0'
Given a CF-syntax $\Sigma = (V_t, V_n, \mathscr{I} \in V_n, R)$, let Δ be the set of all trees in Σ whose roots are labelled with the initial symbol $\mathscr{I}$; then the root ρ of each member of Δ is called 'initial node a_0' with respect to Σ iff there is no path which enters ρ. $\Delta^{\oplus} \subset \Delta$ is then the set of all trees which have the initial node a_0 as root.

DEFINITION 2: 'recursive symbol of Σ'
A symbol $A \in V_n$ is called a 'recursive symbol' iff there is at least one $\delta \in \Delta$ in Σ such that there is at least one path sequence in which more than one node is labelled A.

DEFINITION 3: 'recursion sequence'
Let $s = a_i, \ldots, a_k$ be a path sequence in $\delta \in \Delta$; then s is called a 'recursion sequence' iff a_i and a_k are labelled with the same symbol $A \in V_n$, and there is no a_j in s $(0 \leqslant i < j < k)$ which is likewise labelled A.

DEFINITION 4: 'a_i-distance of a symbol at a node a_j'
Let $s = a_i, \ldots, a_j$ be a path sequence in $\delta \in \Delta$ and a_j labelled $A \in V_n$. Then the length of s is called 'a_i-distance of A at a_j'.

DEFINITION 5: 'Minimal a_i-distance of a symbol'
Let $s = a_i, \ldots, a_k$ be a path sequence and $A \in V_n$ the label of a_k. Then the length of s is called 'minimal a_i-distance of A' iff there is no node a_j in s ($i < j < k$) which is likewise labelled A.

DEFINITION 6: 'absolute minimal root distance of a symbol'
Let m be the smallest minimal a_0-distance of a symbol $A \in V_n$ in Δ. Then m is called the 'absolute minimal root distance of A'.

DEFINITION 7: 'strictly recursive symbol'
Let $A, B \in V_n$ be recursive symbols. A is called 'strictly recursive symbol' with regard to Σ iff conditions (i) through (iv) are satisfied:

(i) there is at least one recursion sequence $a_i, \ldots, a_k$ in Δ;
(ii) a_i and a_k are labelled A;
(iii) $m(a_0, \ldots, a_i) = i$ is the absolute minimal root distance of A;
(iv) there is no node a_j ($i < j < k$) such that
 (a) a_j is labelled B, and
 (b) the absolute minimal root distance of B is less than that of A.

DEFINITION 8: 'rule block'
Let $\varphi \to \psi$ be the general form of the rules of Σ. The set of R_A of all rules which have one and the same symbol $A \in V_n$ for φ are called a 'rule block'.

DEFINITION 9: 'minimal rule'
Given a rule block R_A, then every member r_a of R_A is called a 'non-minimal rule' iff ψ_a of r_a contains a symbol $Q \in V_n$ which appears likewise in ψ_b of a rule r_b ($a \neq b$) in R_A. All other rules of R_A are called 'minimal rules' relative to R_A.

DEFINITION 10: 'self-embedding'
Given a tree $\delta \in \Delta^{\oplus}$ and a path sequence $s = a_i, \ldots, a_j$ ($0 \leqslant i < j$) in δ. A symbol $A \in V_n$ is a self-embedding at a_j iff A is strictly recursive, and both a_i and a_j are labelled A.

DEFINITION 11: 'parasitic self-embedding'
Provided that $A, B, C, D \in V_n$, let $s = a_i, \ldots, a_k$ $(0 \leqslant i < k)$ be a path sequence in $\delta \in \Delta^{\oplus}$, and a_i and a_k labelled with one and the same symbol A. Then A is called 'parasitic self-embedding' at a_k iff conditions (i) and (ii) are satisfied:

(i) Σ contains a binary minimal rule $r_a = \varphi_a \rightarrow \psi_a$ in which A and B appear in ψ_a, and a_k is labelled by means of r_a;
(ii) there is no node a_j in s $(i < j < k)$ which is labelled in one of the following ways:
  (a) B;
  (b) a strictly recursive symbol C, whose absolute minimal root distance is less than that of A;
  (c) D by application of a non-minimal rule $r_b = \varphi_b \rightarrow \psi_b$, D appearing in ψ_b, but not in any unary rule of the same rule block.

DEFINITION 12: 'annex node'
Given a tree $\delta \in \Delta^{\oplus}$ within which two nodes a_{i_j} and a_{i_k} $(j \neq k)$ are immediately dominated by a_{i-1}; and given $A, B \in V_N$ appearing in ψ of a binary rule $r = \varphi \rightarrow \psi$, $r \in R_Q$, then a_{i_j} is called an 'annex node' if a_{i_j} is labelled A, a_{i_k} is labelled B and one of the conditions (i) through (iv) is satisfied:

(i) r is a minimal rule, and B is a parasitic self-embedding at a_{i_k};
(ii) r is a minimal rule, A is not a parasitic self-embedding at a_{i_j}, B is not a parasitic self-embedding at a_{i_k}, and one of the following two conditions is satisfied:
  (a) B is strictly recursive, and A is not;
  (b) B is recursive, and A is not.
(iii) r is not minimal, and there is no unary rule in R_Q with $\psi = A$, but there is one with $\psi = B$, and there is no non-minimal rule in R_Q with $\psi = CB$ or $\psi = BC$ if there is a minimal rule in R_Q with $\psi = C$;
(iv) r does not satisfy any condition (i) through (iii), but one of the following:
  (a) B is a parasitic self-embedding at a_{i_k}, but A is not a parasitic self-embedding at a_{i_j};
  (b) B is strictly recursive, but A is not;
  (c) B is recursive, but A is not.

Following current terminology, we shall call A 'optional' if condition (iii) is satisfied. If a_{i_j} is an annex node, a_{i_k} is called a 'central node'.

A non-optional node a labelled with a symbol $S \in V_t$ will be called 'neutral' if:

S is not a parasitic self-embedding at a,
S is not a self-embedding at a,
S is not strictly recursive,
S is not recursive.

6. Definition 12 enables us to distinguish between a scope node and a non-scope node for every pair of labelled nodes, which firstly are dominated by one and the same labelled node (in the following called 'neighbour nodes') and secondly, fulfill one of the conditions marked by a plus in table (17).

(17)

label (a_{i_k}) = B / label (a_{i_j}) = A	parasitic self-embedding	self-embedding	strictly recursive	recursive	optional	neutral
parasitic self-embedding	–					
self-embedding	+	0				
strictly recursive	+	+	0			
recursive	+	+	+	0		
optional	–	+	+	+	–	
neutral	+	+	+	+	+	0

The definitions 1 through 12 exclude the case that a pair of neighbour nodes are labelled in such a way that for either node the labelling symbol is a parasitic self-embedding or optional in the sense of Definition 12.

There are, however, four cases in which the desired distinction is not met by our definitions. These are marked by 0 in table (17).

It is obvious that (iii) of definition 12 is a reformulation of the idea underlying the conception of one type of endocentric phrase, introduced by Bloomfield (1933: 194ff.). But the other configurations are more complicated.

They may be taken as a reformulation of the ideas connected with the terms quoted in section 0.

Provided that an appropriate syntax Σ_l for a larger section of a given natural language l has been constructed, our definitions make it possible to distinguish scope and non-scope parts even in cases of Bloomfieldian exocentric constructions. "An exocentric phrase, such as *in the house*, contains some characteristic constituent (as, in our example, the preposition *in*) which determines its form-class" (Bloomfield 1933: 268). If it is possible to describe *in the house* by means of Σ_l in such a way that *the house* corresponds e.g. to a node whose label is a recursive symbol in Σ_l whereas *in* corresponds to a neighbouring node whose label is not a recursive symbol in Σ_l, then the desired distinction can be made according to (iv) (c) of Definition 12.

It should be clear that the definitions we have given refer first of all to symbols, i.e. to elements of a syntax. To this extent the application of the terms introduced is restricted to corresponding properties of a formal language. Taking them as reformulations of ideas connected with scope distinction as applied to natural languages involves having a method of assigning expressions of a natural language or properties of such expressions to expressions of a formal language or to properties of such expressions. One well-known such method, although nowadays not really in vogue, is so-called distributional analysis. We are convinced that this method yields the most reliable basis for syntactical work, although details require further investigation.

The aim of this paper is to outline one possible approach to the elimination of the intuitive way in which we ourselves have handled the conception of scope (explicitly e.g. in Clément & Thümmel 1976; cf. also François 1979).

If, as we assume, a CF-syntax can serve as a useful instrument when describing some aspects of a natural language and therefore has to be systematically confronted by expressions of that natural language for which it provides structural descriptions, it seems reasonable to support that there should be certain combinatorial properties within the set of the NL-expressions in question. It goes without saying that not all combinatorial properties which are observable in a given set of NL-expressions can be dealt with adequately by a CF-syntax.

Assuming that such correspondences should be established involves the assumption that the application of the concept introduced by Definition 12 depends not only on linguistic data in general, but above all on the state of our knowledge of the combinatorial properties of the natural language under analysis. To this extend we are dealing with an empirical matter.

Leaving aside the four – empirically less important – cases where, as mentioned above, the distinction between annex node and central node cannot be made according to our definitions, we find other cases where complications may arise, and this presumably because of a deficiency in our knowledge about the phenomena analysed (cf. Clément 1979). These complications concern the choice between alternative possible scope/non-scope divisions. However, they do not lead us to doubt that such a division can be made.

REFERENCES

Bally, Charles: 1965, *Linguistique générale et linguistique française*. Quatrième édition revue et corrigée, Berne: Francke. [Bally 1944/65].

Bierwisch, Manfred: 1963, *Grammatik des deutschen Verbs*, Berlin: Akademie-Verlag. = Studia grammatica. 2.

Bloomfield, Leonard: 1962, *Language*, London: George Allen & Unwin. [Bloomfield 1933/62].

Chomsky, Noam: 1965, *Aspects of the Theory of Syntax*, Cambridge, Massachusetts: The M. I. T. Press.

Clément, Danièle: 1979, 'Einige regelmäßigkeiten der verwendung von *freilich* und *jedoch* und deren beschreibung im rahmen einer teilsyntax der deutschen standardsprache', in *Die Partikeln der deutschen Sprache*, Hrsg. von Harald Weydt, Berlin & New York: Walter de Gruyter, pp. 109–120.

Clément, Danièle & Thümmel, Wolf: 1976, *Syntaxe de l'allemand standard. esquisse d'une base générative*, Paris: Librairie Larousse.

Cresswell, M. J.: 1973, *Logics and Languages*, London: Methuen.

François, Jacques: 1978, 'A propos de la "relation d'incidence" dans la *Syntaxe de l'allemand standard* de D. Clément et W. Thümmel', *Cahiers d'allemand* **14**, 92–102.

Gabelentz, Georg von der: 1875, 'Weiteres zur vergleichenden Syntax. Wort- und Satzstellung, *Zeitschrift für Völkerpsychologie und Sprachwissenschaft* **8**, 129–165.

Gabelentz, Georg von der: 1887, 'Zur chinesischen Sprache und zur allgemeinen Grammatik', *Internationale Zeitschrift für allgemeine Sprachwissenschaft* **3**, 92–109.

[Gladkij] = Gladkiĭ, A. V.: 1970, *Leçons de linguistique mathématique*. (*Kurs matematičeskoj lingvistiki*). ⟨1er Fascicule⟩. (Édition bilingue russe-français préparée par D(aniel) Hérault). (Paris): Centre de linguistique quantitative de la Faculté des sciences de l'Université de Paris (1970), Document de linguistique quantitative, 5.

Grunig, Blanche-Noëlle: 1978, *Structure sous-jacente: sur les fondements théoriques*. [Thèse pour le doctorat d'Etat soutenue à l'Université de Paris X le 28 janvier 1978], Paris [Mimeographed].

Hansen, Aage: 1933, *Sætningen og dens led i moderne dansk*, Kjøbenhavn: Nyt Nordisk Forlag, Arnold Busck.

Harris, Zellig S.: 1970, 'The elementary transformations', in Harris, Z. S.: *Papers in Structural and Transformational Linguistics*, Dordrecht: Reidel, pp. 482–532. [Harris 1964/70].

Kratzer, Angelika, Pause, Eberhard and von Stechow, Arnim: 1974, *Einführung in Theorie und Anwendung der generativen Syntax*. Einbändige Gesamtausgabe. (Erster Halbband: Syntaxtheorie), (Frankfurt/M.): Athenäum.

Lang, Ewald: 1979, 'Zum Status der Satzadverbiale', *Slovo a slovesnost* **40**, 200–213.

Lehrberger, John: 1974, *Functor Analysis of Natural Language*, The Hague & Paris: Mouton (Janua linguarum, Series minor, 197).

Levelt, W. J. M.: 1973, *Formele grammatica's in linguïstiek en taalpsychologie*, Deel III: *Toepassingen in de taalpsychologie*, Deventer: Van Loghum Slaterus.

Martinet, André: 1975, 'The foundations of a functional syntax', in Martinet A.: *Studies in functional syntax. Études de syntaxe fonctionnelle*, München: Wilhelm Fink (= Internationale Bibliothek für allgemeine Linguistik, 15), pp. 111–122.

Mathesius, Vilém: 1941, 'Základní funkce pořádku slov v češtině', *Slovo a slovesnost* 7, 169–180.

Meiner, Johann Werner: 1971, *Versuch einer der menschlichen Sprache abgebildeten Vernunftlehre oder Philosophische und allgemeine Sprachlehre*. (Leipzig: Johann Gottlieb Immanuel Breitkopf 1781.) Faksimile-Neudruck der Ausgabe Leipzig 1781 mit einer Einleitung von Herbert E. Brekle, Stuttgart-Bad Cannstatt: Friedrich Frommann.

Moreau, René: 1975, *Introduction à la théorie des langages*, Paris: Hachette.

ARNIM VON STECHOW

TOPIC, FOCUS AND LOCAL RELEVANCE*

SUMMARY. T. Reinhart (80) has claimed that the naive identification of topic information with old information and of focus information with new information is inconsistent.

I shall try to reconstruct the old versus new information approach in such a way that no inconsistency can arise.

My topic information will be what Chomsky (71) calls presupposition. The focus information of a sentence will be the material implication between its topic information and its content (its truth-conditions). The focus-information is 'the meaning' of the sentence *qua* focus-structure.

The usefulness of these concepts is illustrated because they are needed to show claims like the following.

1. Different focus assignment does not affect the truth conditions of a sentence, but it is responsible for the fact that the same sentence expresses different assertions, if it has different foci.

2. Topichood is one essential notion for the definition of the concept of the 'local relevance' of one utterance for another.

3. The relation between answers and questions should be described in terms of local relevance. Such an approach will provide a much more general account of the relation of being an answer to a question than commonly found in the literature.

4. Negative sentences with different foci express diffferent assertions although they have the same truth-conditions. It makes a difference whether the negation belongs to the focus or not. The phenomena to be discussed can't be explained by differences in the scope of the negation.

5. We are able to explain the difference between questions like 'Who called, JOHN or MARY?' or 'Did JOHN call or did MARY call?' on the one hand and the corresponding alternative question without focus, 'Did John or Mary call?' on the other hand.

The approach developed in this paper belongs to truth-conditional semantics. It is assumed that propositions determine truth-conditions. But we argue for something more: Propositions should be regarded as structured entities. They should at least have a topic-focus structure.

I. WHAT IS NEW INFORMATION?

Mostly the topic of an utterance is defined as the old information of the utterance. And the focus is the new information of the utterance.[1]

The concept of 'new information' is omnipresent in the 'functionalistic' literature. When I tried to find out how this notion is semantically defined I was very surprised to discover that there doesn't seem to exist a commonly

W. Klein and W. Levelt (eds.), Crossing the Boundaries in Linguistics, 95–130.

accepted definition. One could think that this is so for trivial reasons: We have a clear intuitive understanding of old and of new information. Therefore there is no need to define these notions.

Tanya Reinhart's paper 'Pragmatics and linguistics: An analysis of sentence topics' shows however that the notions of old and new information are far from being unproblematic. A problem arises as soon as we admit that being old or new information is a property of referents.

Imagine that we are talking about Hans-Robert and you want to know whether anyone likes him. I say then:

(1) Hans-Robert likes himself.

Now, **Hans-Robert** and **himself** obviously are coreferential, by the rules of English grammar. So both words denote Hans-Robert. Next, let us assume that **Hans-Robert** is the topic of (1). Therefore Hans-Robert is old information. Let us further assume that he himself is the focus expression of (1). Therefore, the denotation of **himself**, *i.e.*, Hans-Robert, is new information. Thus, Hans-Robert is both old and new information.

T. Reinhart concludes from an argument of this kind that topichood (and, presumably, focushood, too) can't be defined in terms of referents. I think this observation is correct, but I believe that it would be premature to draw the same conclusion from it as T. Reinhart does. She gives up the identification of topichood with old information in favour of the notion of 'aboutness'.[2] It may be a matter of personal taste whether one finds this latter notion very illuminating. As for myself, I find it rather obscure.

I prefer the old information approach, despite the inconsistency discovered above. The inconsistency can easily be eliminated. Let us see how. Consider the following small text.

(2) a. Hans-Robert has admirers.
b. He admires himself.

Let us ask ourselves what the new information of (b) with respect to (a) is. In other words, what does (b) tell us in addition to (a)?

I think the answer is this. In the configuration (2), (b) excludes the possibility that (a) holds but (b) does not hold.

To put it using different words: The new information of sentence (b) with respect to sentence (a) is the information that given (a) is true, (b) is true. So the new information of (b) with respect to (a) is the material implication between (a) and (b).

I will make this idea more precise in a moment. But let us show first how it may help us to avoid puzzles of the kind discussed by T. Reinhart.

Let us assume that the only thing I know about Hans-Robert is the following proposition:

(3) a. Hans-Robert exists.

Then you tell me:

b. Hans-Robert likes himself.

The new information of (b) with respect to (a) is the proposition

(4) If Hans-Robert exists then he likes himself.

The essential idea I will promote in this paper is that the information of a constituent like **himself** *qua focus* is not a referent[3] but a conditional of the above kind. (It will turn out that (4) is not the 'focus information' of **himself** but of **likes himself**.) Once we take this line, none of Reinhart's puzzles can arise. But the idea itself may seem awkward. One could ask: What has all this to do with the usual notions of topic and focus? I claim that it has something to do with them. Before I show this, let me first make the notions introduced so far a bit more precise.

In what follows, I will avoid all unnecessary technicalities. I will assume a very primitive possible-world-semantics framework, just rich enough for my purposes.

1.1. DEFINITIONS. Let W be a set of possible worlds.

(a) A proposition is a subset of W.
(b) The proposition p is *true* (*false*) in the world w iff $w \in p$ ($w \notin p$).
(c) The proposition p *entails* the proposition q iff $p \subset q$.
(d) The proposition p is *compatible* with the proposition q iff $p \cap q \neq \emptyset$. p is *incompatible* with q iff $p \cap q = \emptyset$.

These are usual notions which are found in one or another shape in almost any kind of semantics. The next definition concerns the topic of this section.

1.2. DEFINITION. Suppose (p, q) is a sequence of propositions. Call p the *old information* of (p, q). The *new information* of q with respect to p is the material implication between p and q, $p \Rightarrow q$, where $p \Rightarrow q$ is that proposition r such that for any world w:

$$w \in r \text{ iff } \sim(w \in p \;\&\; w \notin q).$$

Notice that this notion of old *viz.* new information doesn't presuppose any semantical connection between the propositions p and q. The only thing that matters is the linear order of p and q. Consider some examples.

(5) a. The sky is blue in Katmandu.
b. The kiwis dwell in Wellington.

The new information of (5 b) with respect to (5 a) is the entirely contingent proposition p which is true in any world w iff (if the sky is blue in Katmandu in w, then the kiwis dwell in Wellington in w).

More pathological cases of new information are exhibited by (6) and (7):

(6) a. The captain lives in Marlinspike.
b. The captain lives somewhere.

(7) a. Ruth has children.
b. Ruth has no children.

The new information of (6 b) with respect to (6 a) is zero, *i.e.* the necessary proposition W:

(6) c. If the captain lives in Marlinspike, he lives somewhere,

i.e.

{w: If the captain lives in Marlinspike in w, then he lives somewhere in w}.

The new information of (7 b) with respect to (7 a) is (7 b) again. This follows from the fact that the proposition $p \Rightarrow \sim p$ is $\sim p$, where $\sim p$ is the complement of p, *i.e.* the negation of p.

The situation illustrated by (5) can never arise in connection with sentence topcis. But the cases (6) and (7) are quite common as we will see later.

Let me introduce next the notions of sentence topic and sentence focus.

2. FOCUS AND TOPIC

Let us take the simplistic view that sentences express propositions. We ignore context-dependency, assume that deictic words work like names, that there is no vagueness and so on. We call the proposition expressed by a sentence the *content of the sentence*.

Consider an example. The content of sentence (8 a) is (8 b), no matter how (8 a) is prosodically realized.

(8) a. Wolfgang kocht zwei Eier.
 b. {*w*: Wolfgang is cooking two eggs in *w*}.

Like Jackendoff (72), I am assuming that there is one (or several) rule(s) of focus assignment. In spoken language, the foci of a sentence are determined to a large extent by prosodic features. Consider the following (mostly unnatural) questions and their natural full answers.[4]

(9) a. What is going on?
 b. Wolfgang kocht zwei Eier.
(10) a. Wolfgang is doing what?
 b. Wolfgang kocht zwei Eier.
(11) a. Wolfgangis cooking what?
 b. Wolfgang kocht zwei Eier.
(12) a. Wolfgang is cooking two what?
 b. Wolfgang kocht zwei Eier.
(13) a. Wolfgang is cooking how many eggs?
 b. Wolfgang kocht zwei Eier.
(14) a. Wolfgang is doing what to two eggs?
 b. Wolfgang kocht zwei Eier.
(15) a. Who is cooking two eggs?
 b. Wolfgang kocht zwei Eier.
(16) a. Who is cooking what?
 b. Wolfgang kocht zwei Eier.
(17) a. Who is cooking how many what?
 b. Wolfgang kocht zwei Eier.

For the representation of the pitch pattern I have been using the following notation:

High level pitch:
Middle level pitch:
Low level pitch:
Rising pitch:
Falling pitch:

If we look at these examples, we see that the intonation pattern of the (b)-sentence is different in each case. We express this difference by saying that the sentences exhibit a different focus-structure, *i.e.* they have different focus constituents. It is possible to describe the focus-constituents by means of the intonation features given above. But I do not want to go into the details here.[5]

Let me mention instead some typical pitch contours of focus-constituents in German sentences:

(18) + rising – high – falling +
(+ marks the beginning and end of the focus constituent)

Example:

+ zwei Eier +

(19) + rising – high + step
+ Wolfgang + kocht

(20) ‡+ high-falling +
(‡ marks the beginning of the sentence).
+ Wolfgang + kocht

Whenever a constituent has one of these prosodic forms, we call it a focus-constituent.[6] We will represent the foci of a sentence by means of brackets labelled with an *F*. Thus (9 a) to (17 a) are prosodic realizations of the following focus-structures (9 c) to (17 c).

(9) c. $[\text{Wolfgang}]_F [\text{kocht}]_F [\text{zwei Eier}]_F$.
(10) c. Wolfgang $[\text{kocht}]_F [\text{zwei Eier}]_F$.
(11) c. Wolfgang kocht $[\text{zwei Eier}]_F$.
(12) c. Wolfgang kocht zwei $[\text{Eier}]_F$.
(13) c. Wolfgang kocht $[\text{zwei}]_F$ Eier.
(14) c. Wolfgang $[\text{kocht}]_F$ zwei Eier.
(15) c. $[\text{Wolfgang}]_F$ kocht zwei Eier.
(16) c. $[\text{Wolfgang}]_F$ kocht $[\text{zwei Eier}]_F$.
(17) c. $[\text{Wolfgang}]_F$ kocht $[\text{zwei}]_F [\text{Eier}]_F$.

These examples show that I am assuming that a sentence may have more than one focus. (I share this view with Jackendoff). I will even admit that every minimal constituent of a sentence is a focus. Thus, in addition to (9 c), I will also assume the existence of the focus-structure (9 d).

(9) d. $[\text{Wolfgang}]_F [\text{kocht}]_F [\text{zwei}]_F [\text{Eier}]_F$.

Such a multiplication of focus-structures won't cause any harm, because it will turn out that (9 c) and (9 d) are equivalent in a sense to be explained: both of them have no topic.

In the examples given above we made the assumption that focus can be defined prosodically. However, I don't want to commit myself to the claim that this can always be done in spoken language. Usually, it is assumed that sentences with "normal intonation" are ambiguous as to focus.[7] For instance, the sentence

(18) Wolfgang kocht zwei EIER

is supposed to have any of the following focus-structures:

(18) a. Wolfgang kocht zwei $[\text{Eier}]_F$.
b. Wolfgang kocht $[\text{zwei Eier}]_F$.
c. Wolfgang $[\text{kocht zwei Eier}]_F$.

In written language, information about focus is mostly absent. But sometimes we have syntactic clues (word order, dislocations, clefts etc.). Generally speaking, a notation may underdetermine the focus structure of a sentence. It might be the case that also in actual utterances, the focus structure is not fully determined, as Chomsky (71) assumes.[8] In this case we would have focus-ambiguity. I will, however, ignore this possibility and assume that focus-structure is a formal property of a sentence, defined prosodically (and syntactically), *i.e.* each of our sentences has one and only one focus structure.

I will further assume that a sentence may have no focus at all, disregarding the question how such a sentence is prosodically realized.

The focus-structure of a sentence determines *the topic* (*expression*) of the sentence in this way: Replace the focus-constituents of the sentence by a 'corresponding' variable and form a property by λ-abstraction from the open sentence which is obtained by the replacement.

So the topic of a sentence is what Chomsky (71) or Jackendoff (72) call the presupposition of the sentence.

I don't want to make precise the concept of λ-abstraction, since this would require the introduction of a formal language. For my purposes, a "λ-categorial language" as in Cresswell (73) would do. Let me clarify only one terminological point, namely the way I am using the word 'property'.

2.1. DEFINITIONS. (a) Let $A_1, \ldots, A_n$ be a sequence of sets of entities. An *n-place property over* $A_1, \ldots, A_n$ is a function from $A_1 \times \ldots \times A_n$ into the set of propositions.

(b) Let ω be an n-place property over $A_1, \ldots, A_n$, and let $a_1, \ldots, a_n$ be in $A_1, \ldots, A_n$ respectively. Then ω is *true of* $a_1, \ldots, a_n$ in the word w iff $w \in \omega(a_1, \ldots, a_n)$.

Otherwise, ω is *false of* $a_1, \ldots, a_n$ in w.

Let me illustrate this terminology. Consider the following focus-structure.

(19) **[Ede]$_F$ admires [Senta]$_F$.**

The topic of (18) is the following λ-abstract.

(20) $\lambda < x, y > [x$ **admires** $y]$.

The semantic value of this two-place λ-abstract is that two-place property $\omega_{\mathbf{admires}}$ which is true of any two individuals a, b in the world w iff a admires b in w. Call this property the *topic-value* of sentence (19).

Next, what is the *focus-information* of sentence (19)? Well, it is the material implication between existential closure of (19)'s topic-value and its content.

Let us make this more explicit.

2.2. DEFINITIONS. (a) Let ω be an n-place property over $A_1, \ldots, A_n$. The *existential closure* of ω, $\exists\omega$, is the proposition $(\exists x_1) \ldots (\exists x_n) [\omega(x_1, \ldots, x_n)]$, where $x_1, \ldots, x_n$ are in $A_1, \ldots, A_n$ respectively.

(b) Suppose we are given a focus-structure s, and ω is the topic-value of s. Call $\exists\omega$, *i.e.* the existential closure of ω, the *topic-information* of s, $t(s)$.

(c) Suppose we are given a focus-structure s whose content is the proposition $c(s)$. Then, the *focus-information* of s, $f(s)$, is the proposition $t(s) \Rightarrow c(s)$.[9]

Apply these definitions to our example (19). The topic-value of (19) is $\omega_{\mathbf{admires}}$. Therefore, the topic-information of (19) is the existential closure of $\omega_{\mathbf{admires}}$, *i.e.* the proposition that someone admires someone, *i.e.* $\{w: (\exists x_1)(\exists x_2)(x_1 \text{ admires } x_2 \text{ in } w)\}$.

Now, at the beginning of this paragraph, I said that the content of a sentence does not depend on its prosodical realization. Therefore, it does not depend on the focus-structure in particular. The content of (19) is the proprosition

$c(19)$: that Ede admires Senta,

i.e. that set of worlds w, such that Ede admires Senta in w.

The focus information of (19) is the material implication between the topic information and the content of (19), *i.e.* the following proposition:

f(19): If someone admires someone, then Ede admires Senta

This is the set $\{w\text{: If } (\exists x_1, x_2)\ (x_1 \text{ admires } x_2 \text{ in } w)\text{, then Ede admires Senta in } w\}$.

Notice that this explication of focus-information is closely connected with the concept of new information, as introduced in definition *1.2*. Indeed, the focus-information of a sentence *s* is the new information of the content of *s* with respect to the topic-information of *s*.

One could also introduce the notion of *focus-values*. Since a sentence has in general more than one focus, its focus-value should be a sequence of values. For instance, the focus-values of sentence (19) should be the sequence

Ede, Senta,

since these are the contents of the focus-constituents of (19),

Ede, Senta.

Focus-values in this sense seem to be the usual interpretation of foci (*vide, e.g.*, Jackendoff (71)). But I will argue that this concept is not an interesting one.

3. FOCUS-INFORMATION AND ASSERTION

What is asserted when we utter the following sentence (focus structure)?

(21) **Ede ate [raw meat]$_F$ yesterday**

I will argue in this section that the assertion made by this utterance is the focus-information of (21), *i.e.*, the following proposition:

(22) If Ede ate something yesterday, then he ate raw meat yesterday.

At first sight, this seems surprising. But I believe that such a move helps to explain some puzzles arising in connection with assertions. Before going on, I will say a few words about assertion.

I don't want to try a general account of assertive speech-acts. For my purposes it suffices to make a few, highly idealized assumptions about an "assertive language game".

3.1. *Assertive Language Games*

First, we are considering only those contexts where a *common ground* is given. The common ground contains that information (true or not) which is accepted by the participants of the conversation for the purposes of the conversation. (Cf. Stalnaker (75)).

I assume that the information in the common ground is consistent and closed with respect to entailment. Hence we can identify it with a proposition.[10]

Second, an utterance of a sentence (which has a focus-structure) is *appropriate* at a context only if the topic-information of the sentence is entailed by the common ground of the context. If S is uttered appropriately at a context k, then call the focus-information of S the *assertion* made by S (in k).

Third, suppose S is uttered appropriately in the context k. Then the speaker of S is obliged to act as if the assertion made by S were true.

Fourth, if S is uttered appropriately and none of the participants objects, then the assertion made by S is added to the common ground, *i.e.* if p is the common ground and q is the assertion made by S, then p is replaced by $p \cap q$.

This is more or less as in Stalnaker (75), with one exception: The assertion of a sentence is in general a hypothetical proposition, the material implication between topic-information and content.

The advantage of these definitions is seen, if we compare it to the one given in Jackendoff (72, p. 246).

If we disregard the differences in terminology – Jackendoff calls 'presupposition' what I call 'topic-value'; he speaks of 'focus' where I use the term 'focus-value' and he has nothing that corresponds to 'focus-information' – then Jackendoff says:

(23) The assertion made by a sentence S is the proposition that the topic-value of S is true of the focus-value(s) of S.

According to Jackendoff, the assertion made by our focus-structure (21) is the following proposition p_{24}:

(24) $w \in p_{24}$ if λx_{NP} $\{w$: Ede ate x yesterday in $w\}$ is true of raw meat in w, for any $w \in W$.

By definition 2.1 and λ-conversion this is equivalent to

(25) $p_{24} = \{w$: Ede ate raw meat yesterday in $w\}$.

No, take a different focus-structure for the same sentence.

(26) **$[\text{Ede}]_F$ ate raw meat yesterday.**

I think Jackendoff's motivation for the introduction of the notion of assertion is that he wants to say that (26) expresses a different assertion than (21) does. But this doesn't come out from his account of assertion. According to Jackendoff, the assertion made by (26) is the proposition p_{27}:

(27) $w \in p_{27}$ *iff* the property λx_N $\{w: x$ ate raw meat yesterday in $w\}$ is true of Ede in w.

Obviously, p_{27} and p_{24} are the same. This shows that Jackendoff's notion of assertion and the notion of content (truth-conditions) collapse. I guess this is not a consequence wanted by him.

On the other hand, I have no difficulty in expressing the idea that one and the same sentence may express different assertions, depending on what the focus assignment is. Consider our examples again:

(28) [= (21)] **Ede ate $[\text{raw meat}]_F$ yesterday.**
(29) [= (26)] **$[\text{Ede}]_F$ ate raw meat yesterday.**

The content of these two is the same , namely the proposition p_{24}.

The topic informations of (28) and (29) are p_{28a} and p_{29a} respectively:

p_{28a}: = $\{w$: Ede ate something yesterday in $w\}$;
p_{29a}: = $\{w$: Someone ate raw meat yesterday in $w\}$;

The focus informations of (28) and (29) are p_{28b} and p_{29b} respectively.

p_{28b}: = $\{w$: If Ede ate something yesterday in w, then Ede ate raw meat yesterday in $w\}$;
p_{29b}: = $\{w$: If someone ate raw meat yesterday in w, then Ede ate raw meat yesterday in $w\}$.

Clearly p_{28b} and p_{29b} are different propositions, and since I take them to be the assertions made by (28) and (29), my terminology accounts for the intuition that (28) and (29) express different assertions.

It remains to show that the above notion of assertion is also intuitively sensible. At first sight, it seems more appropriate to say that the asserted proposition is the content of the sentence, and if the assertion is successful, then the content is added to the common ground. Call such an approach a *content-adding-game*.

Now, in a content-adding-game we could not say that (28) and (29) express different assertions. But the definition *3.2* allows us to say this and it can in addition account for the fact that, after a successful assertion, the content of the sentence is added to the common ground as a content-adding-game assumes, too.

In order to see this, let us assume that we are given a sentence S which is uttered appropriately with respect to a common ground g. Assume that the topic information of S is t and the content of S is c. Then the assertion made by S is $t \Rightarrow c$. Since S is an appropriate utterance, t is entailed by g. Suppose now that the assertion is successful. Then g is changed to $g' = g \cap (t \Rightarrow c)$.

It is easily proved that $g' = g \cap c$.[11]

So our rule of common ground change has exactly the same effect as the simple addition of the content would have.

What is gained then by the introduction of our more complicated notion of assertion? Consider the following two cases.

(30) **Ede ate [raw]$_F$ meat.**
(31) **Ede ate [raw meat]$_F$.**

The point is that (31) is a stronger assertion than (30) is. Let us show this in some detail. (30) is appropriately uttered at the context g_1 and (31) is appropriately uttered at g_2. Hence g_1 entails the topic information of (30), *i.e.* the proposition

t_{30} := Ede ate raw meat (having some property),
whereas g_2 entails the topic information of (31), the proposition
t_{31} := Ede ate something.[12]

The assertion made by (30) is the proposition

f_{30} := If Ede ate meat, then he ate raw meat.

The assertion made by (31) is

f_{31} := If Ede ate anything, then he ate raw meat.

Suppose not that $g_1 = t_{30}$ and $g_2 = t_{31}$. If the assertions made by (30) with respect to g_1 and by (31) with respect to g_2 are successful, then the change of the respective common ground amounts to the same thing:

$g_1 \cap f_{30}$ = Ede ate meat & (If Ede ate meat, then he ate raw meat).
$g_2 \cap f_{31}$ = Ede ate something & (If Ede ate anything, then he ate raw meat).

I take it that these two propositions are the same. And we could have obtained this information state by a content adding game, *i.e.* by adding the content of (30) and (31) to g_1 or g_2, where the content of (30) (and of (31), too) is this:

c_{30} = Ede ate raw meat.

By adding c_{30} to g_1 or g_2 we obtain:

$g_1 \cap c_{30}$ = Ede ate meat & Ede ate raw meat.
$g_2 \cap c_{30}$ = Ede ate something & Ede ate raw meat.

At the end we have obtained in each case the proposition g' = Ede ate raw meat.

But the history of these assertive games is different. In a content adding approach, it makes no difference whether we utter (30) or (31). In our approach, however, focus assignment plays a crucial role. Compare the two assertions f_{30} and f_{31}:

f_{30}: If Ede ate meat, then he ate raw meat.
f_{31}: If Ede ate anything, then he ate raw meat.

The antecedent of these implications is in each case that part of the assertion which is already in the common ground. Hence the speaker is not responsible for this part. No-one is permitted to object to it. The listener is allowed to object to the consequent only. This shows that f_{31} is a much stronger assertion than f_{30} is. If f_{31} is asserted with respect to g_2, then I can object:

(32) But Ede didn't even eat meat!

(32) is not a possible objection against the assertion f_{30} with respect to g_1, because g_1 entails that Ede ate meat.

4. LOCAL RELEVANCE AND THE THEORY OF QUESTIONS AND ANSWERS

In this section I propose a definition of 'local relevance'. This will be a relation connecting appropriate sentences. The connection works partly via topic, partly via content. I will argue that local relevance is the essential "semantical" connection between questions and answers. There is no "logic of questions and answers".[13]

(33) a. **Did Tanya come [by train]$_F$?**
b. **No, she came [by car]$_F$.**

(b) is a locally relevant answer to (a). It has the same topic.

(34) a. **Ich [habe im Lotto gewonnen]$_F$**
b. **Das [freut mich]$_F$**

(b) is locally relevant to (a). It is about the content of (a).

(35) a. **[Who knows B. Traven]$_F$?**
b. **[Elisabeth knows everyone]$_F$.**

(b) is locally relevant to (a), because it entails what I will call the content-information of the question (a), *i.e.* the proposition that someone knows B. Traven.

(36) a. **[Have you lost your horns]$_F$?**
b. **I [never had horns]$_F$.**

(b) is locally relevant to (a) because its content is incompatible with the content of (a).

These examples show already the most important instances of pairs of propositions connected by local relevance. The pairs (33) and (34) are connected by topic, (35) and (36) are connected by content.

In order to be able to give a more general account of these connections, let me introduce some notions concerning the interpretation of interrogatives.

Yes-no-interrogatives are analysed exactly as indicatives, at least as to content and topic.[14] We are ignoring for a moment the "illocutional" force of interrogativity versus indicativity.

The content-value of a *wh*-question is a property. In order to get it, we replace the *wh*-words by appropriate variables and form the corresponding λ-abstract.[15] The topic value of an interrogative is determined exactly as for indicatives. We only have to take into account that *wh*- phrases can be focus-constituents (which, in fact, they mostly are). Consider an example.

(37) **[Who]$_F$ invented the powder?**

Both the content and the focus-value of (37) are (38).

(38) λx_N [x invented the powder].[16]

For technical reasons, I will also introduce the notion of content-information for interrogatives. For *Yes-No*-questions, the content-information is just that what we have called content so far. For *wh*- interrogatives, the content-information is the existential closure of the content-value. So, the content-information of (37) is the following proposition:

(39) Someone invented the powder.

The *focus-information* of interrogatives is the material implication between the topic-information and the content-information of the interrogative. The focus-information of (37) is the proposition

(40) If someone invented the powder then someone invented the powder.

This is the necessary proposition. Thus the focus-information of (37) is zero.

Contrast (37) with (41):

(41) **[Did anyone invent the powder]** $_F$?

The topic of this *yes-no*-question is zero, *i.e.* the necessary proposition. The content-value and the content-information of (41) both are (42):

(42) Someone invented the powder.

The focus-information of (40) is the material implication between the necessary proposition and (42), and this is (42) again. Thus, we can account for an essential difference between the *wh*-question (37) and the *yes-no*-question (41): the focus-information of (37) is zero, whereas the focus-information of (41) is the contingent proposition (42), *although (37) and (41) have the same content-information.*

This explains why we can react to (41) by saying "Yes", whereas we can't so react to (37). Suppose namely that *yes* means that I agree that the focus-information is added to the common ground. Now, it is trivial to agree that the necessary proposition is added to the common ground, since its addition does not change the common ground.

Now I am in a position to propose a general definition of local relevance of a sentence for another sentence.

4.1. *Local relevance*. Suppose we are given a pair of sentences $< S_1, S_2 >$ where S_1 is an indicative or an interrogative and S_2 is an indicative. Then S_2 is locally relevant for S_1 iff at least one of the following conditions obtains.

(a) S_1 and S_2 have the same topic-value.
(b) The topic-value of S_2 is the content-value of S_1.
(c) The content-value of S_2 entails the content-information of S_1.
(d) The content-value of S_2 is incompatible with the content-information of S_1.

In case S_1 is an interrogative and S_2 is an indicative and S_2 is locally relevant for S_1, we say that S_2 *is an answer to* S_1.

In order to see that these definitions give us a nice typology of answers, let us introduce some further terminology.

4.2. (a) The proposition q is *informative with respect to* p iff q is not entailed by p.

(b) The proposition q *specifies* p iff q entails p but not vice versa.

We are now in a position to give a typology of answers which makes use of the notion of local relevance.

4.3. *A typology of answers*. Suppose we are given an interrogative S_1 and an indicative S_2 such that S_2 is an answer to S_1.
Let tv(s_j) be the topic-value of s_j,
ti(s_j) be the topic-information of s_j,
cv(s_j) be the content-value of s_j
and let
ci(s_j) be the content-information of s_j,
$j = 1, 2$. We say the following.

(00) S_2 is a *direct but uninformative answer to* S_1 iff tv(S_1) = tv(S_2) and ci(S_1) $\subset$ ci(S_2), *i.e.* ci(S_1) entails ci(S_2).

(010) S_2 is a *direct informative and specifying answer to* S_1 iff tv(S_1) = tv(S_2), ci(S_1) $\not\subset$ ci(S_2) and ci(S_2) $\subset$ ci(S_1).

(0110) S_2 is a *direct, informative, unspecific and compatible answer to* S_1 iff tv(S_1) = tv(S_2), ci(S_1) does not entail ci(S_2), ci(S_2) doesn't entail ci(S_1) and ci(S_2) is compatible with ci(S_1).

(0111) S_2 is a *direct, informative, unspecific, incompatible answer to* S_1 iff tv(S_2) = tv(S_1), ci(S_1) doesn't entail ci(S_2) and ci(S_2) does not entail ci(S_1) and ci(S_2) is incompatible with ci(S_1).

This is only part of the classification. The sequences of numbers at the beginning of each subclassification may be thought of as the branches of a "classificatory tree" in the style of Porphyrius. As it is directly seen, the classification is incomplete. There is no sequence beginning with "1". I will come back to this.

Let us first consider some examples:

(42) Direct uninformative answer:
a. **Ede sleeps [in a chair]$_F$?**
b. **Yes, Ede sleeps [in a chair]$_F$.**

The topic of both (a) and (b) is $\lambda x_{loc.\ Adv}$ [Ede sleeps x]. ci(a) is the proposition that Ede sleeps in a chair, and so is ci(b). ci(a) entails ci(b).

(43) Direct specifying answer:
a. **[Wie]$_F$ geht es dir?**
b. **[Mies]$_F$! (= Mir geht es[mies!]$_F$)**
(44) Direct, unspecific but compatible answer:
a. **Did Bill kill [the judge]$_F$?**
b. **Bill killed [a man from Whanganui]$_F$.**
(45) Direct, unspecific and incompatible answer:
a. **[Which girl from Munich]$_F$ loves Ede?**
b. **Ede loves [no Bavarian at all]$_F$.**

Certain unspecific and compatible answers may be called 'eliminative'.

(46)a. **Wem fühlt sich Ede landsmannschaftlich verbunden?**
b. **Den Bayern nicht.**

Since I haven't distinguished between positive and negative propositions (and I know of no way in which they can be distinguished) I can't account for the intuitive difference between compatible positive answers and compatible negative (= eliminative) answers. It would be nice to have such a distinction.[17]

Let me extend the typology of answers a bit more.

4.4. *Typology of answers extended*

(100) S_2 is an *uninformative comment to* S_1 iff tv(S_1) ‡ tv(S_2) but tv(S_2) = ci(S_1) and ci(S_1) entails ci(S_2).

(1011) S_2 is an *informative and specifying comment to* S_1 iff tv(S_1) ‡ tv(S_2), tv(S_2) = ci(S_1), ci(S_1) does not entail ci(S_2) but ci(S_2) entails ci(S_1).

(10110) S_2 is an *informative, unspecific but compatible comment to* S_1 iff tv(S_1) ‡ tv(S_2), tv(S_2) = ci(S_1), ci(S_1) $\not\subset$ ci(S_2), ci(S_2) $\not\subset$ ci(S_1) and ci(S_2) is compatible with ci(S_1).

(10111) S_2 is an *informative, unspecific and incompatible comment to* S_1 iff $\mathrm{tv}(S_1) \neq \mathrm{tv}(S_2)$, $\mathrm{tv}(S_2) = \mathrm{ci}(S_1)$, $\mathrm{ci}(S_1) \not\subset \mathrm{ci}(S_2)$, $\mathrm{ci}(S_2) \not\subset \mathrm{ci}(S_1)$ and $\mathrm{ci}(S_2)$ is incompatible with $\mathrm{ci}(S_1)$.

(110) S_2 is an *indirect, noninformative answer to* S_1 iff $\mathrm{tv}(S_2) \neq \mathrm{tv}(S_1)$, $\mathrm{tv}(S_2) \neq \mathrm{ci}(S_1)$ and $\mathrm{ci}(S_1)$ entails $\mathrm{ci}(S_2)$.

(1110) S_2 is an *indirect, informative compatible answer to* S_1 iff $\mathrm{tv}(S_1) \neq \mathrm{tv}(S_2)$, $\mathrm{tv}(S_2) \neq \mathrm{ci}(S_1)$, $\mathrm{ci}(S_1) \not\subset \mathrm{ci}(S_2)$ and $\mathrm{ci}(S_2)$ is compatible with $\mathrm{ci}(S_1)$.

(1111) S_2 is an *indirect, informative, incompatible answer to* S_1 iff $\mathrm{tv}(S_1) \neq \mathrm{tv}(S_2)$, $\mathrm{tv}(S_2) \neq \mathrm{ci}(S_1)$, $\mathrm{ci}(S_1) \not\subset \mathrm{ci}(S_2)$ and $\mathrm{ci}(S_2)$ is incompatible with $\mathrm{ci}(S_1)$.

This looks scholastic and so it is. But it illustrates my point: The relation of being an answer to a question is a complicated, perhaps gradual thing, not definable by just one condition. This typology could be made finer and finer. Yet, I stop here and illustrate the definitions by some further examples.

(47)a. **[Are there cows with white ears]**$_F$?
b. **That['s possible]**$_F$.

I take it that **that** refers to the content-information of the question. Then (b) is an example of an uninformative answer that comments (a), given an appropriate reading for **possible**, of course.

(48)a. **[Do you believe in God]**$_F$?
b. **[You know]**$_F$ **that I do!**

Maybe, this is an informative, specifying and commenting answer to (a).

(49)a. **[Do you want to marry me]**$_F$?
b. **[Ede believes]**$_F$ **so.**

Perhaps this is a case of an informative, unspecific, compatible commenting answer to (a).

(50)a. **[Are there unicorns]**$_F$?
b. **That['s impossible]**$_F$.

(b) is an informative, unspecific and incompatible comment to (a).

I stop here with the discussion of further examples which illustrate the above typlogy, because I don't know whether the branch of answers introduced in **4.4** is very interesting. The general point should have become clear: One could define a lot of different kinds of answers starting from the idea, that answers are connected to questions either by topic or by content-relation. I have called this kind of connection 'local relevance' (cf. Manor (80)).

5. NEGATION

Consider the following sentences:

(52) **Ede DIDN'T kiss Senta in Rome**
(53) **Ede didn't KISS Senta in Rome**
(54) **Ede didn't kiss SENTA in Rome**
(55) **Ede didn't kiss Senta IN ROME.**

We have to explain two things:

First. These sentences express different assertions although they have the same truth-conditions.

Second. (52) to (55) have certain implicatures, namely the following.

(53) a. Ede did something else in Senta in Rome other than kissing.
(54) a. Ede kissed someone else other than Senta in Rome.
(55) a. Ede kissed Senta somewhere else other than in Rome.

We would like to explain these implicatures by means of the methods developed so far. But we have to face a problem neglected up to this point. It is this.

Suppose the topic-value of (53) is (53)b:

(53) b. λx_{TV} [Ede x-ed Senta in Rome], where x_{TV} is a variable for two-place-properties.

Suppose further that the topic information of (53) is (53)c:

(53) c. $(\exists x_{TV})$ [Ede x-ed Senta in Rome]

Then the topic-value of (53) should be the conditional (53)d.

(53) d. $(\exists x_{TV})$ [Ede x-ed Senta in Rome] $\Rightarrow$ Ede did not kiss Senta in Rome.

At first sight, this looks good, because it seems to be the case that we obtain a different proposition for each of the focus-structures (52)–(55) (putting aside the problem what the exact procedure for determining the topic-value is). For instance, the focus-information of (54) should be (55)d:

(55) d. $(\exists x_{IAV})$ [Ede x (kissed Senta)] $\Rightarrow$ Ede did not kiss Senta in Rome.

(53)d and (54)d look different. Thus we seem to be able to explain, why (53) and (54) express different assertions despite the fact that they have the same truth-conditions. But this appearance is treacherous. (53)d and (54)d are exactly the same proposition, because the antecedent is the necessary proposition in each case and the consequent is the same. Since this might not be obvious from these examples, I will show this by discussing a simpler case.

Consider the following focus-structure.

(56) **Udo [ist doof]** $_F$.

According to procedure described in section 2, (56) has the following topic-information:

(56) a. $\exists P$ [P is true of Udo]

where P is a variable for one-place properties. But there is always a property which is true of Udo, take *e.g.* the universal property ω_U which is true of any individual what so ever: $w \in \omega_U(x) \Leftrightarrow x \in U$, for any $w \in W$ and any $x \in U$. U is our universe of discourse.

Therefore, (56) a is true in every world w.

For the same reason, the topic-information (57) b of the focus-structure (57) a is a logical truth:

(57) a. **Ede [loves]** $_F$ **Senta**
b. $(\exists x_{TV})$ [x(Ede, Senta)],

where x_{TV} is a variable for a two-place property. In order to prove the necessary truth of (b), take the two-place universal property. Obviously, this situation is given whenever we existentially quantify over higher-order things like properties or operators. A case of quantification over an operator would be the determination of the topic-information of (52) under the assumption that the negation belongs to the focus. The topic-information of (52) would then be:

(52) d. $(\exists x_{S/S})\, x$ (Ede kissed Senta in the bathroom),

whereas $x_{S/S}$ is a propositional operator like 'it is the case that', 'it is not the case that', 'possibly' or the like. Clearly, (52) d is a logical truth, too.

These considerations show that the procedure for the determination of the topic-information that was given in section 2 can't be quite right. But we wan't to keep the spirit of this procedure, if possible.

What the best way is out of this little debâcle I am not sure. We have to make sure somehow that the existential propositions that express the topic information are contingent.

One possibility of guaranteeing this would be to take a sort of Davidsonian approach: We forbid the quantification over higher-order entities, at least for the purposes of the determination of topic-information. Perhaps, the topic-informations of (58)a to (60)b are (58)b to (60)b respectively.

(58) a. **Tristan [is an ass]$_F$.**
b. $(\exists x)$ (x is a natural kind and Tristan is a member of x).

(59) a. **Udo [ist doof]$_F$.**
b. $(\exists x)$ (x is a state and Udo is in x).

(60) a. **Ede [hits]$_F$ Senta.**
b. $(\exists x)$ (x is a transitive action and Ede does x to Senta).

These paraphrases of the topic-information might be wrong but they illustrate the essential point: it is necessary to somehow restrict the existential quantifiers which correspond to the topic positions. It is doubtful to me whether this restriction can be formulated purely semantically. It seems to me that it is determined partly by the context of utterance and partly by the semantical class of the constituent focussed on. I have no idea what the exact conditions determining the restrictions are. For the aims of this paper, it is enough to imagine that we are given for each focus constituent or rather for each focus position a set of *focus alternatives*. For instance, the focus alternatives of **[hits]$_F$** in (60) a might be the set of all two-place properties expressible by transitive verbs. We will restrict the existential quantification over properties just by saying that we are quantifying over focus alternatives only. The quantification over operators (adverbs, adjectives and the like) seems easier. We just replace the operator by the identity operator. This seems to work. The quantification over ordinary individuals does not need to be restricted.

These considerations lead us to the following new definitions of the procedure for determining the topic-information.

5.1. *Determination of Topic-Information*

Suppose we are given a sentence s whose topic-value is the n-place property ω over $A_1, \ldots, A_n$.

Suppose that any A_i is a set of first-order properties, a set of individuals or one-place operations over some set B. Then the topic-information of s is the proposition $(\exists x_1) \ldots (\exists x_n)$ $[\omega_1(x_1)$ & $\ldots \omega_n(x_n)$ & $\omega(x_1, \ldots, x_n)]$, where

$$\omega_i = \begin{cases} \text{the property of being an individual, if } x_i \text{ is an individual,} \\ \text{the property of being a focus-alternative, if } x_i \text{ is a first-order property,}^{18} \\ \text{the property of being an identity operation over } B, \text{ if } x_i \text{ is a one-place operation over } B.^{19} \end{cases}$$

This definition does not cover every case possibly occurring but a lot of cases. Let us apply it to our examples (52) to (55). Suppose these sentences have the following focus structures.

(52) e. **Ede did [not]$_F$ kiss Senta in Rome**
(53) e. **Ede did [not]$_F$ [kiss]$_F$ Senta in Rome**
(54) e. **Ede did [not]$_F$ kiss [Senta]$_F$ in Rome**
(55) e. **Ede did [not]$_F$ kiss Senta [in Rome]$_F$.**

Suppose **not** is a one-place propositional operator and **in Rome** is a one-place predicate modifier. Then the topic-information of (52)e. to (55)e. is (52)f to (55)f respectively.

(52) f. $(\exists x_{S/S})$ [x is the identity mapping & x(Ede kissed Senta in Rome)].
(53) f. $(\exists x_{S/S})$ $(\exists y_{TV})$ [x is the identity mapping & y is a focus-alternative & x(Ede y-ed Senta in Rome)].
(54) f. $(\exists x_{S/S})$ $(\exists y_{N})$ [x is the identity mapping & y is an individual & x(Ede kissed y in Rome)].
(55) f. $(\exists x_{S/S})$ $(\exists y_{IV/IV})$ [x is the identity mapping & y is the identity mapping & x(Ede y (kissed Senta))].

I think that this time the topic-informations express what we want them to express. (52)f to (54)f can be restated in ordinary speech in the following way (neglecting the restrictions of the existential quantifiers):

(52) g. Ede kissed Senta in Rome.
(53) g. Ede did something to Senta in Rome.
(54) g. Ede kissed something in Rome.
(55) g. Ede kissed Senta.

These examples show that the operators focussed on are simply dropped when we determine the topic-information.

Now, we are in a position to give the explanations we have required at the beginning of this section.

First. Clearly, (52)e to (55)e express different assertions. To give two examples:

(53)e expresses the assertion (53)h whereas (54) expresses the assertion (54)h. This is compatible with the assumption that all of these sentences have the same truth-conditions.

(53) h. If Ede did something to Senta in Rome, then he did not kiss her there.
(54) h. If Ede kissed someone in Rome, then he did not kiss Senta there.

Second. We get the different implicatures carried by (53) to (55) just by conjoining the topic-information and the content. Let us show this for two cases.

The topic-information of (53) is (53)g, the content of (53) is (53)i:

(53) **Ede did [not]$_F$ [kiss]$_F$ Senta in Rome.**
(53) g. Ede did something to Senta in Rome.
(53) i. Ede did not kiss Senta in Rome.

The conjunction of (g) and (i) is (j):

(53) j. Ede did something to Senta in Rome and Ede did not kiss her in Rome.

And this is equivalent with

(53) a. Ede did something else to Senta in Rome than kissing.

(53)a is the implicature of (53) we wanted to explain. It should be clear why we can explain this implicature by conjoining the topic-information with the content. We could have taken the topic-information plus the focus-information as well. That would have given us the same result, because $p \mathbin{\&} (p \Rightarrow q) \equiv p \mathbin{\&} q$.

Sentence (53) behaves a bit differently as to implicature.

(53) **Ede did [not]$_F$ kiss Senta in Rome.**

This sentence presupposes that the proposition that Ede kissed Senta in

Rome is "under discussion".[20] But, unlike the other sentences, (53) carries no implicature of the kind discussed. If we applied the same procedure as before, *i.e.*, if we conjoined the topic-information of (53) with the content-information of (53), we would obtain a contradiction.

(61) Ede kissed Senta in Rome and Ede didn't kiss Senta in Rome.

Notice that the differences in meaning of (52) to (55) could not be explained by differences of the scope of the negation because there are no quantifiers in these sentences. But the difference of scope of the negation matters only in connection with genuine quantifiers. On the other hand, I don't want to dispute that scope ambiguities of the negation are important in order to account for certain phenomena. But not for the examples discussed here.

In the sentences given above, the negation always was part of the focus. Therefore, it wasn't present any more in the topic.

Consider now a case where the negation does belong to the topic-value.

(62) a. **Wolfgang doesn't like [what]$_F$?**
b. **He doesn't like [fish]$_F$.**

The topic-value of (b) is the content-value of (a), *i.e.* the property λx_N [Wolfgang doesn't like x].

This example connects with the so called question-test (vide Hatcher (1956)), according to which the topic of a sentence is the question it answers.[21] I could have introduced the intuitive concept of topic(-value) by means of the question test from the beginning on, but this would not have been advisable, because the question test works for indicatives only. Questions don't answer questions, but they have a topic.

Let me finish this section with some remarks about intonation. In the examples (53) to (55) we tacitly assumed that the unstressed clitic negation word belonged to the focus. This premise is sensible only if we assume that the relation between prosody and focus-structure is much more complicated than it was suggested in section 2.

This raises the question how focus is defined exactly in terms of prosody. I don't know yet, but since I believe in the 'reality' of this concept, I believe that it is definable somehow. (52) and (55) were cases where an unstressed constituent was a focus constituent. But there are also cases where a stressed constituent, even the constituent bearing the intonation center is not a focus-constituent. Consider this case:

(63) a. **[Schätzt Ede Wagner]$_F$?**
b. **Ja, er SCHÄTZT ihn.**
c. **Nein, er schätzt ihn NICHT.**

The 'schätzt' in (b) is not a focus-constituent. It is not the *verb* 'schätzen' that is focussed on in (b). It is the *position* of the finite verb that is focussed on in order to express the idea that the answer is positive.[22] Correspondingly, the intonation center of the negative answer is the negation particle 'nicht'. The topic of (b) and (c) is the same. It is (a).

6. ALTERNATIVE QUESTIONS AND *WH*-QUESTIONS

The preceding section was supposed to illustrate once more the usefulness of our notions of topic and focus. I have to come back to questions and answers, because some of the classical problems are still open.

Let me say first something as to the semantics of answering particles like **yes** and **no**. In German, we have a richer system of answering particles than in English.[23] We have three particles, namely, **ja, nein** und **doch**. Their use can be illustrated by the following matrix:

	Agreement	Disagreement
Positive question	**ja**	**nein**
Negative question	**nein**	**doch**

The terms agreement and disagreement may be confusing in connection with questions. What is meant by them is this: If I agree to a question, I agree that the focus-information of the question be added to the common ground. If I disagree with the question, this means that I am not willing to add the focus-information of the question to the common ground. And it means something more: I assert the opposite of the focus-information of the question.

Let me illustrate this.

(64) a. **Wolfgang mag [keinen Fisch]$_F$?**
b. **Nein.**
c. **Doch.**
d. ***Ja.**

The focus-information of (64) is (65)a.

(65) a. If Wolfgang likes something, then he doesn't like fish.

Suppose, (64)a is uttered appropriately. Then the premise of (65)a is in the common ground. Saying **nein** has the effect that the proposition

(66) Wolfgang doesn't like fish

is added to the common ground. If I say **doch**, I do not want to have (65)a in the common ground. I rather want to have the opposite of (65)a in the common ground. This is the proposition (65)c.:

(65) c. Not (If Wolgang likes anything, then he doesn't like fish)

i.e.,

Wolfgang likes something and he likes fish.

Thus, if the other participants agree with my **doch**, this will have the impact that the proposition

(67) Wolfgang likes fish

is added to the common ground.

Notice that saying **ja** is really out of place when (64)a is asked. (This is a reason why I always have difficulties with negative questions in English. I don't know how to react.)

Consider the reaction to a positive question.

(66) a. **Mag Wolfgang [Goethe]**$_F$?
b. **Nein, er mag [Eisbein]**$_F$.

(66)b. is a sequence of two different speech-acts. By saying **nein**, I disagree with the claim

(68) If Wolfgang likes anything, then he likes Goethe.

Furthermore, my claim is that the negative of (68) should be added to the common ground. So, saying **nein** is a sort of complex speech-act: I react negatively to an assertion and make the opposite assertion.

The second speech-act is a positive claim, namely (69):

(69) If Wolfgang likes anyone, then he likes Eisbein.

A notoriously difficult problem for any theory of question and answers is represented by questions with *or*-tags.[24]

(70) **Who slept in my bed, John or Mary**?

The topic of this question seems to be the same as the topic of the corresponding *wh*-question without the *or*-tag.[25]

(71) **Who slept in my bed?**

Furthermore, it seems to be clear that the NPs occurring in the *or*-tag are foci, *i.e.*, (70) has this focus-structure:

(72) **[Who]$_F$ slept in my bed, [John]$_F$ or [Mary]$_F$?**

(72) is a genuine *wh*-question. We can't answer it by saying **yes** or **no**. A good answer would be either **John** or **Mary**. This observation makes Rainer Bäuerle think that the *or*-tag is a sort of restriction for the *wh*-phrase, it tells us what the possible answers are. If I understand him correctly, then Bäuerle would analyse (72) roughly in this way:

(73) Question: λx_N [x_N slept in my bed]
Answers: {John, Mary}.

A question with a simple NP-tag like

(74) **Who slept in my bed, Mary?**

would be analysed as something like

(75) $<\lambda x_N$ [x slept in my bed], Mary$>$.

This analysis could explain why we can answer (74) by saying **yes** or **no. Yes** would mean that the property of having slept in my bed is true if Mary did so, **no** that it is false of her.

I have several worries against such a procedure. I don't know whether Bäuerle's approach is general enough to be able to cover any sort of tag. What about the following example?

(76) **Who loves Senta, if not Ede?**

Second. The same phenomenon as in (74) arises with alternative questions which have a very different structure from *wh*-questions with *or*-tags.

(77) **Did [Mary]$_F$ sleep in my bed or did [John]$_F$ sleep in my bed?**

I think (77) means exactly the same as (72). We can't answer it by **yes** or **no.** But if we change the focus-structure a bit, we can.

(78) **[Did Mary or John sleep in my bed]$_F$?**

This is a good **yes-no**-question. We are only interested whether the alternative is true. A clumsier way of expressing (78) would be (79):

(79) **[Did Mary sleep in my bed or did John sleep in my bed]** $_F$?

We have to explain the difference between (77) and (79) anyway. It is the same as the difference between (72) and (79) (or (78)). It doesn't seem natural to think that the meaning of (77) should be analysed via the restriction of a variable, because there isn't any element in (77) that could be regarded as a natural candidate for a variable (there is no *wh*-word).

Third. The direct analysis of questions given by Bäuerle, which is in the tradition of people like Hamblin, Belnap or Keenan-Hull, is not compatible with the more general approach developed in this paper.

I have no fully satisfactory analysis of *wh*-questions with *or*-tags. For the moment, I propose to take this line. Regard (72) as a sequence of two questions:

(80) **[Who]** $_F$ **slept in my bed? Did [John]** $_F$ **sleep in my bed or did [Mary]** $_F$ **sleep in my bed?**

This amounts to the same as

(81) **Did [John]** $_F$ **sleep in my bed or did [Mary]** $_F$ **sleep in my bed?**

What should be the analysis of (81)? I think Dieter Wunderlich is right when he assumes that the speaker of (70) or (81) is committed to the hypothesis that either John or Mary slept in my bed.[26] But I think this view is not compatible with the assumption that (70) or (81) have the same topic as the corresponding simple *wh*-question (71), which has no *or*-tag.

It seems to me that the situation is more complicated. Let me propose this tentative solution.

The topic-*value* of (81) is

(82) $\lambda < x_N, y_N >$ [x slept in my bed or y slept in my bed]

But the topic-*information* of (81) is the proposition:

(83) John slept in my bed or Mary slept in my bed.

Since (83) is also the content of (81), the focus-information of (81) is the necessary proposition, *i.e.* it is zero.

This solution would explain, why (81) behaves exactly as a *wh*-question. Saying **yes** to (81) would be an agreement to the necessary proposition. This is trivial. A good answer would be "**Mary!**", or "**John!**", since this would specify the content of (81).

Notice that this account would leave open the possibility to answer something like "both of them", which doesn't seem natural. But here a sort of 'Gricean device' could help. We have to look at the history of the assertion game. Maybe, we accepted the claim that John or Mary slept in my bed only under the supposition that not both did. This is a very common supposition for the acceptance of an alternative, as Gazdar has argued in his remarks about **or**.[27]

The solution sketched here, if workable at all, requires a redefinition of the procedure for the determination of topic information (cf. Definition 5.2.).

Let me say for sake of completeness that (79) is analysed exactly as one would expect. It has no topic, whereas focus and content are the same, namely the proposition (83).

I still have to say something about indirect questions.

(84) **Elisabeth knows who invented the powder.**

(85) **Elisabeth knows whether Bill or Rainer or Ede loves her.**

(86) **Elisabeth knows that Ede loves Senta.**

In order to analyse the meaning of these sentences, we have to introduce two subcategorizations for 'to know', namely 'knowing wh' and 'knowing that'.

The truth conditions roughly are these:

(87) 'x knows $_{\text{wh}}$ p' is true *iff* x knows all the true answers to p, where p is the content information of an interrogative.

(88) 'x knows $_{\text{that}}$ p' is true *iff* p belongs to x's knowledge.

(87) is a very strong condition, of course. But I am not too worried about that at the moment. It gives us some correct predications. For instance, (85) entails the following proposition:

(89) *If* Elisabeth knows whether Bill or Rainer or Ede loves her, *then* she knows that Bill loves her, if he loves her.

It should be clear that the definitions (87) and (88) are more than crude. The relation of answerhood involves the parameters topic-value, content-value and content-information, and not only content-information. Nevertheless, let us apply the same brutal method for a semantics for 'asking'.

(90) 'x asks$_{\text{wh}}$ p' is true *iff* x wants to know the true answers to p.

This semantics, as crude as it may be, explains the entailment between (91)a and (91)b:

(91) a. **Elisabeth asks whether Paul or Bill likes her.**
b. **Elisabeth asks whether Paul likes her.**

Since 'Paul likes Elisabeth' is more informative than 'Paul or Bill likes Elisabeth', it is an answer Elisabeth asks for. Of course, there are strong pragmatic restrictions for 'good' or 'relevant' answers. And we ask for these answers, not for all answers. But this is not my concern in this paper.

7. CONCLUDING REMARKS

In the preceding sections I have tried to show that my distinctions concerning the notions of topic and focus are useful for explaining some important phenomena of semantics and pragmatics.

At the beginning of the paper I said that I would defend a definition of topic in terms of old information and I mentioned that Tanya Reinhart believes that such an approach is empirically falsifiable. She has in mind cases like the following:[28]

(92) **Pat McGee, I don't know if you know him, lives in Palisades** . . .

She thinks that **Pat McGee** is in a topic position. Therefore, Pat McGee is the topic of (92). But (92) is said in a context where it can't be presupposed that the hearer has any knowledge about Pat McGee. Therefore, the topic-information which corresponds to Pat McGee, say 'that Pat McGee exists' can't belong to the common ground. Hence, the topic can't be old information. In a lot of cases, we introduce 'new referents' which nevertheless are topics.

I do not want to go into the question whether **Pat McGee** is the only topic expression in (92). Let us grant that. My reaction would then be that (92) is not fully appropriate. We could interpret 'I don't know if you know him' as an excuse of the speaker for possibly inappropriate speech.

In practice, we very often neglect rules of conversation. For such a case we have 'rules of accommodation', as D. Lewis calls them.[29] If something should be old information (*i.e.* a presupposition contained in the common ground) but it isn't there, we tacitly change the common ground and act as if the information were old information. That much to T. Reinhart's objection.

Another problem is the relation of my notions of topic to aboutness. Clearly, Mary can be the topic a sentence is about. Now, Mary is an individual. Therefore our sentence should be about an individual. But according to the definitions of the notions of topic, a topic is never an individual. It is a property or a proposition. So our approach couldn't be adequate. The objection can be refuted in the following way. Take the sentence

(93) **Mary [is tired]** $_F$.

The topic-value of (93) is

(94) λPP (Mary),

where P is a property-variable. But this is the set of properties possessed by Mary and you may identify this set with Mary.[30] So the topic is Mary. On the other hand, there are clear cases where the topic can't be an individual but must be a property.

(95) **Jetzt schon aufhören, dazu habe ich keine Lust.**

The left-dislocated phrase is an infinitival, hence it expresses a property.

Another objection against my approach is possible against the identification of topic-information with presupposition and of focus-information with assertion, as I did in the assertive language game 3.2. There are clear cases where the asserted information is not the focus-information but rather the content.[31] Consider the following dialogue.

(96) I: **Ede is rich.**
You: **That's possible.**

Suppose that the focus-structure of the second sentence can be represented in the following way:

(97) **That Ede is rich [is possible]** $_F$.

The focus-information of (97) is the proposition (98):

(98) If Ede is rich then possibly so.

But this is not what you asserted in (96). Given an appropriate interpretation of **possibly**, (98) is even fully trivial, namely the necessary proposition. You wouldn't assert that. What you asserted rather is (99):

(99) That Ede is rich is possible.

This is the content of (97).

The language-game 3.2 does not cover such cases. It is concerned only with "initiative" assertions. But (96) is an example where the second assertion is a reaction to the first one. Notice that your statement is connected to mine by local relevance: my statement is the topic of your statement. There is a clear analogy between reacting to a claim and answering a question. This has pointed out at several occasions by R. Manor. I believe that the relation of local relevance developed above will be very useful for the description of such reactions. So far I didn't say anything about them in this paper.

Let me mention another thing. Is it really necessary to distinguish between topic-value and topic-information? Consider the following case.

(100) a. **[Who]$_F$ knows someone?**
b. **[Elisabeth]$_F$ knows someone.**
c. **Someone knows [Bill]$_F$.**

Intuitively, (b) is a direct answer to (a) but (c) is not. We account for this fact, by saying that (b) has the same topic-value as (a) has, whereas this is not so with (c). The topic-value of (a) and (b) is (101), whereas the topic-value of (c) is (102).

(101) λx_N [x knows someone].
(102) λx_N [someone knows x].

The topic-information is, however, the same for (100) to c. It is the proposition

(103) Someone knows someone.

In (103) the information about the order of the arguments is lost. Nevertheless, (103) is needed, in order to determine the focus information of (100) to c. It is clear that the topic-*value* is needed. It would be nice if we could dispense with the notion of topic-information, but I don't yet see, how.

A remark to the relation of this approach to truth-conditional semantics. In a way, everything we did is classical. In particular, there are no truth-value gaps. The method developed so far is inspired by the more-dimensional semantical approach to 'implicature' found in Karttunen & Peters (79).[32] I believe, however, that my approach is something else. I do not introduce a new level of meaning as this seems necessary for an analysis of implicatures. The analysis of topic and focus is situated on the content-level only. I think my procedure links with something else namely with the idea of conceiving the proposition as something structured. There are lot of arguments in the literature for such a view, which ultimately go back at least to Carnap's

'Meaning and necessity'. (I have in mind Lewis (72), Kaplan (77) and Cresswell (80)). What I said is essentially this: the proposition is at least structured as to topic and focus. So a proposition would be an ordered pair $\langle P, \langle a_1, \ldots, a_n \rangle\rangle$, where P is an n-place property (the topic-value) and $\langle a_1, \ldots, a_n \rangle$ are arguments of the right type (the focus-value). From these two you can derive the content, but not vice versa. A formal theory that realizes these ideas has still to be be worked out, of course.

The last remark is connected with Manfred Bierwisch's work. Since his pioneer-article about German intonation[33] not much progress has been made in this field (I am speaking of studies about *German* intonation, not of studies about intonation in general). I hope that this situation is changing rapidly. Like Bierwisch's work, most of the current literature about intonation are 'autonomous' studies (*e.g.* the dissertation of M. Libermann).[34] My contribution is almost entirely semantical or pragmatic, hence an 'autonomous' study, too.

I think the time has come to combine the two views.

Universität Konstanz

NOTES

* Acknowledgements. I profited from discussions with Irene Heim, Ruth Manor, Tanya Reinhart and Wolfgang Klein. Last but not least I wish to thank our secretary Sonnya Borho for patiently typing the manuscript. Thanks also to Josef Baier, Wolfgang Skonefeld, Christa Hauenschild, Dieter Wunderlich and Ede Zimmermann, who commented on an earlier version.

[1] There is a systematic ambiguity in the notions of topic and focus. Sometimes we understand these notions as referring to certain aspects of the meaning of a sentence, sometimes as referring to certain formal properties of the sentence. Whenever confusion may arise from this ambiguity, I will use a self-explanatory terminology.

[2] There is another 'empirical' refutation of the old information approach to topichood which I will disregard for a while.

[3] It doesn't make much sense anyway to say of a referent like Hans-Robert that it is information.

[4] These data are fully impressionistic.

[5] Cf. for instance, Jackendoff (1972). Rules that account for the above examples are given in Stechow (1980).

[6] This is not a serious definition. The facts are much more complicated. *Vide*, for instance, section **5** of this article.

[7] Cf. Chomsky (71).

[8] See also Höhle (1979).

[9] For the definition of the material implication $\Rightarrow$, cf. **1.1.**

[10] This picture is too simple. Irene Heim has argued that the common ground should be an open proposition. I am ignoring this complication. Cf. Heim (80).

[11] More precisely, we have to show the following claim: If $g \subset t$, then $g \cap (t \Rightarrow c) = g \cap c$.

Proof: Suppose $g \subset t$. "$\subset$": Assume $w \in g \cap (t \Rightarrow c)$. Then $w \in g$ and $w \in (t \Rightarrow c)$. Hence, by supposition, $w \in t$. Hence $w \in c$, by definition of $\Rightarrow$. Therefore $w \in g \cap c$. The direction "$\supset$" is fully trivial.

[12] When speaking of propositions, I will henceforth mostly avoid the tedious set-theoretical notation used above. Think of 'Ede ate something' as short for $\{w$: Ede ate something in $w\}$.

[13] Most of the ideas found in this paragraph are inspired by Manor (80). But I am not sure whether R. Manor would agree with me on the last claim in the text. On the other hand, I am in agreement with Wunderlich (76). On page 190, he writes: "Der propositionale Gehalt der Frage kann deshalb nicht durch die Menge der möglichen Antworten bestimmt werden, sondern umgekehrt bestimmt er, was eine mögliche Antwort ist."

[14] This analysis is proposed in Cresswell (73), but practically nowhere else in the literature about questions. Clearly, this analysis is the simplest possible and I see no reason for not taking this line. The usual interpretation of the content of a *yes-no*-interrogative α is Karttunen's '$\lambda x_S\, [x_S \,\&\, (x_S = \alpha \vee x_S = {\sim}\alpha)]$' where x_S is a proposition.

One consequence of this account is that positive and negative questions have the same content. I find this counterintuitive. Furthermore, it is hard to explain why we react differently to positive questions than we react to negative questions. See the discussion in section 6.

[15] This procedure is found in Egli (74) and in other places as well.

[16] I am using a sloppy notation for properties. (38) is short for $\lambda x_N \, \{w$: x invented the powder in $w\}$.

[17] The importance of eliminative answers is stressed in Manor (80).

[18] It should be clear from the above remarks that this qualification needs further clarification.

[19] A one-place operator over B is a function whose domain is B and whose values are in B. The identity operator or mapping over B is the function f over B such that for any $x \in B: f(x) = x$.

[20] Vide Jackendoff, at several places.

[21] Vide A. G. Hatcher, 'Syntax and the sentence', *Word* **12** (1956), pp. 234–50.

[22] Wolfgang Klein has pointed out to me that this becomes particularly clear if we consider a perfect tense: compare: (a) "er hat ihn geschätzt' – (b) 'er hat ihn nicht geschätzt'. As to topichood, the two sentences should be exactly equivalent. This wouldn't come out if "hat" were a focus in (a) but not in (b).

[23] Vide Bäuerle (79).

[24] Cf. Bäuerle (79).

[25] Cf. the two Wunderlichs (80).

[26] *Vide* Wunderlich, loco citato.

[27] Cf. Gazdar (76).

[28] Cf. Reinhart, p. 40.

[29] Cf. Lewis (79).

[30] Cf. *e.g.* Montague's PTQ, where such a procedure is adopted.

[31] I owe this insight to Reis (77), p. 221ff.

[32] Or Gazdar (76).
[33] Cf. Bierwisch (1966).
[34] M. Libermann: *The Intonational System of English*. PhD-dissertation, M. I. T. 1975.

REFERENCES

R. Bäuerle: 1979, 'Questions and answers', in Bäuerle et al.

R. Bäuerle, U. Egli and A. v. Stechow (eds.): 1979, *Semantics from Different Points of View*, Berlin-Heidelberg-New York, Springer.

J. Bayer: 1980, 'Comments on Tanya Reinhart's *Pragmatics and Linguistics: An Analysis of Sentence Topics*; Manuscript, Konstanz.

M. Bierwisch: 1966, 'Regeln für die Intonation deutscher Sätze', in *Studia Grammatica* 7, 99–201.

N. Chomsky, 1971, 'Deep structure, surface structure, and semantic interpretation', in *Semantics: An Interdisciplinary Reader in Philosophy*; D. Steinberg & L. Jakobovits (eds.).

M. Cresswell: 1973, *Logics and Languages*, London, Methuen.

M. Cresswell: 1980, 'A highly impossible scene. The semantics of visual contradictions', manuscript, Wellington.

U. Egli: 1974, *Zur Integration der Semantik in die Grammatik*, Kronberg/Tr, Scriptor.

E. Engdahl: 1980, *The Syntax and Semantics of Questions in Swedish*, PhD-dissertation, Amherst (Mass.).

G. Gazdar: 1976, *Formal Pragmatics for Natural Language*, PhD-Thesis, University of Reading.

C. L. Hamblin: 1976, 'Questions in Montague English', in *Montague Grammar*, B. Partee (ed.), New York etc. Academic Press.

R. S. Jackendoff: 1972, *Semantic Interpretation in Generative Grammar*, M.I.T. Press, Cambridge (Mass.).

A. G. Hatcher: 1956, 'Syntax and the sentence', *Word* **12**, 234–50.

I. Heim: 1980, 'Reference and open propositions', Part I (July); Part II (October); unpublished manuscript, Amherst (Mass.).

T. N. Höhle: 1979, *'Normalbetonung' und 'Normale Wortstellung': eine pragmatische Explikation*. Katholieke Universität Leuven, Voorlopige Publikatie Nr. 66, October.

D. Kaplan: 1977, *Demonstratives. An Essay on the Semantics, Logic, Metaphysics and Epistemology of Demonstrations*. Unpublished manuscript, March.

L. Karttunen and S Peters: 1979, *Conventional Implicature*. In *Syntax and Semantics*, Vol. II: *Presupposition*. Academie Press.

L. Karttunen and S. Peters: 1980, Interrogative Quantifiers; in *Time, Tense and Quantifiers*; Ch. Rohrer (ed.), Tübingen.

W. Klein: 1980, 'Ellipsis and intonation', manuscript, Nijmegen.

A. Kratzer: 1978, *Semantik der Rede*, Kronberg, Scriptor.

D. Lewis: 1972, 'General semantics', in D. Davidson and G. Harman (eds.), *Semantics of Natural Language*, Dordrecht, Reidel.

D. Lewis: 1977, 'Index, context and content', manuscript.

D. Lewis: 1979, 'Score-keeping in a language game', in *R. Bäuerle et al.*

M. Libermann: 1975, *The Intonational System of English*, PhD-dissertation, M. I. T.

R. Manor, 1980, 'Answers and other reactions', manuscript.

R. Manor: 1980, 'Dialogues and the logics of questions and of answers', manuscript to appear in *Linguistische Berichte*.

R. Manor: 1980, 'Positive and negative sentences and their use', manuscript.

R. Montague: 1974, *Formal Philosophy*, R. H. Thomason (ed.).

T. Reinhart: 1980, 'Pragmatics and linguistics. An analysis of sentence topics', to appear in *Philosophia*.

M. Reis: 1977, *Präsuppositionen und Syntax*, Tübingen, Niemeyer.

P. Sgall, E. Hajivocá and E. Benesová: 1973, *Topic, Focus and Generative Semantics*; Kronberg/Ts.

R. Stalnaker: 1974, 'Pragmatic presupposition', in: Munitz, M. K. and Unger P. M. (eds.): *Semantics and Philosophy*, New York Univ. Press, N. Y.

R. Stalnaker: 1975, 'Assertion', manuscript.

A. v. Stechow: 1978, 'Presupposition and context', *Working papers of the SFB 99*, Konstanz. To appear in *Aspects of Philosphical Logic*; U. Mönnich (ed.).

A. v. Stechow: 1980, 'Modification of noun phrases. A challenge for compositional semantics', *Working Papers of the SFB 99*, Konstanz. To appear in *Theoretical Linguistics*.

A. v. Stechow: 1980, 'Notes on topic and focus of interrogatives and indicatives', *Working Papers of the SFB 99*, Konstanz.

D. Wunderlich: 1976, 'Fragesätze und Fragen', in D. Wunderlich, *Studien zur Sprechakt-theorie*, Frankfurt.

D. Wunderlich: 1979, *Fragen und Antworten*. 1979. To appear in *Energeia*.

D. Wunderlich: 1980, *Fragen und Antworten*, manuscript, Nijmegen.

DIETER WUNDERLICH

QUESTIONS ABOUT QUESTIONS*

Mit Fragen kommt man nach Rom.

1. WHY SHOULD QUESTIONS BE A MATTER OF CONCERN FOR LINGUISTS?

Though questions play an important role in our daily life, they do not have that prominent a position within linguistic theory. We ask for information, confirmation, or deliberation, for help, support, or advice; we ponder hypotheses and inquire into problems. One who aims towards building up a theory is best advised to proceed by asking one question after another. We cannot even imagine an activity where we are not engaged, in some way or the other, in deliberating questions.

Let us take for granted that linguists are concerned with the sentences of a language and their respective meanings. We can now observe that, for every indicative sentence in a language, a whole battery of interrogatives can be construed. For instance, from (1) we can formally derive interrogative sentences such as (2):

(1) Manfred has to pay for it.
(2) a. Does Manfred have to pay for it?
b. Who has to pay for it?
c. What does Manfred have to pay for?

(The formal operations which are needed here include inversion, substitution by a question-word and modification of the intonational contour.)

We first have to build up the linguistic structure connected with an indicative sentence such as (1) before we can consider the derivational mechanisms that can be applied to it. Hence, from the syntactical point of view interrogative sentences are, in a way, secondary. It is yet uncontested that the formal means for marking an interrogative sentence in a language constitute a proper subpart of the study of syntax.

Now, notice that (1) can represent a (full, redundant, or non-elliptic) answer to both of the questions that can be posed by uttering (2a) and (2b). If we characterize a question by the set of answers it can induce, it

W. Klein and W. Levelt (eds.), Crossing the Boundaries in Linguistics, 131–158.

becomes clear that the study of indicative meaning, that is, of propositional content, is inevitable, even if we are really more concerned with questions. Again, from the semantic point of view the study of questions is somewhat supplementary.

Sentence (2c) above requires a special remark. It expresses a question invited by (1), but is not answered by (1). It makes us aware that the pronoun *it* in (1) relates to a particular context. We may consider (2c) as just pointing out one of the semantic properties of (1). Again, we are drawn back to considerations about indicative meaning.

On the whole, the study of questions seems nothing but an extension of ordinary grammarian's work. It presupposes a thorough study of indicatives. Most of the interesting semantic problems already arise in connection with indicative meaning, hence the semantician, too, is not forced to go into questions.

From the point of view of illocutionary force or interactional setting the situation is, however, quite different. A question is the most prominent kind of initiative speech act, that is, it invites a verbal response. Many adjacency pairs of utterances, as well as many tripartite sequential patterns, begin with a question. A question can serve there in many different pragmatical or communicative functions. It will not, however, be my concern here to go into this matter. Thus, I do not want to dispute whether it is reasonable to exclude illocutionary force completely from semantic considerations, or at least to provide for some counterpart of illocutionary force on the semantic level.

I wish to select only two points from this whole field of inquiry – be it properly linguistic or not. The first point is that the semantic status of an interrogative cannot be identified with that of an indicative. If we take the position that an indicative designates a proposition (which can be true or false), we must admit that the content of a question is something else, since a question cannot be true or false.

The second point is that the linguistic structure of a sentence often reflects the possible position of that sentence within a sequential pattern. This phenomenon has been accounted for by introducing such notions as topic and focus. These are related to the problem of question and answer insofar as a question may define the topic of a subsequent indicative. And it is just this which seems to reflect the initiative nature of a question.

Another interesting feature of questions is their close connection with both the state of knowledge and uncertainties and the state of preferences a person may have. Such attitudes, taken alone, would be the subject of a psychological inquiry rather than of a linguistic one. But attitudes do not lie fully outside of the field of linguistics. If we were concerned with speech acts, we could, for instance, partly define illocutionary force in terms of the attitudes a speaker conventionally conveys in a particular kind of speech act.

Even in an account of the more specific properties of questions, we make use of certain notions with respect to the attitudes involved. For instance, the focus of a question can be related to a specific interest of and an assumption made by a speaker. We also distinguish between more or less informative answers. This notion of informativeness has to be explicated in terms of the corresponding states of knowledge. Beside this, informativeness is connected with the possible sequencing of questions and answers. We expect the less informative questions and answers at the beginning of a discourse and not at the end. In a way, it is easier to ask a less informative question (with fewer background assumptions) than a more informative one. And it seems that a yes/no-question is easier to answer than a wh-question, for the former divides the set of possible states of affairs into just two subsets. A well-known technique for sequencing questions consists in a stepwise partitioning of the set of all possible alternatives into progressively smaller subsets.

If we find ourselves, when reading a detective story, confronted with a corpse in the fog, one question above all comes to mind: "Who is the murderer?" ("Whodunit?"). Given the event that somebody murders somebody, it could just as well be the question: "Who is the victim?" In fact, some detective stories focus just on the victim, taking the murderer for granted. This is a possible linguistic option given the structure of a sentence about killing.

In the following, I will say nothing about pragmatical aspects of questions, including illocutionary force. By the term 'interrogative', or 'question sentence', I refer exclusively to linguistic means, whereas 'question' is used for the meaning of interrogatives. More specifically, a question is what someone puts forth by uttering an interrogative under the proper circumstances. I take an interrogative as always having been uttered 'literally', without investigating just what the proper circumstances might be. I also exclude any consideration about the context dependence of interrogative meaning. If no confusion can arise, 'question' covers both the sentence and its meaning. 'Content of a question' is used for only a part of the interrogative meaning, for I am aiming at a multiple approach, where focus and topic also belong to interrogative meaning.

2. WHICH KINDS OF QUESTIONS SHALL WE CONSIDER?

In a first inspection we can distinguish at least three kinds of questions: yes/no-questions, wh-questions, and alternative questions. Examples are (3)–(5):

(3) Is pragmatics a proper part of linguistic theory?
(4) What is the semantic type of an interrogative sentence?
(5) Is presupposition a semantic or a pragmatic phenomenon?

There is nothing new about this classification. Moreover, I believe every language can make the distinction by appropriate intonational, syntactical, or lexical means.

A yes/no-question sentence is derived from an indicative sentence by some technique of formal marking peculiar to a given language. Some languages mark yes/no-questions by a final rising intonation (often in combination with other means), others use particles (usually at the beginning or at the end of a sentence) or prefixes or suffixes (usually attached to the verb or the whole predicate). There are also languages which mark yes/no-questions in their system of verbal inflexion, and finally we have languages, such as English and German, which use word order (inversion of the subject and the finite verb). A yes/no-question can properly be answered with a *yes* or *no* (or the respective equivalents) or by repetition of some part of the predicate in its given or in the negated form. Consider the answer to (3):

(6) No, it isn't.

where both techniques are applied.

A wh-question sentence is distinguished by the occurrence of a question word or phrase which is always specific for a certain syntactic category. It either takes the position of that category in a corresponding indicative sentence, or it is moved, usually into a frontal position. This kind of question can properly be answered with some expression of the same category as the question word. Such an expression may, however, be complex, e.g. consisting in a Boolean function on the set of expressions of the appropriate kind.

Finally, an alternative question sentence (which, however, shares some characteristics of the yes/no-question sentence) is marked by the explicit enumeration of the alternatives which have to be considered. Accordingly, the alternative question is properly answered by any one of these alternatives or by a complex expression which is a Boolean function on the set of the alternatives given.

Is There Any Deeper Reason For Having Just These Three Kinds Of Question?

I think so. We could speculate along the following lines: A speaker can try to build up a hypothesis about what the state of affairs he is interested in might be, and then try to find out his listener's opinion, be it consenting or dissenting. The speaker might, however, come up with a certain set of alternatives which are equally viable and wish to make a decision with respect to these alternatives. A rather different kind of problem solving behaviour is to restrict a range of 'entities' that could fit a certain matrix; in this case, the speaker is interested in a specification within that range. The only further possibility I can think of is that the speaker both restricts a range and ponders certain hypotheses or alternatives within that range. Then he may come up with a so-called focus question, which turns out to be a 'mixed type' of question. Examples are:

(7) a. *What* is the simplest kind of question, *the yes/no-question*?
b. Is the *yes/no-question* the simplest kind of question?

I consider (7a) and (7b) to be semantically equivalent.

3. CAN ALL QUESTIONS BE TREATED ALIKE?

Linguists and philosophers often seem to be fascinated by the idea of a semantic approach general enough to cover all three kinds of question considered thus far. If one is concerned only with the propositional content of questions, it is quite natural to aim for a uniform approach within this domain. When you have discovered, however, that there is a common speaker attitude or a common speaker-hearer relationship which you can associate with all kinds of questions mentioned, the search for a common semantic approach becomes less important. Of course, there are pragmatically different questions, e.g., real information questions, examination questions, didactic questions, surprise questions, and so on – but each of these goes with any of the kinds of questions thus far considered. Given that we want to justify the common denomination of 'question', if we can show that there are common features on the speech-act level, there is no real need for a uniform semantic approach.

Moreover, in my opinion, the fact that each language has developed such different formal means for marking questions reflects semantic rather than pragmatic differences. This view does not, however, rule out the search for a common semantic approach, provided we do not simply extend some feature of one of the types of questions to the others.

But some of the familiar approaches do just this. There are two such approaches, recently discussed by Bäuerle (1979): the propositional approach, and the categorial approach.

According to the propositional approach, every answer provides a proposition, and a question can be considered to be the set of possible direct answers. Hence, every question sentence denotes a set of propositions. A yes/no-question S? denotes the set whose members are the propositions p and $\sim p$, given that S denotes p. A wh-question wh$_A$-S'? denotes the set whose members are the propositions $p_1, p_2, \ldots$, given that $a_1, a_2, \ldots$ are members of the category A and that a_1-S', a_2-S', ... denote $p_1, p_2, \ldots$, respectively. An alternative question S_1 or S_2 or ...? denotes the set whose members are the propositions $p_1, \sim p_1, p_2, \sim p_2, \ldots$, given that $S_1, S_2, \ldots$ denote $p_1, p_2, \ldots$, respectively. Clearly, this approach can be elaborated further. One should also keep in mind that each of the denotation functions must be relativized to a certain context. Generally, S denotes an open proposition, that is, a function from contexts into propositions. The denotation set of an interrogative can also be restricted pragmatically.

(8) Whom did you talk to?

Excluded from the relevant category set of persons are, in any case, people who are already dead and people who live elsewhere and don't have telephones.

The problem with the propositional approach is that every categorial answer must be considered elliptic: one always has to construe a full answer by taking into account the content of the question. Undoubtedly, this *can* be done. If you are asked, for instance, what a particular answer means with respect to a given question, you can make such a propositional reconstruction. But this does not seem to be the way most languages proceed.

On the other hand, according to the categorial approach, every question is somewhat incomplete with respect to some category, and it is the answer that delivers an entity of the appropriate kind. It is only the pair of a question and an answer which is equivalent to a proposition. Hence every interrogative denotes a function from categorial answers into propositions. This approach works quite well for wh-questions. It is, however, problematic for yes/no-questions and for alternative questions.

Egli (1974, 76) has proposed an approach in which the needed category is the modus of the assertion, which can be indicated by *yes* or *no*. Another solution within the categorial approach has been proposed by Bäuerle himself (1979). He considers every yes/no-question and every alternative question to be equivalent to a focus question, and he states that the answer always focusses on the same category. As for yes/no-questions – leaving aside for a moment the alternative questions – Bäuerle's argumentation hinges on three points: First, he rejects the idea that *yes* and *no* are real answers to a yes/no-question. Second, he argues that a focus can be determined for every yes/no-question. Third, he argues that, if the categorial answer to a yes/no-question is not overtly present, it can nevertheless easily be derived. Though I sympathize somewhat with Bäuerle's first point, I disagree with his second and third points. (Incidentally, the two approaches – the propositional and the categorial – are not as different as Bäuerle would have us believe. We can describe a function in terms of a characteristic set of values. A proposition can be true or false. If we now fix the true propositions as the interesting values, we can describe the question as it is understood in the categorial approach in terms of a set of true propositions.)

4. WHAT DO *YES* AND *NO* MEAN IN ANSWERS?

Yes and *no* are in no way restricted to a question response. They can also be used in responding to an assertion or request. We can observe similar phenomena in many languages, but the way in which the lexical equivalents of *yes* and *no* can be used differ somewhat from language to language. Therefore, let us consider some examples from German.

(9) Gibt es Elefanten im Zoo? ('Are there elephants in the zoo?')
– Ja, natürlich. ('Yes, of course.')
– Nein. ('No.')

(10) Gibt es keine Elefanten im Zoo? ('Aren't there any elephants in the zoo?')
– Doch, natürlich gibt es welche. ('Yes, of course there are.')
– Nein, aber Giraffen. ('No, but giraffes.')

(11) Das Wetter ist heute doch prima. ('The weather is fine today.')
– Ja, aber windig. ('Yes, but windy.')
– Nein, mir ist es zu kalt. ('No, it's too cold for me.')

(12) Das Wetter ist heute gar nicht gut. ('The weather is not very good today.')
– Doch, ich mag's gerne kalt. (lit. 'Yes it is, I like it cold.', i.e., 'It isn't so bad')
– Nein, aber wenigstens regnet es nicht. ('No, but at least it isn't raining.')

(13) Gib mir mal dein Fahrrad. ('Let me have your bike.')

– Ja, natürlich, gerne. ('Yes, of course, gladly.')
– Nein, ich brauch's selber. ('No, I need it myself.')

(14) Laß das Fahrrad nicht im Regen stehen. ('Don't leave the bike out in the rain.')
– Doch, es soll mal sauber werden. (lit. 'But it should get clean.', i.e., 'It could use a wash')
– Nein, natürlich stell ich's rein. ('No, of course, I'll take it in.')

The examples show that *ja, doch,* and *nein* can equally be used in responding to a question (as in (9) and (10)), or an assertive remark (as in (11) and (12)), or a request (as in (13) and (14)). I conclude that they are general response words with different uses, but with a unique meaning. Similarly, *yes* and *no* in English and their respective equivalents in other languages mark a general form of response behaviour.

What is the content of the response? From the use of *ja, doch*, and *nein*, we can reconstrue what the respective speaker is ready to assert if we take into account the proposition expressed in the preceding utterance. We can, therefore, call these words propositional agreement markers.

On the other hand, the use of *natürlich* ('of course') shows that the respective responding speaker is willing to agree with a certain attitude of the preceding speaker. This explains why in (10), where the questioner rather assumes that there are elephants in the zoo, *natürlich* goes with *doch*, whereas in (14) where the requesting speaker wants the bike to be taken in, *natürlich* goes with *nein*. Other attitude agreement markers in English are *sure* and *OK*.

Although (e.g. in examples (10) and (12)) we could consider *nein* ('no') as an expression of disagreement with an attitude, this cannot be maintained throughout. Example (14) clearly shows that *nein* can also be used where there is agreement with an attitude.

Ja ('Yes') always indicates the acceptance of a preceding non-negated proposition; *doch* indicates the negation of a previously negated proposition, whereas *nein* ('no') indicates either the negation of a non-negated proposition, or the acceptance of a negated proposition.

I take the great variation in the conditions for using *yes* and *no* and their equivalents in different languages as an indication that these words were not designed for expressing answers. This is merely one of their possible functions, provided there is a preceding question that seeks agreement or disagreement.

As Pope (1973) has pointed out, one can differentiate between languages where the response words are always sensitive to the kind of precedingly expressed proposition (i.e., negated or not negated) and languages where they are not. In the latter – one example is Japanese – the response words always indicate agreement or disagreement with an attitude, independent of the kind of precedingly expressed proposition. Thus, the agreement marker *ee* in Japanese can be translated 'yes' only if the preceding proposition is not negated, and the disagreement marker *iie* means 'no' only if the preceding proposition is negated (cf. Kitagawa 1980).

I wish to draw a further conclusion from the foregoing remarks. If it is true that in so many languages one either agrees or disagrees with the proposition expressed in a yes/no-question, there is hardly room for recognizing it as an implicit alternative question. Contrary to the position taken by Katz and Postal (1964), Karttunen (1977) and many others, I sympathize with Bolinger, who claims that what a yes/no-question advances is "a hypothesis for confimation" (Bolinger 1978, p. 104). For if

(15) Will you have a beer?

is treated like

(16) Will you have a beer, or not?

than (15) should also be equivalent to

(17) Won't you have a beer?

We know, however, that (15) and (17) are not alike. And this asymmetry calls for an explanation. As I will show below, the difference between (15) and (17) lies in their respective foci (and, triggered by the foci, in different speaker assumptions associated with them), whereas their contents are the same. The answer to a question is determined by the focus, not by the content. Thus, in a way I subscribe to both positions: Katz-Postal's – in that I reconstrue it as a content-oriented position, and Bolinger's – in that I reconstrue it as a focus-oriented position.

5. IS EVERY YES/NO-QUESTION A FOCUS QUESTION?

The essence of Bäuerle's proposal lies in the assumption that every yes/no-question sentence is ambiguous to the extent that it allows for different focus questions. Thus, for instance,

(18) Are you Dr. Livingstone?

turns out to be ambiguous between (19) and (20):

(19) Are *you* Dr. Livingstone?
(20) Are you *Dr. Livingstone*?

where the italics indicate the focussed part of the sentence. Before coming back to Bäuerle's suggestion, let us first examine the notion of the focus question.

A constituent of a sentence can be focussed by a particular intonation pattern, which differs somewhat from language to language. In German, for instance, we have some kind of rising or high pitch, depending on the whole pitch contour. A focus can, however, be realized by grammatical means as well. Some languages mark the focus constituent of an interrogative by means of a particle or by moving that constituent. English and German have cleft sentences, where the cleft constituent is always the focussed constituent. Consider

(21) Is it you that is Dr. Livingstone?
(22) Is it Dr. Livingstone that you are (called)?

(Let us disregard the fact that these particular instances are not good English – because of the pragmatical circumstances of an utterance of (18)–(20).)

As many linguists have pointed out, a focus question such as (19) or (20) is connected with a particular topic, sometimes also called a presupposition (Rohrer 1971) or a background assumption (Kiefer 1980).

If we consider a yes/no-question as advancing a certain hypothesis, we can easily find the hypotheses which underlie (19) and (20). They are:

(23) *You* are Dr. Livingstone.
(24) You are *Dr. Livingstone*.

We can then find the topic which is common to the focus question and the corresponding focus assertion by replacing the focussed constituent of the indicative sentence with an indefinite (or existential) pronoun of the corresponding category. We thus get:

(25) Someone is (called) Dr. Livingstone.
(26) You are (called) something.

Someone and *something* determine the focus category. Given an assumption such as (25) or (26): in a focus question the speaker asks whether a particular entity of the focus category fits with this assumption, and in a focus assertion the speaker asserts that this particular entity is fitting.

Under what circumstances can a focus question properly be uttered? They are as follows: The speaker takes the topic for granted (as being shared by his audience), and he also has some reason to believe that the focussed entity fits with the topic. Thus, we might say that there is a topic assumption being shared by speaker and hearer as well as a focus assumption on the part of the speaker alone. In a *yes* or *no* response to a focus question the answerer either agrees or disagrees with the focus assumption, whereas in both cases he accepts the topic assumption.

Besides the type of focus question just considered, there is another type – the 'mixed' question – which is similar to it in many respects. Consider

(27) Who is Dr. Livingstone, *you*?
(28) Who are you, *Dr. Livingstone*?

(Again, I am not concerned here with the most appropriate formula for asking somebody's name.)

(27) and (28) consist of two parts: a wh-question and a yes/no-question concerning the focussed constituent. One can argue that any answer to (27) or (28) is at the same time an answer to (19) or (20) respectively. (27) and (28) do not differ in this respect from (19) and (20). The two types of question share their respective focus elements. But do they also share their topic? This depends on how we conceive of wh-questions. I shall discuss this matter below. At the moment, note that it need not be the case that a speaker of (27) assumes that the topic previously discussed – that someone in the vicinity is called Dr. Livingstone – is shared by his audience.

The wh-part of the mixed question shown in (27) and (28) plays an impartant part in Kiefer's investigation into yes/no-questions as wh-questions (Kiefer 1980). He observes that, if it is not indicated otherwise in the context, a 'pure' focus question such as (19) or (20) can be interpreted as a wh-question. This wh-question is obtained by replacing the focussed constituent with the corresponding interrogative pronoun. Thus we get for (19) and (20), respectively:

(29) Who is (called) Dr. Livingstone?
(30) You are (called) what? ⇒ What are you called?

In a way, we can say that (29) and (30) lie behind (or sequentially before) such questions as (19) and (20), and just this has been explicated in the mixed type of focus question. If we answer (27) with *no*, we are still expected to answer the wh-question which is part of (27), e.g., by responding

(31) No, it's the man over there with the green hat.

And, if not indicated otherwise in the context, such an answer – instead of a blunt *no* – is also expected in response to (19), as Kiefer has convincingly shown.

Now I wish to return to Bäuerle's claim that every yes/no-question can be treated as a categorial question. As proof of this he takes the position that a question such as (18) is always meant as a mixed question such as (27) or (28). Furthermore he states that if one properly responds to a yes/no-question such as (18), (27), or (28) respectively, a categorial answer, even if not uttered 'on the surface', can always be derived. For instance, with respect to (27) we can derive a categorial answer as follows:

(32) Yes ⇒ It's *me*. (*I* am.)
No ⇒ *I* am not.

This claim is, however, simply not correct. Though in some cases we may have a categorial answer – see Bäuerle's example:

(33) Hast du das im Radio gehört? ('Did you hear that on the radio?')
– Ja, im Radio. ('Yes, on the radio.')

– with respect to a more 'simple' question such as (18) or (27) one repeats a part of the predicate as well. In many languages where there are no agreement expressions such as *yes* and *no*, it is quite natural to repeat a part of the predicate when answering a yes/no-question. And what we derive from an agreement or disagreement or from an answer which in some respect is incomplete, is a propositional answer. In a case such as (33), the categorial answer may be stipulated by a rather high accessibility to the focus position in the sense Kiefer has introduced. (33) seems to be an example of an unmarked focus question, that is, if the focus is not marked otherwise, it lies on the adverbial *im Radio* regardless of whether or not we give a particular intonation contour to it.

Having rejected the idea that a yes/no-question quite naturally has a categorial answer, let me consider the other part of Bäuerle's 'proof'. Is every yes/no-question a focus question? Consider

(34) Is Arnim going to Wellington this summer?

Clearly, we may have a focus on *Arnim*, or on the place adverbial, or on the time adverbial, and so on. *This* and possibly even *going* can also be focussed constituents. These details, however, are not significant here.

We can also have a multiple focus question, e.g.

(35) Is *Arnim* going to *Wellington* this summer?

Compare (35) with

(36) Is *Arnim* going to Wellington this summer?

In a way, the speaker of (36) wants his addressee to consider the range of possible persons based on the assumption that someone is going to Wellington this summer, whereas the speaker of (35) wants his addressee to consider the range of possible pairs ⟨a person, a place⟩ based on the assumption that someone is going somewhere this summer. This can easily be elaborated further. Let us consider one last example:

(37) Is *Arnim going to Wellington this summer*?

The speaker seems to be interested in the range of possible quadruples ⟨a person, an activity, a place, a time⟩ based on the assumption that someone is doing something somewhere sometime, and, as before, he advances a certain hypothesis for one of these quadruples. But isn't this a rather artificial situation which requires very peculiar pragmatic circumstances to come into being?

I assume that (34) is not an unmarked focus question, that is, there is no single constituent of (34) which is more easily accessible to focus position than the others. If we simply utter (34) without marking a focus, the utterance will, however, not be ambiguous in the sense that one of the several possible focus questions is meant. The most unlikely reading would be to identify this unfocussed utterance with the maximally focussed utterance of (37), since the latter would require a very strong pragmatic restriction. Hence we arrive at the result that (34) can be a yes/no-question without any focussed constituent.

Is (34), then, focus undetermined? In a way, yes, if we always use 'focus' to mean the rendering prominent of a sentence constituent. But we are free to extend the notion of focus. A speaker who utters (34) without marking a focus advances a hypothesis towards the whole proposition

(38) (that) Arnim is going to Wellington this summer.

Therefore we can consider (38) to be the focus of that utterance, or of sentence (34) itself. This fits with the conception that a focus assumption is always speaker-based. If the focus of a yes/no-question is the corresponding proposition, then there is no topic in that question, and henceforth no topic assumption can be made. In a way, in a simple utterance of (34) the whole proposition is new to the hearer, and there is nothing in that sentence that is shared by speaker and hearer except the names.

There are two kinds of yes/no-questions which can never be turned into a constituent focus question.

(a) *Existential Questions*

(39) a. Has anybody seen Pim?
b. Do you have any connection with astrology?
c. Is there a Loch Ness monster?
d. Didn't you ever get a letter from Santa Claus?

It would make no sense to consider the indefinite pronoun as being focussed, since there are no such questions as

(40) a. *Who has seen Pim, anybody?
b. *Is it anybody that has seen Pim?

In these cases there is no topic that can be assumed. Existential questions ponder, instead, a possible topic. To consider another constituent as being focussed hardly makes sense. Consider

(41) a. Whom has anybody seen, Pim?
b. Is it Pim that anybody has seen?

These cases are grammatical but ruled out on pragmatic grounds. We would rather expect a double focus question like

(42) Who has seen whom, *Veronika Pim*?

I cannot think of even one appropriate situation for uttering (41).

(b) *Questions Without A Subject-Predicate Structure, Or Without A Second Focusable Constituent*

(43) a. Is it snowing?
b. Does it help?

In these cases, there is only one constituent that can be focussed upon. This, however, cannot be done, since there would then be no topic left. One condition for a constituent-focus question is that there are at least two constituents that it is possible to focus on.

A third kind of question is simply for pragmatical reasons resistant to focussing.

(44) a. Are you angry?
b. Do you feel sick?

In the normal course of affairs one doesn't want to find out persons who are angry or feel sick. People are, instead, interested in the feelings or views of their interlocutors, that is, they presuppose 'that's about you'. But notice that this is not a grammatical property of questions such as (44). It is easy to think of situations where *you* in (44) will be focussed upon. (Compare also with example (19) above.)

6. WHAT IS THE QUESTION TOPIC, AND WHAT IS THE QUESTION CONTENT?

According to Höhle (1979), the topic of an indicative sentence is the set of questions it answers. This leads us to a somewhat different conception of topic. The topic of an indicative sentence is some property which is satisfied by the focussed element. Consider

(45) Mit *Manfred* bin ich nach Berg en Dal geradelt. ('With Manfred, I rode to Berg en Dal by bike.')

With (45), I can answer the question

(46) Mit wem bist du nach Berg en Dal geradelt? ('With whom did you ride to Berg en Dal?')

Let us abbreviate R = ride, b = Berg en Dal, I = Speaker 1, m = Manfred, and let us assume that R is a three-place predicate. The topic of (44) is then the property

(47) $\lambda x\, R(I, x, b)$

(I will leave out all the otherwise necessary intensionality indicators.)

This property is satisfied by the focussed element, that is, m. The content of (45) is then as follows:

(48) $\lambda x\, R(I, x, b)\,(m)$, which is equal to $R(I, m, b)$

Besides the topic, we have the topic assumption of (45), which the speaker apparently shares with the questioner:

(49) $\exists x\, R(I, x, b)$

To make sure that the topic of (45) is the question it answers, I take the position that (47) is the content of (46) as well. In other words, asking a wh-question means to bring in a property which has to be satisfied by an entity of the appropriate type, delivered within an answer.

Now, we have two options for determining the topic of a wh-question.

(a) The topics of a direct answer and its corresponding question are always the same. Hence, the topic of a wh-question is identical with its content.

(b) The topic of a direct answer to a wh-question is always the content of this question, as pointed out above. The topic of a wh-question, however, is different from its content; it is, rather, the topic assumption the answerer shares with the questioner.

According to option (a), (47) is the topic of (46), whereas according to option (b), (49) is the topic of (46).

Von Stechow (1980), in his notes on topic and focus of interrogatives and indicatives, subscribes to option (a). In an earlier version, he identifies the common topic of a wh-question and the corresponding answer with an existential proposition such as (49). He then revises his attempt, in order to avoid certain unwanted corollaries, by taking the common topic to be the corresponding property, as in (47). I cannot, however, see any reason why the topic of an answer-question pair should remain the same.

In what follows, I myself shall argue for option (b). (Note that I considered (46) as a focussed wh-question. We shall have to examine whether there is any difference from a wh-question in which the interrogative pronoun phrase is not focussed.)

I will base my further considerations on an observation of the sequencing of questions. Since this will, in a way, constitute the climax of my attempt, I am giving it the number 50.

(50) – Did anybody call up? (a)
– Yes. (b)
– *Who* called up? (c)
– *Wolfgang.* (d)

This little dialogue could have gone on, for example, with questions such as "What did he want?", "Why?", etc., but this will not be my concern here. (In fact, this whole article came out of this dialogue.)

(50) seems to be a natural sequence of two questions with their respective answers. In a way, (50c) – "*Who* called up?" – presumes a *yes*-answer to

the existential question (50a) – "Did anybody call up?" – and (50b), the *yes*-answer to an existential question, invites the following focus question. Someone who begins a dialogue with (50c) runs the risk that his addressee might disagree with the corresponding existential proposition, whereas someone who begins with (50a) does not run such a risk. It turns out that (50a) is a 'safe' question, but (50c) is not.

We can explain this property of questions in terms of their topic. The most natural way is that a speaker takes the content of a preceding utterance as the topic of his own utterance. (Of course, he need not proceed in this way. The topic may be some part of the content of one of the preceding utterances, or it can be inherent in the speech situation.) I take it that (50) is a sequence of the most natural kind:

(50a) has no topic;
(50b)'s topic is identical with the content of (50a);
(50c)'s topic is identical with the content of (50b); and
(50d)'s topic is identical with the content of (50c).

So, far, nothing has been said about the content of a yes/no-question. I think this is also a property, namely, a property of propositions. A yes/no-question does not, however, show its content on the surface; we have to reconstrue it by taking into account its possible answers. When a yes/no-question advances a hypothesis towards the proposition p, the opposite could also turn out to be the case. Therefore, we can always construe the content as follows:

(51) $\lambda\alpha(\alpha = p \vee \alpha = \sim p)$

(This could be refined by adding an intensionality operator and the condition that the proposition of the answer should be true – see Wunderlich (1976, 1978), Karttunen (1977).)

Notice, however, that this conception of what the content of a yes/no-question is does not mean that it is an implicit alternative question. As I have pointed out above (examples (15)–(17)), the content of a question is a rather abstract notion. The different foci (of a yes/no-question and an alternative question) determine the kind of answer to be given.

Let C be the one-place predicate "call up', and w = Wolfgang, and let us disregard the tense. Then we can construe the content-topic relationship involved in the dialogue (50) as follows:

	topic	content
(50a)	–	$\lambda\alpha(\alpha = \exists xCx \vee \alpha = {\sim}\exists xCx)$
(50b)	$\lambda\alpha(\alpha = \exists xCx \vee \alpha = {\sim}\exists xCx)$	$\exists xCx$
(50c)	$\exists xCx$	λxCx
(50d)	λxCx	$\lambda xCx(w)$

A subsequent question "Why?" would just take the content of (50d) for its topic.

I am fully aware that this notion of topic and content requires some apparatus to work out the context dependences involved. The answer *yes*, for instance, takes both its topic and its content from the preceding utterance. The same holds true for the answer *Wolfgang* in (50d). (50c), "*Who* called up?", however, overtly marks a focus within a sentence; thus we can derive the corresponding topic from the sentence itself.

There is one serious objection which could be made. Compare the following question-answer pairs:

(52)	– *Who* called up?	(a)
	– *Wolfgang* called up.	(b)
(53)	– Did *Wolfgang* or *Pim* call up?	(a)
	(=*Who* called up, *Wolfgang* or *Pim*?)	(aa)
	– *Wolfgang* called up.	(b)
(54)	– Did *Wolfgang* call up?	(a)
	(=*Who* called up, *Wolfgang*?)	(aa)
	– (Yes), *Wolfgang* called up.	(b)

The (b)-answers to the three questions (52a)–(54a) seem to be identical. It might be questioned whether (54b) should be identified with the other two answers, since we expect a *yes* in this answer and *Wolfgang* to be unstressed. In any case, (52b) and (53b) are equally good answers.

The three questions (52a)–(54a) have different contents. Now, if the topic of an answer is identified with the content of the preceding question, then the sentence

(55) *Wolfgang* called up.

can be given three (or at least two) different topics within the given question-answer pairs. Moreover, (55) could have an infinite number of different topics, since *Pim* in (53a) could be replaced by any other name. With regard to its topic, sentence (55) would then be just as context dependent as the propositional agreement marker *yes*. This result is somewhat counterintuitive.

We can, however, avoid this unwanted corollary if we consider (53a) to be equivalent to (53aa), and (54a) equivalent to (54aa). The topic of the answer might then be retraced to the matrix of the question, which in all three cases is the same, namely

(56) $\lambda x Cx$.

(56) represents just the content of (52a) and of the first parts of (53aa) and (54aa). Both of the latter questions contain an addition to this matrix. Hence, their full content is as follows:

For (53) = (53aa):

(57) $\lambda x(Cx \wedge (x = w \vee \sim(x = w)))$

For (54a) = (54aa):

(58) $\lambda x(Cx \wedge (x = w \vee x = m))$

The topic of the answer is then sensitive only to the matrix condition and not to the list of alternatives given.

7. HOW DOES THE FOCUS OF A QUESTION CONTROL THE ANSWER?

Having shown that the topic has to do with the natural sequencing of utterances, I would like to come back to the notion of focus. In a natural sequence, no two consecutive utterances should have the same focus, since having the same focus would mean, in a way, that the second utterance does not contribute anything new.

In the preceding sections I indicated that it is the focus of a question which controls the answer. To see how this general principle works, we again have to distinguish among the different kinds of questions.

In a yes/no-question, the speaker seeks agreement or disagreement. Is it the focus of the question the answerer agrees or disagrees with? Consider these possible dialogue fragments:

(59) – Did *Wolfgang* call up? (a)

– { Yes. (b)
Yes, he did. (c)
Yes, *Wolfgang* called up. (d)
No. (e)
No, he didn't. (f)
No, *Pim* called up. } (g)

The focussed part of (59a) is *Wolfgang*. One cannot, however, agree or disagree with a single constituent. What is agreed or disagreed with is, instead, the whole proposition advanced in the question, which the focus is a part of. (In a yes/no-question without a focussed constituent, this proposition is identical with the focus.) Thus the proposition of (59a) to which propositional agreement can be applied, can be represented by $\lambda x Cx(w)$ (which is equal to Cw).

This proposition should not be confused with the speaker's focus assumption. As I pointed out above, *yes* and *no* mark agreement or disagreement with a proposition, but not with an attitude. In the case of (59a), there is no difference between the proposition expressed and the focus assumption. But consider

(60) Didn't *Wolfgang* call up?

The proposition expressed is $\sim\lambda x Cx(w)$, whereas the focus assumption is the opposite, namely $\lambda x Cx(w)$. (I shall ignore the fact that a focus assumption can more or less be biased – this is a purely pragmatical matter.)

(59b) and (59e) indicate pure agreement/disagreement; these are non-focussed answers. And so are (59c) and (59f): The use of the pronoun *he* shows that no focussing takes place. The answers (59d) and (59g), however, do focus. In the disagreement example (59g) the former focus has been replaced with a new one (of the same category, thus showing that the topic of the question has been accepted). Only in the agreement example (59d) do both the focus of the question and the focus of the answer turn out to be the same. This redundancy seems to rule out (59d) as a natural answer; we would at least expect *Wolfgang* to be somewhat defocussed, that is, to have a less pronounced stress on it.

Next, I shall consider the wh-question. In this case, the speaker looks for a specification. Let us compare the focussed and the non-focussed wh-questions.

(61) – *Who* called up? (a)
– { *Wolfgang* (did). (b)
Not *Wolfgang*. (c)
Somebody. (d)
Nobody. } (e)

(62) – Who called up? (a)

– { *Wolfgang* (did). | (b)
Not *Wolfgang*. | (c)
Somebody. | (d)
Nobody. } | (e)

Is there any difference in the dialogue fragments presented in (61) and (62)? (61a) is a focussed wh-question with the topic $\exists xCx$. Let us assume that there is also a topic assumption on the part of the questioner regarding this very topic. The answerer seemingly accepts this assumption in (61b) and (61c). (Note that the topic assumption of an answer refers back to the topic of the question, whereas the topic itself is the content of that question.) The foci of both (61b) and (61c) lie within the range of the focus of (61a); thus, both are specifying answers – although (61c) is clearly less informative then (61b). (61d) is not informative at all, since it just renames the topic of the question. And (61e) rejects the topic, so it is not an answer at all.

(62a), the non-focussed counterpart of (61a), has a peculiar property: The only constituent that can be focussed upon is the interrogative pronoun, or, more generally speaking, the phrase that contains it. Consider these questions:

(63) Wolfgang called up *when* from Nijmegen?
(64) ?Who called up *yesterday* from Nijmegen?
(65) *Was it yesterday that who called up?
(66) Who called up, *Wolfgang*?
(67) *Who called up, *yesterday*?
(68) If someone called up, *who*?
(69) ?If someone called up, *when*?

The interrogative phrase must be focussed if it is not fronted. (In this case a pragmatical condition holds – that is, (63) has to be used as a echo question – which ensures that the corresponding topic can be assumed.) No other constituent can normally be focussed, as is shown by (64) and (65) and, again, by (67). It is, however, possible to focus some entity within the range of the wh-word, that is, of the same category as the wh-word – see (66). And, finally, it is as a rule possible to focus on a wh-word following an existential *if*-clause only if it is of the same category as the existential pronoun in that clause – compare (68) and (69).

This leads us to the idea that a non-focussed wh-word nevertheless tends to become focussed, that is, (62a) and (61a) easily become the same. This is true for ordinary conversation, where differences only rarely occur. It is also assumed in some theories of interrogatives; Åqvist (1965), among others, simply identifies (62a) with (61a). I think, however, that there is a difference. If not indicated otherwise in the context, a non-focussed wh-question does not share a topic with its focussed counterpart. For reasons just outlined, I shall say that the unstressed wh-word designates a weak focus.

(62b) introduces a focus within the range of the wh-word; this is a specifying procedure in the same way as in the mixed question (66). (62c) now poses a problem: though it also focusses on *Wolfgang*, it does not seem to be an acceptable answer. The explanation I would offer is this: (62b), in the context of (62a), entails that someone called up, hence *Wolfgang* has been properly focussed. But (62c) does not, in this context, entail that someone called up, nor can this be presumed. Therefore, the focus on *Wolfgang* is somewhat misleading.

(62d) could be informative with respect to (62a), but it lacks any specification. (62d) can nevertheless be made acceptable by adding some explanation as in

(70) Somebody did call up, but I don't know who.

With respect to (61a), however, the first part of (70) would not be possible. Finally, (62e) seems to be a perfectly good answer. If the whole range is taken out of perspective, any specification becomes superfluous.

The same difference in the acceptability of a *nobody*-answer shows up with regard to (66) as opposed to (59a). Let me repeat the two questions with this kind of answer as (71) and (72):

(71)	– Did *Wolfgang* call up?	(a)
	– No, nobody called up.	(b)
(72)	– Who called up, *Wolfgang*?	(a)
	– No, nobody called up.	(b)

(71b) is less acceptable than (72b), provided that (71a) does not have a rising final intonation.

Example (68) – repeated here for convenience –

(68) If someone called up, *who*?

– is a rather interesting kind of question. It has been discussed in the literature as a typical example of a 'safe' question. We can represent this lack of risk by the tautological topic:

(73) $\exists xCx \rightarrow \exists xCx.$

where the consequens is induced by the focussed wh-word.

Similarly, in the case of the mixed question (72a), we may consider the proposition advanced by the focus (which in this case is identical with the focus assumption) to be conditional:

(74) $\exists xCx \rightarrow \lambda xCx(w)$

(A similar proposal has recently been made by von Stechow (1980, p. 80); he calls the proposition advanced the 'new information'.) This explains why (72b) is a good answer. (74) does not commit the speaker to the antecedens that someone called up (and the answerer need not reject). But if the questioner's focus assumption is simply $\lambda xCx(w)$ – as is the case in (71a) – he is committed to the view that someone called up, hence, if the answerer disagrees, he has to reject this view explicitly. Instead of (71b), he may then give a response like this:

(75) No, in fact, nobody at all called up.

This approach can now be extended for a simple unfocussed wh-question. Considering its lack of a topic and the weak focus on the wh-word, we can construe the proposition advanced by the focus as a tautological conditional. In case of (62a) we get then exactly the same conditional as in (73):

(73) $\exists xCx \rightarrow \exists xCx.$

– but now as a focus-proposition, not as a topic. This explains why a *yes*- or *no*-response to such a question is not sensible, but any response which asserts or rejects the antecedens (e.g., (62d) or (62e)), or which specifies the consequens (by replacing the existential pronoun with an expression of the same category) is sensible.

Finally, some brief remarks have to be made about alternative questions. In this kind of question, the speaker always looks for a selection from a given list. For the sake of simplicity I shall assume that the alternatives are equally focussed. This is, however, not always the case. Consider questions where the list remains somewhat open, which is also indicated in the whole intonation contour of the sentence.

(76) a. Did Wolfgang call up, or Arnim, or anybody else?
b. Who called up, Wolfgang, or Arnim, or . . . ?
c. Hat Wolfgang angerufen, oder Arnim, oder wer?

The alternatives may be propositionally or categorially given. Compare

(77) Would you like to come over for a drink, or is it too late for you?
(78) Did *Wolfgang* or *Pim* arrange this awful time schedule?

The focus of (77) is the ordered set of propositions $\{p, q\}$, where p and q stand for the two propositions expressed in (77); the focus of (78) is the ordered set of persons $\{w, m\}$, where w = Wolfgang and m = Pim. The addressee is expected to select from the respective focus sets, whereas in the 'weaker' cases such as (76) any Boolean function on the set of alternatives is acceptable.

In the strong version of an alternative question, such as (78), the speaker seems to take the focussed elements to be exclusive. Thus the proposition advanced by the focus, and assumed by the speaker, is a disjunction. The speaker does not seek agreement or disagreement, but a decision. If we compare (78) with a question like it but without any focus marking:

(79) Did Wolfgang or Pim arrange this awful time schedule?

we see the difference. To some extent (79) shares with (78) the proposition advanced, but it differs with respect to focus and content. We can answer (79) with *yes* or *no*, whereas (78) is properly answered with either *Wolfgang* or *Pim*. This shows, again, that the focus controls the answer. Nevertheless, a convincing theoretical treatment still remains to be worked out.

According to what has been said regarding yes/no-questions, (77) has no topic; and (78) has the topic 'someone arranged this awful time schedule' ($\exists xAx$). The content of an alternative question can be construed from the given alternatives, thus we get (80) for (77), and (81) for (78):

(80) $\lambda\alpha(\alpha = p \vee \alpha = q)$

(81) $\lambda x(Ax \wedge (x = w \vee x = m))$
$= \lambda\alpha(\alpha = \lambda xAx(w) \vee \alpha = \lambda xAx(m))$

Putting together the various pieces of analysis, we arrive at the Table I:

TABLE I

	topic	focus	proposition advanced by the focus
(82) Are you leaving?	–	You are leaving.	You are leaving.
(83) Aren't you leaving?	–	You are not leaving.	You are not leaving.
(84) { *When* are you leaving? / You are leaving *when*? }	You are leaving sometime.	when	You are leaving sometime.

TABLE I (Continued)

	topic	focus	proposition advanced by the focus
(85) When are you leaving?	–	when (weak focus)	If you are leaving sometime, you are leaving sometime.
(86) When are you leaving, *tomorrow*?	–	tomorrow	If you are leaving sometime, you are leaving tomorrow.
(87) *When* are you leaving, *tomorrow*?	You are leaving sometime.	{when, tomorrow}	You are leaving tomorrow.
(88) Are you leaving *tomorrow*?	You are leaving sometime.	tomorrow	You are leaving tomorrow.
(89) *What* do you want, *tea* or *coffee*?	You want something.	{what, tea, coffee}	You want either tea or coffee.
(90) Do you want *tea* or *coffee*?	You want something.	{tea, coffee}	You want either tea or coffee.
(91) Do you want tea or coffee?	–	You want tea or coffee.	You want tea or coffee.

With the exception of a negated question such as (83), the proposition advanced by the focus is always the content of the speaker's assumption. (In (83), the focus assumption is most likely that you are leaving.)

The table shows that I consider (86) and (87), for instance, to be different questions. The argument for this has been given earlier. We might, however, assume that the difference is due only to pragmatic matters. In this case we could suggest that both (86) and (87) advance the conditional proposition expressed in

(92) If you are leaving sometime, you are leaving tomorrow.

A similar suggestion could be made regarding (88)–(90). We would then have to consider the respective antecedens as a possible topic. It would depend on pragmatical factors whether or not it would actually become the topic. To date, however, I have found no conclusive arguments to decide on this issue.

8. HOW CAN ANOTHER QUESTION BE INVITED?

Let us consider these two cases:

(93) (a) – Bist du mit dem Zug gekommen? ('Did you come by train?')
(b) – Nein. ('No.')
(c) – Womit *denn*? ('Then how?')
(94) (a) – Ist irgendetwas passiert? ('Has anything happened?')
(b) – Ja. ('Yes.')
(c) – *Was* denn? ('What?')

The plain (b)-answers are, in a way, incomplete; we expect something more. Thus, the (c)-questions are invited by these responses. The German *denn* clearly shows that the desideratum has not been satisfied.

I consider (93a) to be an unmarked focus question, hence it has the topic 'you came by some means'. As I pointed out earlier, Kiefer (1980) has shown that the question may then be interpreted as a wh-question. This conception can now be supported. According to my analysis, (93a) is equivalent to

(95) *How* did you come, by *train*?

If we answer *yes*, the first part has been answered, too; but if we answer *no* (without any indication that the topic has not been accepted), the first part of the question still remains open. It is, then, quite natural that this is the question which is invited. Of course, one need not add just this question – we can think of situations where this is not done. Therefore, the invitation of a subsequent question is a matter of pragmatics.

The explanation for this phenomenon is, however, fairly straightforward, since we can relate it to a semantic property of the focus question. In a way, the invited question backtracks to the matrix presumed for the focus question.

With (94), the situation is quite different. In this case a blunt *no* is a good answer, whereas a blunt *yes* invites another question. How does this come about? At this point, we should remember the possible sequencing of questions. An existential question ponders something which can become the topic of some subsequent question. If one wants to find out something specific, it is always safe to start with an existential question. Given that the existential proposition has been accepted, the only question with no further assumption is the wh-question of the corresponding category. Hence we can say that the invited question progresses along a possible sequence of questions in the most natural way.

The same thing happens with requests. For instance, if we go into a shop looking for grapes we can start with a question like

(96) Do you have grapes?

and then continue.

The existential proposition can also become the antecedens of a conditional question or request:

(97) If something has happened, please tell me what?
(98) If you have grapes, please give me two bunches.

Now, if we analyze the proposition advanced in a focus question as a conditional, we can even find a semantic background for more remote invited questions. Consider the following back-trace:

(99) Was this paper written to honour *Manfred*?
(100) If this paper was written to honour somebody, than it was written for Manfred.
(101) Was this paper written to honour someone?

Yes, it was. Therefore, the antecedens of (100) is true. And therefore, (99) was in a way invited.

University of Düsseldorf

NOTE

* It is due to the persistent efforts of Wolfgang Klein that this paper has ultimately been written. I want to dedicate it to my friend and teacher Manfred Bierwisch. Arnim von Stechow's notes on topic and focus have inspired me; we arrived at some similar conclusions. I am grateful to Constance Guhl, who corrected my English.

REFERENCES

Åqvist, Lennart: 1965, *A New Approach to the Logical Theory of Interrogatives*, Uppsala.

Bäuerle, Rainer: 1979, 'Questions and answers', in R. Bäuerle, U. Egli, and A. v. Stechow (eds.), *Semantics from Different Points of View*, Springer, Berlin, Heidelberg, New York, pp. 61–74.

Bierwisch, Manfred: 1980, 'Semantic structure and illocutionary force', in J. R. Searle, F. Kiefer, and M. Bierwisch (eds.), *Speech Act Theory and Pragmatics*, Reidel, Dordrecht, pp. 1–35.

Bolinger, Dwight: 1978, 'Yes-No questions are not alternative questions', in Henry Hiż (ed.), *Questions*, Reidel, Dordrecht, pp. 87–105.

Egli, Urs: 1974, *Ansätze zur Integration der Semantik in die Grammatik*, Scriptor, Kronberg.

Egli, Urs: 1976, 'Zur Semantik des Dialogs', SFB 99 Linguistik Universität Konstanz, *Working Papers*.

Höhle, Tilman N.: 1979, '"Normalbetonung" and "Normale Wortstellung": eine pragmatische Explikation', *Leuvense Bijdragen* **68**, 385–437.

Karttunen, Lauri: 1977, 'Syntax and semantics of questions', *Linguistics and Philosophy* **1**, 3–44.

Katz, Jerrold J., and Paul M. Postal: 1964, *An Integrated Theory of Linguistic Descriptions*, The M.I.T. Press, Cambridge (Mass.).

Kiefer, Ference: 1980, 'Yes-No questions as Wh-questions', in J. R. Searle, F. Kiefer, and M. Bierwisch (eds.) *Speech Act Theory and Pragmatics*, Reidel, Dordrecht, pp. 97–119.

Kitagawa, Chisato: 1980, 'Saying "Yes" in Japanese', *Journal of Pragmatics* **4**, 105–120.

Pope, Emily, N.: 1973, 'Question-answering systems', in C. Corum et al. (eds.) *Papers from the Ninth Regional Meeting of the Chicago Linguistics Society*, CLS, Chicago (Ill.), pp. 482–492.

Rohrer, Christian: 1971, 'Zur Theorie der Fragesätze', in D. Wunderlich (ed.), *Probleme und Fortschritte der Transformationsgrammatik*, Hueber, München, pp. 109–126.

Stechow, Arnim von: 1980, 'Notes on topic and focus of interrogatives and indicatives', SFB 99 Linguistik Universität Konstanz, *Working Papers* No. 45.

Wunderlich, Dieter: 1976, 'Fragesätze und Fragen', in D. Wunderlich, *Studien zur Sprechakttheorie*, Suhrkamp, Frankfurt, pp. 181–250.

Wunderlich, Dieter: 1978, 'On the semantics of questions', *Proceedings of the Twelfth International Congress of Linguists*, Innsbruck, pp. 243–246.

FERENC KIEFER

QUESTIONS AND ATTITUDES

1. In this paper I am going to discuss certain semantic and pragmatic aspects of questions. It will be assumed that the semantics of questions need not take into account speech situations and that, in contradistinction to semantics, the pragmatics of questions can only be accounted for by taking into consideration speech situations (involving at least two aspects: the interactional setting and the knowledge of the speaker/hearer). I shall mainly be concerned with the problem of how knowledge, more precisely, knowledge about the answer, is involved in the pragmatic interpretation of questions. I am going to stipulate that the various types of questions (information question, rhetorical question, didactic question, examination question, etc.) can best be accounted for by postulating a common semantic structure for *all* questions – apart from the differences in propositional content – and let pragmatics do the rest. The main difference between the various question types will be analyzed in terms of differences in *cognitive attitudes* which, in turn, are based to a large extent on some particular features of knowledge. In the second part of my paper I am going to show that there is an interesting relationship between the cognitive attitudes of questions and the predicate types of the matrix sentences of embedded questions. In addition, I shall try to answer the question of what kind of predicates can occur in these matrix sentences and how they are organized.

2. Any theory of questions has to explain the differences between at least the following types of questions:

(i) *Information questions*

(1) (a) When will you return to Zánka?
(b) Whom have you visited in Tihany?

(ii) *Rhetorical questions*

(2) (a) Shouldn't we help our friends when they are in need?
(b) Which girl would not dream of having such a husband?

W. Klein and W. Levelt (eds.), Crossing the Boundaries in Linguistics, 159–176.

(iii) *Examination questions*

(3) (a) How many syllables does the Hungarian word *Székesfehérvár* contain?
(b) Are the e-phonemes in Hung. *fekete leves* all identical?

(iv) *Didactic questions*

(4) (a) What kind of things are cognitive attitudes?
(b) What is the propositional content of questions?

(v) *Exclamations*

(5) (a) Isn't he a nice guy?
(b) Isn't she pretty?

(vi) *Indirect requests*

(6) (a) Can you help me?
(b) Could you comment on my paper?

(vii) *Indirect offers*

(7) (a) Can I help you?
(b) Would you like some more wine?

Before proceeding, a note of warning seems to be necessary. I assume that the speech situations in which the above questions are uttered are sufficiently specified in order to get the intended interpretations. Other speech situations which would change the above interpretations are, however, equally possible. Notice furthermore that I by no means want to suggest that the list (i)–(vii) is exhaustive.[1] Nor do I want to claim that the categories are distinctive: overlappings are quite possible. What is important in the present context is to recall that questions may have various functions and information-asking is only one of them.

Most theoretical works on questions have so far concentrated on information questions.[2] Accordingly, the "question operator" has been interpreted as "asking for information" or the like. On this approach, of course, each question type has to be accounted for separately either by assigning to the "question-operator" various interpretations or by changing the interpretation 'asking for information' according to various additional conditions. Both solutions seem to overcomplicate things and to lead to counterintuitive results. "What seems to be required . . . is a distinction between asking a question of someone and simply posing the question (without necessarily addressing it to anyone). When we pose a question, we merely give expression to, or externalize, our doubt; and we can pose questions which we do not merely expect to remain unanswered, but which we know, or believe, to be unanswerable. To ask a question of someone is both to pose the question and, in doing so, to give some indication to one's addressee that he is expected to respond by answering the question that is posed. But the indication that the addressee is expected to give an answer is not part of the question itself." (Lyons 1977: 755) Lyons points out that the advantage of this analysis of questions is that "It covers not only information-seeking questions, but various kinds of rhetorical and didactic questions without obliging us to treat these as being in many respect abnormal or parasitic upon information-seeking questions."[3] (ibidem) Consider the following question:

(8) Who is JAKE?

Depending on speech situation (8) can be an information question in which case it is paraphrasable as (9):

(9) I want to know who JAKE is.

However, it is quite easy to imagine situations in which (8) would be interpreted as a rhetorical question. Again in other situations (8) could be used to ask an examination question and so forth. What is left unchanged in these various interpretations is (i) the propositional content of (8) and (ii) the interrogative character of (8).

The propositional content of questions is an *open structure*, i.e. a structure containing one or more variables. By filling in the variables we get a proposition which can be true or false. Yes-no questions and wh-questions, maybe also disjunctive question and so-called open questions, will have to be characterized by different propositional contents. We can neglect all the details here, however. For our present purpose it suffices to assume that each question can be characterized by the propositional content P and the question operator Q. Each question would thus be roughly of the form $Q(P)$. What remains to be done is to assign an appropriate interpretation to Q. As pointed out above Q should not be interpreted as 'I want to know' or 'I ask for information'. Let us introduce the following terminological conventions.

By filling in the variables of an open structure we shall say that we get a *solution* to the question and that the propositional content of the question (= an open structure) will be *closed*. We are now prepared to stipulate the following preliminary interpretation of *Q*.

(10) The speaker (= *S*) poses *P* as an open structure that calls for a solution. (In short: *S poses P*)

Notice that in indirect (embedded) questions such as (11) (a)–(b) the open structure *P* is asserted rather than posed. In addition, of course, the matrix sentences of indirect questions contain specific predicates.

(11) (a) I don't care who came first.
(b) Nobody has told me who came first.

Notice furthermore that the interpretation (10) of *Q* does not presuppose an addressee for questions. Neither is it implied by (10) that questions must always be given a solution or that the solution must be provided by the addressee. The question can be left unanswered, it may already have a solution and this solution may be known to the speaker when he utters it, etc.

To be sure, (10) is not sufficient in order to account for how questions work. In what follows I am going to sketch a framework which will enable us to explain the various functions questions may fulfill. We shall restrict ourselves to speech situations in which there is a speaker and a hearer who are engaged in a cooperative conversation. Speech situations can be classified in many different ways but we have to look for a classification that is relevant for our present enterprise. It would seem that the speaker's knowledge concerning the answer provides us with such an aspect for the classification of speech situations. Accordingly, we can distinguish four types of speech situation.[4]

(i) The speaker doesn't know the answer but he assumes that the hearer knows it.

(ii) Neither the speaker nor the hearer know the answer and the speaker knows that the hearer doesn't know the answer.

(iii) The speaker knows the answer but he is not sure whether the hearer knows it or not.

(iv) Both the speaker and the hearer know the answer and the speaker knows that the hearer knows the answer.[5]

It is easy to see that information questions would belong to questions uttered in speech situation (i). In speech situation (ii) the question formulates a *problem*. By uttering the question the speaker may wish to call the hearer's attention to the problem or to emphasize the importance of the problem or the like. If (12) (a) is uttered in speech situation (ii) it can be paraphased by (12) (b):

(12) (a) What is the propositional content of yes-no questions?
(b) The problem is what the propositional content of yes-no questions is.

Questions uttered in speech situation (ii) will be referred to as *problem questions*.

The various types of didactic questions (including examination questions) are questions uttered in speech situation (iii). For examination qestions we get the paraphrase "I want to know if you know . . . ", for other types of didactic questions we need different paraphrases, for example, "I want you to solve the problem . . . " or the like.

Echo-questions, rhetorical questions, exclamations are questions characteristic of speech situation (iv). Such questions express the speaker's cognitive or emotive states and are in this sense not really questions.

Since the speech situations considered involve only the cognitive states (knowledge) of the speaker, one way of accounting for these speech situations (and, consequently, for the pragmatic interpretation of questions) is to express them in terms of the speaker's *cognitive attitudes.*[6] Let us introduce the following notations: S stands for the speaker and H for the hearer, P denotes the propositional content of the question which, as we know, is an open structure, the corresponding closed structure will be denoted by ${}^{\vee}P$;[7] r stands for any state of affairs. In order to account for the speech situations considered above we shall need the following cognitive attitudes of the speaker:

(13) (a) Epistemic attitudes
KNOW (S, r)
RECOGNIZE (S, r)
(b) Doxastic attitudes
ASSUME (S, r)
(c) Emotive attitudes
EMOT (S, r)
(d) Motivational attitudes
WANT (S, r)
(e) REQUEST (S, r)
OFFER (S, r)[8]

In addition, we need the following predicates:

(14) (a) PROBLEM (*x*) '*x* is a problem
(b) POSSIBLE (*x*) '*x* is possible'

The whole structure of the speech situation reflected by the cognitive attitudes of the speaker will be called *configuration of attitudes*. The speech situations (i)–(iv) can be rendered by the following configurations of attitudes:

(15) (a) ~ KNOW (*S*, $^{\vee}P$)
ASSUME (*S*, KNOW (*H*, $^{\vee}P$))
WANT (*S*, KNOW (*S*, $^{\vee}P$))
(b) ~ KNOW (*S*, $^{\vee}P$)
ASSUME (*S*, ~ KNOW (*H*, $^{\vee}P$))
WANT (*S*, RECOGNIZE (*H*, PROBLEM (*P*)))
(c) didactic questions:
KNOW (*S*, $^{\vee}P$)
ASSUME (*S*, (POSSIBLE (KNOW (*H*, $^{\vee}P$)) & POSSIBLE (~ KNOW (*H*, $^{\vee}P$))))
WANT (*S*, KNOW (*H*, $^{\vee}P$))
examination questions:
KNOW (*S*, $^{\vee}P$)
ASSUME (*S*, (POSSIBLE (KNOW (*H*, $^{\vee}P$)) & POSSIBLE (~ KNOW (*H*, $^{\vee}P$))))
WANT (*S*, KNOW (*S*, (KNOW (*H*, $^{\vee}P$)) v KNOW (*S*, (~ KNOW (*H*, $^{\vee}P$))))
(d) KNOW (*S*, $^{\vee}P$)
ASSUME (*S*, KNOW (*H*, $^{\vee}P$))
EMOT (*S*, $^{\vee}P$)
WANT (*S*, RECOGNIZE (*H*, EMOT (*S*, $^{\vee}P$)))

In the case of (15) (a) we get a simpler configuration of attitudes if we realize that the following implicature holds:

(16) WANT (*S*, KNOW (*S*, $^{\vee}P$)) ⇒ ~ KNOW (*S*, $^{\vee}P$)

As to indirect requests and indirect offers notice first that what is requested or offered are not propositions but rather actions. Let *A* stand for any action. Then we get

(17) (a) REQUEST (*S*, *A*)
(b) OFFER (*S*, *A*)

for requests and offers, respectively. Indirect requests and indirect offers can only occur in speech situations (i) and (iv). That is, problem questions and didactic questions can never be interpreted as indirect requests or indirect offers. Both in speech situation (i) and in speech situation (iv) the hearer knows the solution, in the case of requests the solution is, in general, known to the speaker as well whereas in the case of offers it is not.[9]

It goes without saying that the framework as sketched above does not account automatically for all the various functions of questions. Within each speech situation further distinctions are required in order to do justice to what is really going on.[10] We shall not dwell upon this problem any further, however. It should be clear by now that speech situations (i)–(iv) provide an adequate framework for the explanation of the pragmatic functions of questions. One can easily elaborate on this framework, introduce further distinctions, formulate further conditions etc. but these are matters of detail.

It would thus seem that the semantic characterization of questions does not have to go beyond (i) the characterization of the propositional content of the question and (ii) the interpretation for the question operator as given in (10). The rest can be taken over by pragmatics.

3. Let us now turn to the problem of embedded questions. The term 'embedded question' will be taken here to mean a complex sentence in which the subordinate clause expresses the propositional content of a question, i.e. a logically open structure. The following sentences, for example, contain such structures.

(17) (a) I ask you whether Jake likes swimming.
(b) I wonder whether Jake likes swimming.
(c) I don't know whether Jake likes swimming.
(d) I don't care whether Jake likes swimming.
(e) I know whether Jake likes swimming.
(f) I can tell you whether Jake likes swimming.

What kind of predicates can occur in the matrix sentence? Let us have a closer look at this question. Though my observations are based on Hungarian material, most of them can easily be carried over to English.

The predicates in the matrix sentences of embedded questions seem to fall into the following more or less clearly definable groups:

(18) (a) Verbs of asking
e.g. *ask, inquire, call sy to account*, etc.
I ask you whether Jake likes swimming

(b) Verbs of cognitive search
e.g. *think, analyze, wonder, meditate, ponder, ruminate, speculate*, etc.
I wonder whether Jake likes swimming

(c) Verbs of perceptual search
e.g. *look, nose, listen, feel, watch*, etc.
I am watching how Jake likes swimming

(d) Verbs expressing interest
e.g. *be interested, want to know, would like to know, would like to see/to hear*, etc.
I would like to know whether Jake likes swimming

(e) Verbs expressing lack of knowledge
e.g. *do not know, forget*, etc.
I do not know whether Jake likes swimming

(f) Verbs expressing knowledge
e.g. *know, be aware*, etc.
I know whether Jake likes swimming

(g) Verbs of communication
e.g. *tell, explain, write*, etc.
I can tell you whether Jake likes swimming

(h) Verbs expressing perceptual certainty
e.g. *see, hear, experience*, etc.
I have seen how Jake likes swimming

(i) Verbs expressing 'come to know'
e.g. *realize, discover*, etc.
I have discovered how Jake likes swimming.[11]

(j) Emotive predicates
e.g. *to be astonished, to be surprised, it is astonishing/ surprising*, etc.
It is surprising how Jake likes swimming in cold water.

The predicates in (18) (a)–(j) consistute two different classes. The first class comprises the predicates (a)–(e), the second the predicates (f)–(j). The first class in characterized by the fact that the speaker does not know the answer, the second one by the fact that the speaker does know the answer.[12] To put it differently, the embedded questions containing the predicates of type (a)–(e) are open structures which call for a solution. On the other hand, the embedded questions containing predicates of type (f)–(j) are no longer open structures: the predicates of the matrix sentences turn the originally open structures into closed structures. We can see, then, that knowledge is involved in the semantics of embedded questions, too. Let us now extend the notion of propositional attitude such that it covers 'attitudes' toward the propositional content of questions as well.[13] Then the predicates of the matrix sentences of embedded questions can be characterized by the following propositional attitudes (p stands for any proposition):[14]

(19)	*ASK* (x, p)	for verbs of asking
	THINK (x, p)	for verbs of cognitive search
	LOOK (x, p)	for verbs of perceptual search
	SEE (x, p)	for verbs expressing perceptual experience
	KNOW (x, p)	for verbs involving knowledge
	TELL (x, p)	for verbs of communication
	EMOT (x, p)	for emotive predicates
	DISCOVER (x, p)	for verbs expressing 'come to know'

Verbs expressing interest can be analyzed as a complex attitude:

(20) *WANT* $(x,$ *KNOW* $(x, p))$ for verbs expressing interest

It must be emphasized that the attitudes in (19) and (20), in contradistinction to the cognitive attitudes in (15), belong to the semantics of language, they are realized linguistically as predicates of matrix sentences whereas the cognitive attitudes reflect merely the cognitive states of the speaker when uttering questions and are not necessarily realized in the linguistic structure itself. Again, refinements and further distinctions may be necessary for a more adequate account of propositional attitudes but we shall not go into the details here. Let us rather turn to the following problem: How are the above mentioned propositional attitudes organized? The attitudes (18) (a)–(e) are apparently related to the mental state of 'lack of knowledge' or 'non-knowledge'. Notice that either we may simply state what we do not know, or we may ask for information, or we may state that we are thinking about the solution or looking for some perceptual evidence, or we may express our interest in knowing the solution. And it would seem that this exhausts all possibilities. The mental state of 'non-knowledge' may thus prompt the following propositional attitudes:

(21)

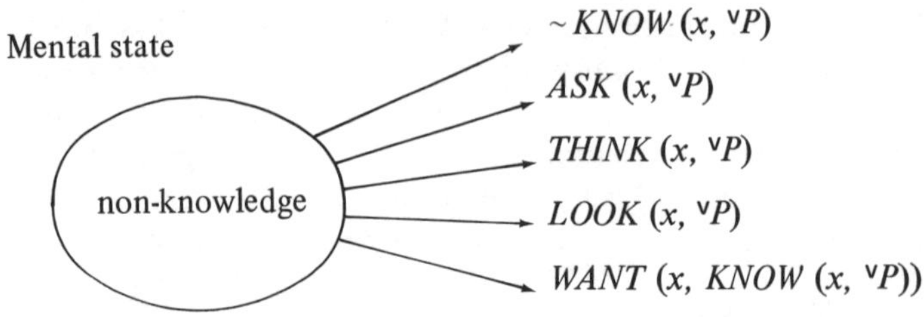

Of course, the speaker may also want to state that he is not asking for the solution, or that he is not thinking about it or looking for it, or that he does not want to know it. The mental state of 'knowledge', on the other hand, may prompt the speaker either to state simply that he knows the solution or to indicate the way in which he has acquired knowledge: (i) he has discovered the solution or (ii) he has perceptually experienced the solution or (iii) somebody has told him the solution. Finally, he may wish to express his emotive reactions toward the solution.[15] We thus receive the following picture:

(22)

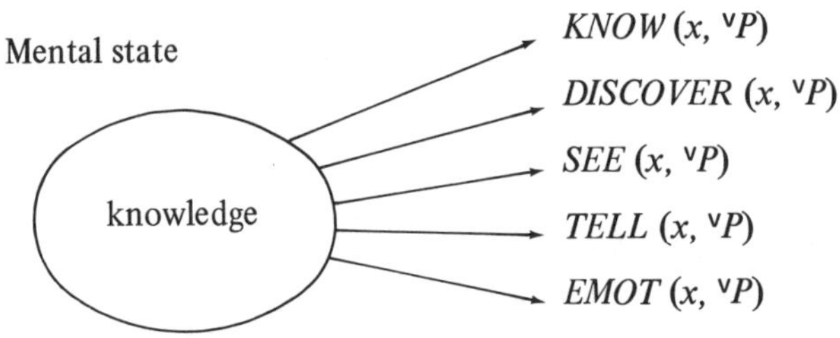

x ranges over persons including the speaker and the hearer and P is the propositional content of questions.

The above observations can be summed up in the following hypothesis:

(23) Only matrix sentences containing predicates that express one of the propositional attitudes (19)–(20) accept embedded clauses of type P.

(21) and (22) seem to represent the linguistically relevant attitudes in connection with questions. (23) is an empirical hypothesis, further inquiries into the structure of language must show if it is correct or if it must be rejected. By comparing (21) and (22) it is not difficult to realize that the propositional attitudes in (21) and those in (22) are related to each other in a fairly obvious way. Unspecified non-knowledge, ~ *KNOW* (x, $^{\vee}P$) is related to unspecified knowledge, *KNOW* (x, $^{\vee}P$); if one asks for a solution, the addressee will, in

general, provide us with it, that is, $ASK\ (x, {}^{\vee}P)$ is related to $TELL\ (x, {}^{\vee}P)$; if one is thinking about the solution, one may discover it, which yields the correspondence between $THINK\ (x, {}^{\vee}P)$ and $DISCOVER\ (x, {}^{\vee}P)$; finally, if one is looking for perceptual evidence, one may get it, that is, the correspondence $LOOK\ (x, {}^{\vee}P)$ and $SEE\ (x, {}^{\vee}P)$ holds. This leaves us in (21) with $WANT\ (x, KNOW\ (x, {}^{\vee}P))$. This attitude, however, is in a way more fundamental than $ASK\ (x, {}^{\vee}P)$, $THINK\ (x, {}^{\vee}P)$ and $LOOK\ (x, {}^{\vee}P)$. Each of them seems to imply the former. In addition, $WANT\ (x, KNOW\ (x, {}^{\vee}P))$ implies $\sim KNOW\ (x, {}^{\vee}P)$. The attitudes in (21) can thus be organized in the following fashion:

(24)
$$\left.\begin{array}{l} ASK\ (x, {}^{\vee}P) \\ THINK\ (x, {}^{\vee}P) \\ LOOK\ (x, {}^{\vee}P) \end{array}\right\} \Rightarrow WANT\ (x, KNOW\ (x, {}^{\vee}P)) \Rightarrow \sim KNOW\ (x, {}^{\vee}P)$$

Similarly, each of the attitudes $DISCOVER\ (x, {}^{\vee}P)$, $SEE\ (x, {}^{\vee}P)$, $TELL\ (x, {}^{\vee}P)$ and $EMOT\ (x, {}^{\vee}P)$ implies knowledge, i.e. $KNOW\ (x, {}^{\vee}P)$:

(25)
$$\left.\begin{array}{l} TELL\ (x, {}^{\vee}P) \\ DISCOVER\ (x, {}^{\vee}P) \\ SEE\ (x, {}^{\vee}P) \\ EMOT\ (x, {}^{\vee}P) \end{array}\right\} \Rightarrow KNOW\ (x, {}^{\vee}P)$$

Notice that the attitudes $ASK\ (x, {}^{\vee}P)$, $THINK\ (x, {}^{\vee}P)$ and $LOOK\ (x, {}^{\vee}P)$ represent the ways in which a solution is sought and the corresponding attitudes $TELL\ (x, {}^{\vee}P)$, $DISCOVER\ (x, {}^{\vee}P)$ and $SEE\ (x, {}^{\vee}P)$ express the ways in which the solution has been found. The latter represent so to speak the results of the corresponding searches. The attitude $WANT\ (x, KNOW\ (x, {}^{\vee}P))$, too, is related to the attitudes in (25) via the attitudes $ASK\ (x, {}^{\vee}P)$, $THINK(x, {}^{\vee}P)$ and $LOOK\ (x, {}^{\vee}P)$ and can thus lead to either one of $TELL\ (x, {}^{\vee}P)$, $DISCOVER\ (x, {}^{\vee}P)$ or $SEE\ (x, {}^{\vee}P)$.

Let us call the attitudes in (24) *question attitudes* and those in (25) *answer attitudes*. The above observations can now be formulated in the following hypothesis:

(26) Each question attitude is related to at least one answer attitude.

The predicate "is related" has been left underfined here but, I think, we have a fairly clear intuitive understanding what it should mean in the present context. In a way, question attitudes and answer attitudes are related to each other as questions and answers are.

If one disregards the attitude $EMOT\ (x, {}^{\vee}P)$ similar things can also be said about answer attitudes, that is

(27) Apart from the attitude *EMOT* $(x, {}^{\vee}P)$ each answer attitude is related to a question attitude.

The two hypotheses, (26) and (27), can be collapsed to (28):

(28) Question attitudes and answer attitudes are not independent of each other. Each question attitude is related to at least one answer attitude and each answer attitude, apart from *EMOT* $(x, {}^{\vee}P)$ is related to a question attitude.

Once again, (28) is an empirical hypothesis which will turn out to be true or false depending on the facts of language.

Let us consider the attitudes in (25) once more. It is not difficult to see that the various attitudes stand for various types of factive predicates. *KNOW* (x, p) and its cognates are clearly factive. *DISCOVER* (x, p) is considered to be semifactive. I have shown elsewhere that the predicates represented by *DISCOVER* (x, p) are factive or nonfactive depending on the topic-comment structure of the sentence.[16] The same holds true for emotive predicates. The verbs of perceptual experience are, at least in Hungarian, always factive. The same holds true for the communicative verbs represented by *TELL* (x, p). Although there are factive predicates that do not occur in (25), *all* predicates in (25) are factive. This explains why they can turn logically open structures (the propositional content of questions) into closed structures. This can only be done by factive predicates. That is, we can formulate the following hypothesis:

(29) The propositional attitudes emanating from the mental state of knowledge represent factive predicates. Only factive predicates can turn open structures into closed structures.

Next, let us compare (24)–(25) with (15). It is not at all surprising that some of the attitudes bear the same label: certain propositional attitudes are simply linguistic realizations of cognitive attitudes. Thus, *KNOW* $(x, {}^{\vee}P)$ is the linguistic realization of KNOW $(x, {}^{\vee}P)$, *WANT* $(x,$ *KNOW* $(x, {}^{\vee}P))$ that of WANT $(x,$ KNOW $(x, {}^{\vee}P))$ and *EMOT* $(x, {}^{\vee}P)$ that of EMOT $(x, {}^{\vee}P)$.

Notice that the speaker's assumptions about the hearer's mental state (knowledge) are not expressed by means of the propositional attitudes (19)–(20). Similarly, the effect that the speaker wants to reach in the hearer by uttering his question cannot be formulated by means of these propositional attitudes either. In neither of these two cases does the speaker's cognitive attitude concern *P* itself but rather various assumptions about the hearer. In sum, then, we get (30):

(30) Only cognitive attitudes concerning $^{\vee}P$ appear as propositional attitudes of questions.

It does not come as a surprise that embedded questions of type (21), but not of type (22), can function as indirect questions. Thus (31) (a) can easily be answered by (31) (b); (32) (a)–(b), however, do not constitute a question-answer pair.

(31) (a) I don't know whether Jake likes swimming.
(b) Of course, he does.

(32) (a) I know whether Jake likes swimming.
(b) Of course, he does.

We can thus formulate the following principle:

(33) Only embedded questions containing propositional attitudes emanating form the mental state of non-knowledge can function as indirect questions.

Finally, one may wonder whether embedded questions can only function as information questions or if other interpretations are equally possible. Already a cursory glance at (21) makes it clear that the only possible candidate for other interpretations is the attitude *ASK* $(x, {}^{\vee}P)$ since all the other propositional attitudes make the speaker's mental state concerning knowledge quite explicit. And, indeed, embedded questions with *ASK* $(x, {}^{\vee}P)$ lend themselves quite easily to various pragmatic interpretations. A sentence such as

(34) I ask you whether Jake likes swimming.

can be interpreted as an examination question, a didactic question, a rhetorical question, etc. depending on the speech situation. Consequently, the propositional attitude *ASK* (x, p) is compatible with any of the configurations of attitudes (15) (a)–(d) whereas the other propositional attitudes in (21) are only compatible with the configuration of attitudes (15) (a). The reason for this seems to be obvious: only *ASK* (x, p) is related to the question operator in a direct way, that is without revealing the mental state concerning knowledge of the speaker.

It follows from what has been said that the implication (24) does not hold for *ASK* $(x, {}^{\vee}P)$. This propositional attitude is only pragmatically related to the propositional attitude $\sim$ *KNOW* $(x, {}^{\vee}P)$: *ASK* $(x, {}^{\vee}P)$ implicates

~ *KNOW* (*x*, $^\vee P$) if and only if it is connected with the configurations of attitudes (15) (a) or (15) (b). Notice furthermore that *ASK* (*x*, $^\vee P$) is related to *TELL* (*x*, $^\vee P$) if and only if *ASK* (*x*, $^\vee P$) is connected with the configuration of attitudes (15) (a). *ASK* (*x*, $^\vee P$) has thus to be erased from (24).

4. In sum, then, it would seem that the function of questions is a matter of pragmatics rather than of semantics and can be accounted for by means of reference to speech situations explicated in terms of the speaker's cognitive attitudes. The speaker's mental states can also be related to the propositional attitudes of embedded questions. I have stipulated that all propositional attitudes which can occur in matrix sentences of embedded questions are relatable to either the mental state of knowledge or to that of non-knowledge. In addition, the cognitive attitudes of the speaker that do not express the speaker's assumptions about the hearer appear as propositional attitudes in embedded questions. The propositional attitudes of embedded questions are organized in various ways. First, the propositional attitudes emanating from the mental state of non-knowledge and those emanating from the mental state of knowledge are related to each other in nontrivial ways. Second, the propositional attitudes emanating from the mental state of knowledge express factive predicates. Factive predicates have the distinguishing property of turning logically open structures into closed structures.

It goes without saying that this paper is only an utterly tentative sketch of the relationships between attitudes and questions and the problems involved. Much further research is needed in order to clarify most of the details.[17]

NOTES

1 "Information question" is a cover term for a rather heterogeneous category which does not only comprise questions asking for information in the strict sense of the word (e.g. *Can you tell me how to get to Zánka*?) but also questions such as

(a) Is it true that you will get a big appartment? (Truth value questions)
(b) Do you think that it is a good idea to write a paper about questions and attitudes? (Questions asking for somebody's opinion)
(c) May I have a look at your manuscript? (Questions asking for permission)
(d) Did not Julia tell you that I was ill? (Questions asking for confirmation)
(e) Shall I talk to your boss? (Questions asking for advice)

and so forth.

Similar considerations hold true for rhetorical questions. Quintilian mentions rhetorical questions among the figurative uses of questions which are the following (cited by Wikberg, op. cit., p. 44); (a) asking for emphasis, (b) asking that which cannot be denied, (c) asking a question to which it is difficult to reply, (d) asking in order to throw odium on the person to whom it is addressed, (e) asking to excite pity, (f) asking to embarrass, (g) asking to express indignation, (h) asking to express wonder, (i) asking to express sharp command, (j) asking ourselves, (k) one question is asked and another is answered, (l) the answer makes defence precede confession, (m) dissimulatory reply serving to raise a laugh, (n) putting the question and answering it oneself, (o) to ask a question and not wait for the reply.

2 This is true of linguistic tradition since *Katz and Postal 1964* and of most logical works since *Åqvist 1965.*

3 *Wunderlich 1976* argues along similar lines (p. 213 and passim) though his conclusions are slightly different from the approach advocated here. In particular, Wunderlich seems to argue for a broader interpretation of semantics than what I myself would subscribe to. On p. 220, for example, he claims that the illocutionary type of question belongs to the meaning (i.e. semantics) of the question.

4 We neglect here all further information about the speech situation.

A similar framework for the pragmatic interpretation of questions was proposed several years ago by P. Ladányi (*Ladányi 1965*).

5 The speech situations as formulated here are speaker-oriented since the pragmatic interpretation of questions (i.e. the functions of questions) does not depend on the hearer's assumptions. Of course, the hearer will recognize the intensions ("attitudes") of the speaker in a cooperative conversation.

6 "The mental state of the speaker reflecting a situational context (= speech situation, FK) is structured. The elements of a structure representing a mental state of that kind are called *attitudes* (= cognitive attitudes)" (*Motsch* 1980: 159). See also *Wunderlich 1976*: 73–4. I will use here the term 'cognitive attitude' in order to distinguish the attitudes considered from propositional attitudes (see further below). Recall that cognitive attitudes need not be realized in linguistic structure.

Cognitive attitudes which I have in mind here are also discussed in *Bierwisch 1980*: p. 20 and passim. Bierwisch stipulates that the question operator (Qu in Bierwisch's notation) determines the cognitive attitude Q (= 'the utterer intends to know'). This may be true of information questions, in general, however, Q is determined by Qu together with other factors including the interactional setting and the speaker's knowledge.

7 It is not accidental that I use here the extension operator to denote closed structures. The way in which closed structures are obtained resembles what we do by applying the extension operator. Since I have said nothing here about the propositional content of questions it seems to be more prudent to use a less technical term for extensional structures in this paper.

8 It should be made clear that each of these attitudes stands for a class of attitudes and should be considered as shorthand devices only. Notice also that it is quite possible that these attitudes are not elementary, i.e. that at least some of them can further be decomposed into more elementary ones. (Cf. the pertinent discussions in *Miller-Johnson-Laird 1976*).

9 Of course, the situational background for indirect requests and indirect offers as sketched here in terms of cognitive attitudes is not sufficient in order to explain these

speech acts. Principles along the lines discussed, for example, in *Searle 1975* cannot be dispensed with.

10 Compare Note 1.

11 It goes without saying that the first person subjects of the matrix sentences can freely be replaced by second or third person subjects.

Wunderlich 1976 discusses similar problems (pp. 185–189), his classification of matrix sentences differs, however, from the one proposed here in several important respects.

12 If the subject noun phrase does not refer to the speaker then, of course, we have to do with the hearer's knowledge or with a third person's knowledge.

13 This move is quite justifiable in cases such as

(a) I know who was here.
I know that Jake was here.
(b) I tell you who was here.
I tell you that Jake was here.
(c) I have discovered who was here.
I have discovered that Jake was here.
(d) I saw who was here.
I saw that Jake was here.

Evidently, the matrix verbs in the two sentences in (a) through (d) do not express different propositional attitudes.

14 Again, most of these attitudes stand for a whole class of attitudes.

15 It should be made clear that the predicates expressing the propositional attitude *EMOT* $(x, {}^{\vee}P)$ behave in many respects differently from the other propositional attitudes discussed here. Without going into the details let me just point out that emotive predicates do not seem to accept the full range of embedded questions. Sentences (a)–(b) are ungrammatical:

(a) +I am happy who was here.
(b) +I am happy whom I saw.

In other cases there seems to be a shift in the syntactic role of the question word. Compare (c) and (d):

(c) I know how Jake likes swimming.
(d) It is surprising how Jake likes swimming.

The two *how*'s are, of course, related but not identical.

It should also be made clear that not all emotive factives can occur in matrix sentences of embedded questions:

(e) +I regret how Jake likes swimming.

In sum, then, it is not at all surprising that emotive predicates [*EMOT* $(x, {}^{\vee}P)$] do not fit so neatly into the system of predicates at hand.

16 Cf. *Kiefer 1978*. In this paper I argue that the following (a)-sentences are factive whereas the (b)-sentences are not:

(A) (a) Péter *rájött* arra, hogy hibát követett el.
'Peter has discovered that he made a mistake'
(b) Péter *arra* jött rá, hogy hibát követett el.
(B) (a) Péter *örül* annak, hogy Anna megérkezett.
'Peter is happy that Ann has arrived'
(b) Péter *annak* örül, hogy Anna megérkezett.

where the italicized words bear the main stress.

In general, semi-factives and emotives are factive if, and only if, the *that-clause* belongs to the topic of the sentence.

As to verbs of communication *mond* 'say' is clearly nonfactive but *megmond* (the perfective variant of *mond*) is always factive. Similarly, *ír* 'write' and *megír*, etc. The nonfactive *mond, ír* do not accept *wh*-clauses, the sentences in (D), on the other hand, are grammatical:

(C) (a) *Péter azt mondta, hogy kit látott.
'Peter said who he had seen'
(b) *Péter azt írta, hogy kit látott.
'Peter wrote whom he had seen'
(D) (a) Péter megmondta, hogy kit látott.
Péter megírta, hogy kit látott.

In the case of perceptual verbs there seems to be no difference between the imperfective and the perfective variant as to factivity: *lát – meglát* 'see', *hall – meghall* 'hear', etc.

For a revealing discussion of the relationship between factivity and *wh*-clauses cf. *Vendler 1980.*

[17] (Added in proof) It would seem that emotive predicates are not as exceptional and irregular as suggested by my paper. They can, in fact, occur in both situations (21) and (22). To be sure, only a rather restricted class of emotives belong here. These emotives seem to express astonishment, amazement, consternation or similar emotions. Consider, for example, the following Hungarian sentences:

(i) Péter csak bámult, hogy mi lesz ebből.
lit. 'Peter was amazed what (all) this would lead to'
(ii) Mindenki csodálkozott azon, hogy hová lett a mennyasszony.
lit. 'Everybody was surprised at where the bride had gone'

The emotives *bámul* 'be amazed' and *csodálkozik* 'be surprised' are not factive in these sentences. That is, $EMOT(x, {}^{\vee}P)$ must also occur among the propositional attitudes (21).

Notice that exactly the same emotive predicates may also be used factively. The factivity of these predicates depends, in addition to the topic-comment structure of sentences, on some aspects of semantic structure. Thus, there seems to be a clear correspondence between emotive question attitudes and emotive answer attitudes though this correspondence is somewhat different from the correspondences discussed thus far. What all this boils down to, however, is a simplification of hypothesis (28).

REFERENCES

Åqvist, Lennart: 1965, *A New Approach to the Logical Theory of Interrogatives*. Almqvist & Wiksell, Uppsala.

Bierwisch, Manfred: 1980, 'Semantic structure and illocutionary force', in *Searle-Kiefer-Bierwisch*, pp. 1–35.

Katz, Jerrold J. and Postal, Paul M.: 1964, *An Integrated Theory of Linguistic Description*, Cambridge, Mass: M.I.T. Press.

Kiefer, Ferenc: 1978, 'Factivity in Hungarian', *Studies in Language* **2**, 165–197.

Ladányi, Peter: 1965, 'Zur logischen Analyse der Fragesätze', *Acta Linguistica Hung.* **15**, 37–66.

Lyons, John: 1977, *Semantics* Vol. II., Cambridge: Cambridge University Press.

Miller-George A. and Johnson-Laird, Philip N.: 1976, *Language and Perception*, Cambridge, Mass.: Harvard University Press.

Motsch, Wolfgang: 1980, 'Situational context and illocutionary force', in *Searle-Kiefer-Bierwisch*, pp. 155–168.

Searle, John R.: 1975, 'Indirect speech acts', *Syntax and Semantics* **3**, 59–82.

Searle, John R., Kiefer, Ferenc and Bierwisch, Manfred (eds.): 1980, *Speech Act Theory and Pragmatics*, Dordrecht: D. Reidel Publishing Company.

Vendler, Zeno: 1980, 'Telling the facts', in *Searle-Kiefer-Bierwisch*, pp. 273–290.

Wikberg, Kay: 1975, *Yes-no Questions and Answers in Shakespeare's Plays*, Åbo Akademi.

Wunderlich, Dieter: 1976, *Studien zur Sprechakttheorie*, Frankfurt a. M./Suhrkamp.

JENS ALLWOOD

ON THE DISTINCTIONS BETWEEN SEMANTICS AND PRAGMATICS

The trichotomy of syntax, semantics and pragmatics is one of the most popular ways of subdividing the study of human languages. It was originally suggested by Charles Morris in Morris (1938) and later again in a revised form in Morris (1946).

The term *pragmatics* was proposed by Morris in 1938 as a tribute to C. S. Peirce's philosophy of pragmatism, to designate the study of signs and their relationship to interpreters. In 1946 Morris changed this slightly to make pragmatics the study of the origin, use and effect of signs. One of the main differences between the two versions is that in the second version the term *use* also includes the production of signs.

The term *semantics* in 1938 was used to designate the more abstract study of the relationship between signs and the objects they signify (leaving out the interpreter). In 1946 this was changed to the study of signification in all modes of signifying. The second version again widens the definition given in the 1938-version. *Syntax* (or *syntactics* (Morris (1938)) in both the 1938 and 1946 version was to designate the even more abstract study of the relationship between signs without taking either their signification, origin, use or effect into account.

Rudolf Carnap (1942) made use of Morris's trichotomy and thus contributed greatly to its becoming widely accepted. In doing this Carnap, however, introduced a distinction of his own, between a pure and a descriptive way of pursuing the three types of study.

A pure study uses normative regimentation and stipulative definitions in order to clarify concepts which are thought to be fundamental to an area. In semantics, for example, such concepts are truth and reference. A descriptive study, on the other hand, tries to capture empirical data in their fullness, thereby describing also phenomena which can be given no clear explications or definitions. For Carnap a pure study was possible both with regard to syntax and semantics but not to pragmatics which seemed to him only open to description. In fact, Carnap, at this stage, regarded all descriptive studies as pragmatical since they all in some sense involve interpretation, origin, use or effect of signs. Later, however, Carnap (1952) came to hold that the analysis of concepts like 'belief' and 'intension' required the development of a pure

W. Klein and W. Levelt (eds.), Crossing the Boundaries in Linguistics, 177–189.

pragmatics. With work such as Bar-Hillel (1954) and R. M. Martin (1959), formal or pure pragmatics came into existence, primarily, as the study of indexicals, i.e. expressions such as personal pronouns, time and place adverbials. This was then further developed in Lewis (1970), Montague (1968) and (1970).

In the trichotomy proposed by Morris, syntax, semantics and pragmatics are seen as successively more abstract levels of enquiry. We can now ask what the abstraction is based on. As far as the distinction between syntax and semantics goes the prevailing view is that syntax disregards meaning in favor of the study of "purely formal phenomena". When it comes to the distinction between semantics and pragmatics this seems mostly to be seen as an abstraction of meaning along the dimension of context and situation dependence. But it has also been argued that it concerns an abstraction of the cognitive aspects of meaning from those of emotion and attitude or as Carnap (1942) seems to have held a distinction between a normative and a descriptive study of meaning. My remarks in this paper will mainly be concerned with situation dependence and only to some extent deal with the latter two ways of establishing the distinction.

The most common way of viewing the distinction between semantics and pragmatics is in terms of situation or context dependence of meaning. Semantics is supposed to be concerned with those aspects of meaning which are situation independent while pragmatics deals with those aspects of meaning which are dependent on situational factors. In pure semantics, situational independence has mostly been achieved through normative, stipulative definitions of such notions as truth, reference and logical form, while in descriptive semantics one has wanted to attain situational independence either by importing notions of pure semantics, claiming that there is no essential difference between a formal language and a natural language (Montague (1970)) or by claiming that meaning which is literal or conventional can be studied independently of context of use. Both of these alternate conceptions of situation independent meaning are supposed to differentiate so-called inherent meaning of linguistic expressions from phenomena such as vagueness, ambiguity, metaphor, suggestion, implicature, emotional and attitudinal associations which all are seen as more fleeting and, accidental and dependent on situation and not characteristic of the "real" meaning of linguistic expressions.

In what follows, I will not be concerned with the pure, normative and stipulative study of meaning, for example through the medium of an artificially constructed language. Since one by fiat can construct most things one can also construct a distinction between semantics and pragmatics this way. I will, instead, be concerned with the extent to which such a distinction can be made for natural languages either via the notions of pure semantics or via the notion of convention.

Let us begin by considering whether pure semantic notions such as reference, truth conditions and logical form when applied to natural languages really can be used to give an analysis of situation independent meaning and thus serve as an instrument in distinguishing semantics from pragmatics. In the tradition of pure or formal semantics the notions of reference and truth are seen as the central semantic notions since they make it possible to achieve what is seen as the central goal of a semantic theory, i.e. linking language to the world. Essentially, this is accomplished by considering only languages with proper names, predicates, sentences, certain operators and variables as basic categories and then, by defining an interpretation, giving every linguistic expression what is known as its extension in a world consisting of individuals, sets, functions and truth values. Sometimes one adds to this so-called intensional entities such as individual concepts, universals and propositions which can either be seen as primitives or analyzed as constructs out of the above mentioned ingredients of the world. These can then also be assigned to linguistic expressions as part of their meaning. Finally, one usually gives a definition of logical consequence and of what it is for the sentences of the language to be true in a certain model of the world.

Since the whole construction of the semantics is achieved by stipulation one can ensure that each linguistic expression gets a fixed and determinate meaning, i.e. intension and extension, and that this meaning is independent of use in different contexts. In the same way truth conditons can be given for sentences in terms of the fixed situation independent intensions or extensions of the constituent expressions of the sentence.

Let us now see to what extent it is reasonable to think that an analysis of meaning in terms of reference, extension, intension and truth can be situation independent in natural language. Since extension and intension for natural language expressions are mostly not stipulatively given, we face an empirical problem. We have to discover the intensions and extensions of natural language expressions in order to give an account of the truth conditions of sentences in natural language. This is clear, since we are not dealing with stipulation. The meanings of expressions must then be determined empirically. However, once we have empirically discovered what the meanings are, can we then not sit back in our chairs and continue as in formal semantics with situation independent meanings? As long as meaning is conceived of in terms of reference, intension, extension or truth conditions I do not think this will be possible since these notions require a precision and specificity of meaning which in natural language cannot be achieved without the help of context. Let me illustrate this thesis by a number of examples some of which are by now quite well known:

(i) I was hungry.

In order to determine the reference and truth conditions of (i) we have to know who the speaker was, (ii) when the speech event occurred, (iii) where the speech event occurred, (iv) whether psysiological or phenomenal hungriness or both was intended. None of the above points are given in the sentence explicitly, but they are necessary for the determination of truth conditions and reference of this sentence. In natural language we don't need to state these factors since we can rely on context to supply them. In a pure semantic approach they would have to be introduced by stipulation such as in Lewis (1970) where we have speaker time and place coordinates or in Montague (1968) where we have indices for speaker and time. In other words pure semantics would be extended with pure pragmatics. The distinction between the two approaches could be maintained by claiming that only certain predicates needed contextual determination and that only a finite number of factors were involved while other predicates would still belong to the domain of pure semantics having extensions determined once and for all independently of all contexts of use. This conviction breaks down, however, if we start to take seriously phenomena such as the predicate indeterminacy of *hungry* between a phenomenal and physiological sense, i.e. a feeling of hunger is not always accompanied by a physiological state of hunger and vice versa.

Other examples are:

(ii) Everyone came to see the small boy.
(iii) It's raining.
(iv) We danced while the band was playing.
(v) 3 men danced with 3 women.
(vi) The picture is beautiful.

In order to assign reference and to determine truth conditions for these sentences we need among other things the following information: For sentence (ii): (1) the universe of quantification for *everyone*, (2) the location of the speaker to determine the deictic reference required by *came*, (3) the veridicality of the predicate *see*, i.e. whether it's phenomenal or not, (4) the universe of comparison for *small*: for sentence (iii): (5) time of speech event, (6) a distinction between rain and fog, mist, hail and snow; for sentence (iv):

(7) the reference of *we*, (8) a delineation of dancing from jumping, (9) specification of contemporality – the duration of the intersection of dancing and playing – could we have danced when the band took a pause? (10) a delineation of playing from practising or tuning instruments; for sentence (v): specification of quantificational distribution (from 3 to 9 women), (11) relational characteristics of the verb to *dance*; for sentence (vi): (12) referential aspects, referred to by *picture*, e.g. colouring or drawing techniques.

The list of factors which are needed for the determination of reference and truth conditions can easily be made much longer. The dependence on context and situation in natural language to make meanings precise and specific enough to determine reference or truth values is pervasive. How many of these factors one will be able to explicate in formal pragmatics by use of stipulative idealization remains an open question. One thing, however, should be clear from what has been said: the study of meaing cannot, if it is taken to be concerned with notions such as reference and truth, be pursued for natural language without continuously drawing on situation for determination. This is true also for formal languages as soon as such languages attempt to model something more than very impoverished aspects of natural language. If we attempt to deal with languages that are not wholly stipulatively defined, the notions of truth and reference as developed within formal, pure semantics do not make it possible to distinguish semantics from pragmatics on grounds of situational independence. This does not mean that the distinction could not be drawn some other way. For example, by keeping the idea that semantics deals with reference and truth whilst excluding the requirement that reference and truth be situation independent.

Pragmatics could then be said to deal with non-referential, non-truth-conditional aspects of meaning whether these be dependent on situations or not. This proposal, however, has its own difficulties which will be discussed below.

The adherent of the idea that meaning could be given a situation independent analysis with the help of pure semantic notions might have another resort, i.e. he could turn to the notion of logical form and claim that at least logical form, if not truth conditions and reference, is situation independent.

This claim, however, leads to several difficulties. First, a common way to characterize logical form is to say that it is an abstract representation of the truth conditions of a sentence which, if what we have said above about the dependence of truth conditions on context is correct, would also make logical form dependent on situational factors. A sentence will have one logical form in one situation and another logical form in another situation.

Second, one might try to make logical form depend not on sentence tokens, i.e. sentences used as statements, but on some more abstract notion of sentence type. Logical form could then be seen as a set of conditions holding for all truth conditional specifications that can be associated with a sentence. The problem with such a characterization of logical form is that it would not be rich enough to yield all the entailments of a sentence, – a job which, after all, is supposed to be done by logical form.

For example, notions such as the scope of quantifiers and modal operators can often not be determined without recourse to context. See example (v) above and Kratzer (1977). In general, any inferences which are dependent on contextual specification and determination cannot be captured.

Third, one can always explicate logical form by stipulation, for example by declaring that logical form is dependent on the meanings of a certain logical vocabulary, such as the sentential connectives, where the meanings have been clarified by formal definitions or by introducing meaning postulates that tell you something about the meaning relations between certain predicates. Both logical vocabulary and meaning postulates can then be indefinitely extended. The problem is, as usual, that the notion of logical form is created by stipulation and that this way of producing situation independence begs the question.

To sum up, therefore, it does not seem as if logical form would be a good candidate for an explication of a notion of situation independent meaning. Either (i) it is just as situation dependent as truth conditions or (ii) it becomes too abstract to give us a rich enough notion to characterize a number of interesting entailments or (iii) it is stipulative in which case its situation independence is restricted to the language for which the stipulation holds.

It might be objected that the argument so far has not sufficiently considered the distinction between intension and extension frequently made in formal semantics. Even if extensions are dependent on contextual determination, intensions need not be. Intensions could be construed as situation invariant meanings which in conjunction with situational factors determine reference. These situation invariant meanings could then in turn be identified with linguistic meaning proper. Thus, even if the reference of an indexical pronoun like *I* varies with situation and speaker, it always has the same intension or linguistic meaning. One could then go on to claim that semantics is the study of intensions while pragmatics deals with how extensions are established.

In order to determine whether this is a reasonable claim we have to investigate whether there is a notion of intension that will serve as a candidate for situation independent linguistic meaning. It is clear that the usual formal semantic approach of characterizing intensions as functions from situations to extensions will not on its own be sufficient, since this characterization does not connect intensions with language. Intensions according to this analysis can be but in no way need to be connected with language. Since we are concerned here with investigating whether there can be an interesting distinction between semantics and pragmatics in the study of natural language meaning, we are interested in intensions only as far as they can be seen as an aid in determining situation independent linguistic meaning. The formal semantic notion of intension does not do this. It only provides a formal functional analysis of something, the determination of which has to be provided on other grounds.

Let us therefore turn from pure semantics to descriptive linguistic semantics in order to see if any notion developed there will help us draw the distinction between semantics and pragmatics along the lines of situation independence. The favorite candidate here is the notion of literal, conventional meaning. The literal meaning of a linguistic expression is its inherent proper meaning. This meaning is either seen as present in all situations of use, due to linguistic conventions dependent on association between form and content only, or as a basic meaning from which the meaning of the linguistic expression in all situations of use can be derived. The role of the literal meaning of a linguistic expression can perhaps be most clearly appreciated when considering written words or sentences out of context. In spite of the fact there is no overt context it seems possible to arrive at an understanding of their meaning. This understanding is claimed to consist of a grasp of the literal meaning.

The question is now whether there is an analysis of literal meaning which can be given without relying on the notions of reference and truth (which as we have seen lead to an analysis of meaning as context dependent). The analysis should also make it possible to show how literal meaning is something that can be differentiated from what is metaphorical, satirical or implied.

There are in principle three types of solutions that have been suggested within descriptive semantics to determine literal meanings:

(1) The intersection or greatest common denominator approach.
(2) The basic meaning or ideal representative approach.
(3) The union or vagueness approach.

The first candidate for the analysis of literal, conventional meaning that I will consider is what one can call the intersection or greatest common denominator

GCD approach or to use a German term the Gesamtbedeutung approach. This is the idea that the literal meaning of an expression is that which is common to all contexts of use, i.e. situation independence by definition. This has the advantage that it suits all types of meaning – referential, cognitive as well as emotive, attitudinal. Further, this type of meaning is totally dependent on conventional use, since the meaning of an expression is the intersection of all its conventional uses. This, as we will see, is not necessarily the case for the next approach.

However, there are other problems with this approach. (i) For many linguistic items there is no intersection of meaning. The greatest common denominator is zero. This is probably true, for example, of the past tense morpheme in English or of the declarative mood markers in English. (ii) Since this consequence is hard to swallow for most people, they, rather than saying that an expression has no meaning, say that it is homonymous. Thus the declarative mood markers in English show ambiguity between a statement, a question or an order, as is illustrated in sentence (vii) below.

(vii) You will be here to-morrow.

Since the risk of ending up with zero meaning is fairly great if we really take all the contexts of use of an expression into account this approach thus leads to an unnecessary multiplication of meanings. (iii) If a greatest common denominator meaning can be found this will have the property of being very general and abstract. This is a consequence of its being what is common to many different contexts of use. Literal meanings will on this approach be so general that they will be very hard to distinguish from so called metaphorical uses of a meaning. This is so since metaphorical uses are among the uses that have to be taken into account in order to arrive at the greatest common denominator meaning, which in turn often will make it impossible to differentiate literal from metaphorical meaning with this approach. What is needed is an approach to literal meaning giving us meanings with more content.

The next approach is that of identifying literal meaning with a basic or ideally representative meaning, in German often referred to as Grundbedeutung. The oldest suggestion of this type is probably that of identifying literal meaning with that which is known as the essence of something, i.e. those qualities that are both necessary and sufficient to make something what is is. There are many problems connected with this proposal: (i) It is very hard to tell which qualities are essential to a certain entity and which are not. (ii) It is not easy to characterize all types of meanings as essences. Consider the essence of *ouch, even though* or *essence*. (iii) Just as with the greatest common denominator approach, the outcome of an analysis of meaning into essences is often an unnecessary multiplication of meaning elements which all represent clear and separable ideas. The word *can* thus be said to mean either permission, ability, possibility or polite request. The word *action* can mean either the intention connected with a certain type of behavior, the behavior itself, the result of the behavior or certain contextual features associated with the behavior. Thus, the price of identifying literal meaning with essence will also be much more widely spread homonymy in language. (iv) Finally, identifying literal meaning with essence has the consequence that the literal meaning is no longer necessarily conventional. Everybody can be wrong about what the essence is or one person can be right and everybody else wrong. For example, when it was discovered that whales were not fish but mammals, for a while there was a majority of people who were wrong about the meaning of whale. This is, of course, unacceptable if one want to hold that the meaning of an expression is conventional, i.e. what the majority take it to be.

Another suggestion which has a lot in common with the above is the suggestion that literal meanings should be thought of as ideal representative types, the latest version of this theory being the so called prototype theory, cf. Rosch (1976) and (1977). This suggestion too is problematic in several ways: (i) How are prototypes established? Do different people develop different prototypes? If this is the case they are not necessarily conventional. If prototypes are not established on purely biological and ontogenetic grounds, but also on such grounds as idealization and abstraction, it seems hard to differentiate them from essence. (ii) In any case, the question of what qualities are prototypical and what qualities are not seems in general just as impossible to settle for prototypes as for essences. (iii) Finally, it seems clear that not all types of meaning are equally amenable to a prototype analysis. We can ask as we did for essences what prototypical meaning corresponds to *ouch, though, prototype, resource* etc. (consider mental resources). In fact, it seems that prototypes are best suited for exactly what they have been tested for, i.e. fruits, vegetables, animals and furniture.

Another possibility would be to combine the greatest common denominator approach with the ideal representative approach by only considering the intersection of a limited number of typical contexts of use. However, the problem with this approach will again be how the representativity of the contexts is established.

The third approach to the problem of literal meaning is to say that it is not the intersection but the union of all uses. This will have the effect of connecting any information that has been conveyed by a linguistic expression with its literal meaning. It will also have the effect of making literal meaning extremely vague and polysemous and will in no way help to differentiate literal meaning from such things as metaphorical or satirical meaning.

In summary, we can see that all three approaches to literal meaning considered so far have drawbacks which in fact will make them unsuitable for a general analysis of conventional literal meaning if this is to be thought of as situation independent:

(1) Basic meanings such as prototypes or essences are not necessarily conventional, not equally suitable for all types of meaning and cannot be determined by any easily definable method of selection.

(2) The greatest common denominator approach and the basic meaning approach lead to a preponderance of homonymy which in turn leads to a need for a mechanism which can select the right meaning. It is very hard to see how one could help introducing context as this point, if one does not want to separate meanings by stipulation and distinguish expressions by little numerical subscripts, which in fact is the course taken in formal semantics.

(3) The greatest common denominator approach runs the risk of ending up with no meaning at all or with such an abstract meaning that it cannot be distinguished from metaphorical meaning, which in turn leads to a need for contextual specification.

(4) The union approach ends up in such vague clusters of polysemous meaning that some type of selection procedure seems necessary if literal meaning is to be determinate at all. The obvious solution is to make use of context here.

Before we leave the descriptive approaches to literal meaning another solution should be mentioned. This is the solution that not all linguistic expressions have a situation independent literal meaning. Only some – the so called syncategorematic or formal and functional expressions of language – do. The others – the categorematic or contentful expressions of language – depend on context for selection and specification. This solution is especially popular within formal semantics where one likes to identify the logical constants, i.e. those expressions whose meaning is said to be independent of any interpreting model or context, with a subset of the syncategorematic terms. The difficulties here are: (i) This is not a general analysis of meaning. (ii) How does one draw the line between categorematic and syncategorematic terms on semantic grounds? Are all auxiliaries, adverbs, conjunctions, prepositions, pronouns syncategorematic and, on the other hand, are all nouns, verbs, adjectives categorematic? A noun like *resource* for example, seems semantically best to be regarded like a pronoun with empty places for agent, goal and activity which is again very like the analysis for *can* and *must* proposed by Kratzer (1977). (iii) Many cases of syncategorematic terms which on the face of it look straight forward, on closer inspection turn out to be problematic. Take, for example, the personal pronouns *you, they* and *we*. In English both *they* and *we* can be inclusive or exclusive. *You* can refer to the listener or everybody including the speaker. *We* can refer to the listener as in the doctor's phrase:

(viii) And how are we today.

In other languages like Swedish additional difficulties attach to pronouns like *he* or *she* (*han* or *hon*) which can be used to refer to the listener. So even if many syncategorematic terms seem to be good candidates for situation independent meaning, it does not in fact seem so clear that the set of syncategorematic terms will be easily determinable from a semantic point of view.

Thus, the approaches of descriptive semantics do not seem to offer us a straight forward way of characterizing a notion of context independent conventional literal meaning. The notion of convention in conjunction with the ideas of intersection, representative type and union just as little as reference and truth enable us to distinguish semantics from pragmatics by abstraction along the dimension of situational dependence. The solution just as with reference and truth seems to be to make literal meaning context dependent by making the meaning conventions sensitive to features of context.

Let us now turn to the relationship between literal meaning and referential, truth conditional meaning. Some authors such as Kempson (1977) have taken them to be the same. Both of them are supposed to be that sort of situation independent meaning which I have tried to show can be achieved for natural language neither by the help of convention nor by the help of reference and truth. It might then be thought that since both referential and conventional, literal meaning seem to be situation dependent Kempson is, after all, right in equating them. This would, however, be a hasty conclusion. Conventional meaning, even though situation dependent, just as is referential meaning, is a notion of much wider application than referential meaning. It is reasonable to talk of the conventional meaning of *ouch* or *mhm* but hardly of their referential meaning. Thus, there is good reason not to equate these notions even though they are both context dependent.

Returning now to the distinction between semantics and pragmatics it might be said that even though it could not be made in terms of context dependence, using notions such as reference, truth or convention, it could perhaps be made in some other way which comes close to Morris' original intentions. One such suggestion is that the distinction should be made in terms of the distinction between cognitive, referential meaning and emotive, non-referential meaning. This approach, however, also has a number of difficulties: (i) It is not clear that everything that is cognitive is referential or vice versa. For example all tautologies are referentially the same yet they seem to be cognitively different. (ii) Nor is it obvious that what is non-referential is emotive or vice versa. The adjective *beautiful* is emotive in some sense. Yet, it is not clear that it is non-referential. The word *well* is non-referential but it is not clear that it is emotive. (iii) It is also very hard to give a set of criteria that distinguish that which is referential from that which is non-referential or that which is emotive from that which is cognitive. Rather there seem to be both referential and non-referential, both cognitive and emotive components in all meanings which means that also with this criterion semantic and pragmatic aspects of meaning will be mixed. For example, the meanings of the adjectives *thrifty* and *stingy* do seem to involve both cognitive, referential and emotive, non-referential aspects. But it is far from evident how these should be separated.

The last way of making a distinction between semantics and pragmatics that I will consider is that of making the distinction equivalent to the distinction between a normative and a descriptive study of meaning, i.e. more or less the opinion that Carnap originally held. Semantics would then be concerned with the normative analysis and explication of concepts that are used in many different and partly inconsistent ways in ordinary language. Pragmatics on the other hand would be concerned with the full richness of empirical data. The trouble with this way of making the distinction is that it is too close to the classical distinction between theory and data. Every science needs a theory through which its data can be understood. This theory to some extent always has to be made up of normative idealizations of data. Thus, if pragmatics is going to be theoretical enterprise at all, rather than just data collection, it will have to be tied to a theory containing normative idealizations. If we like we can call these idealizations semantics but we will then have to accept that many of them have to do with contextual factors.

The conclusions that can be drawn from the arguments presented are that so far we have no theoretically interesting and consistent way of separating semantics from pragmatics and that perhaps the distinction is more of a hindrance than an aid to clarity in the study of meaning in natural languages. Perhaps, it would in fact be better to abandon the distinction in favor of a semantico-pragmatic approach where linguistic meaning has as its primary function contextual adaptability, which would make such things as vagueness, metaphor and contextual determination of meaning central concerns rather than phenomena which are seen as exceptional and therefore safely left for another day.

REFERENCES

Bar-Hillel, Y.: 1954, 'Indexical expressions' in *Mind* **63**, 359–76.

Carnap, R.: 1942, *Introduction to Semantics*, Cambridge, Mass., M I T Press.

Carnap, R.: 1956, *Meaning and Necessity*, 2nd Edition, Chicago, University of Chicago Press.

Kempson, R.: 1975, *Presupposition and the Delineation of Semantics*, Oxford, Cambridge University Press.

Kempson, R.: 1977, *Semantic Theory*, Oxford, Cambridge University Press.

Kratzer, A.: 1977, 'What *must* and *can* must and can mean', *Linguistics and Philosophy* **1**, 337–356.

Lewis, D.: 1970, 'General semantics' in *Syntheses* **22**, 18–67.

Martin, R.: 1959, *Toward a Systematic Pragmatics*, Amsterdam, North Holland.

Montague, R.: 1968, 'Pragmatics' in Thomason, R. H. (ed.), *Formal Philosophy*, Yale University Press, (1974).

Montague, R.: 1970, 'Pragmatics and intensional logic' in Thomason, R. H. (ed.), *Formal Philosophy*, Yale University Press, (1974).

Montague, R.: 1970, 'English as a formal language' in Visentini, B. et al., *Linguaggi nella Società e nella Tecnica*, Milano, Edizioni di Communità pp. 189–224.

Morris, C.: 1946, *Signs, Language and Behavior*, Englewood Cliffs, N. I., Prentice Hall.

Morris, C.: 1938, 'Foundations of the theory of signs', in Morris, *Writings on the General Theory of Signs*, The Hague, Mouton, (1971).

Rosch, F.: 1977, 'Human categorization' in Warren, N. (ed.), *Advances in Cross-cultural Psychology* Vol. 1, London, Academic Press.

Rosch, F., Gray, W., Johnson, D. and Boyes-Braem, P.: 1976, 'Basic objects in natural categories' in *Cognitive Psychology* 8, 382–439.

ÖSTEN DAHL

IN DEFENSE OF A STRAWSONIAN APPROACH TO PRESUPPOSITION

0. The 'Fregean' view of presupposition, and presuppositional failure, according to which there is a logical relation between sentences (or statements) such that if *p* presupposes *q*, *p* has no truth value (or the truth value 'zero') whenever *q* is not true, has, after enjoying a widespread popularity among linguists, been subjected to attacks from several scholars, most notably Allwood 1972, Wilson 1972, 1975, Kempson 1975. In these works, a more orthodox two-valued logic is defended.

In this paper, I shall argue for the following claims: (i) that people's intuitions about the purported counter-examples to the Fregean analysis are not as unambiguous as the critics would have it, (ii) that behavioral data rather support the view of presupposition argued for by Strawson in his later work, (iii) that the argument for a two-valued logic builds on the assumption that natural language sentences can be assigned truth-conditions as types, an assumption that cannot be upheld.

1. We shall consider one major class of purported counter-examples to the Fregean analysis of presupposition, which are the basis for the claim that a presupposition can be 'cancelled' by a following context in which the presupposed statement (sentence) is denied. This claim was apparently first made by Allwood (1972), who gives the following examples:

(1) (said of an astronomer who believes there are nine planets:) I think Jones' theory is incorrect, because we don't know that there are nine planets. (There are in fact ten.)

(2) We will never realize what Jesus strove for us to realize, because his whole theory was based on a misunderstanding.

(3) Molly is not astonished/surprised/amazed that there are only ten million people on earth. Why should she be, when it is not true?

If the predicates *know, realize* etc. are connected with Fregean presuppositions, such discourses should be downright contradictions, since what is presupposed to be true in the first part is denied in the second[1]. Let us specify more precisely what structure this kind of discourse has. It involves a first

W. Klein and W. Levelt (eds.), Crossing the Boundaries in Linguistics, 191–200.

part which is a denial of a proposition p, where p (and consequently also not-p) presupposes q (according to the Fregean view), and a second part, which contains an overt denial of q or a statement which entails not-q. Let us call such discourses PURPORTED PRESUPPOSITION-CANCELLING DISCOURSES (PPCD).

In addition to Allwood 1972, PPCD's are discussed in Kempson 1975 and Wilson 1975. They are more categorical in their claims about the non-deviancy of PPCD's than Allwood, who says that sentences like (2) and (3) 'could probably be made to pass with a little imagination'.

Kempson (1975, 68) says:

> While the implication in a positive sentence of the truth of the complement cannot be cancelled – the resulting sentence is contradictory – in a negative sentence it can be. Witness the distinction between each pair of the following set:
>
> (33a) ?Edward regretted that Margaret had failed even though she knew she hadn't.
>
> (33b) Edward didn't regret that Margaret had failed because he knew it wasn't true. . . .

After listing two more pairs of the same kind, Kempson goes on: 'While the (b) sentences are undeniably not the natural interpretation of the negative sentences in question, they are equally undeniably not contradictory.'

Wilson (1975, 24) list (4) and three other sentences of the PPCD kind:

(4) You won't resent my doing *this* hole in one, since my golfball just landed in the Great White Bunker.

She comments: 'I assume that these sentences are perfectly capable of being true'. On p. 48–49, she compares, among other sentence pairs, 'the odd sentence' (5) with the 'well-formed negative' (6):

(5) ?The archbishop of Manchester read the lesson, but there was no archbishop of Manchester at that time.

(6) The archbishop of Manchester didn't read the lesson, since there was no archbishop of Manchester at that time.

The claim made by both Kempson and Wilson is that while non-negated sentences entail the sentences that on the Fregean view are their presuppositions, the relation between the corresponding negated sentences and the alleged presuppositions is a much weaker and cancellable one, in Gricean terms, an 'implicature'. The non-deviancy of PPCD's is taken to support this claim.

My first reaction when I heard examples like the ones cited above was that they were not well-formed and that those who claimed them to be normal, non-contradictory discourses were simply letting their theoretical prejudices guide their intuitions – not an uncommon case. However, when the same arguments were put forward independently by several people, I had to admit that it seemed as if a sizeable portion of the linguistic community had such intuitions. Of course, I could not entirely get rid of the suspicion that *I* was letting *my* theory guide my intuitions. So I decided to contruct a test which would show what people who have not read Frege or Russell think about PPCD's. Are they felt to be contradictory or not? For this question to be of any value, contradictoriness must be something that you can have reasonably reliable intuitions about. Since 'contradictory' is a theoretical logical term, this need of course not be the case. People might be expected to label as contradictory anything that is ungrammatical, empirically unplausible, contrastive etc. Also, it is clear that since there is no algorithm for deciding upon contradictoriness in general, people cannot be expected to be able to decide whether an arbitrary discourse is contradictory or not. However, the latter objection can be circumvented by choosing sufficiently simple examples. And the former objection need not to be to damaging, either. As far as I understand, at least Kempson and Wilson want to say that PPCD's are completely normal pieces of conversation. Any negative reactions to them would therefore have to be explained.

The following test was carried out: 37 students in an introductory course in linguistics (who had not yet been taught anything about presuppositions) were given a questionnaire, which starts by giving an example of a contradictory statement ('Both my parents are dead but my father is sound and well') and then asks the subjects to mark those of the following ten statements that are contradictory. The statements include (1) two clear cases of contradictions ('There has been no precipitation recently although it has been raining all week', 'Pelle killed Kalle but Kalle did not die'), (b) one (not too well-chosen) example of a breach of a categorial presupposition and (c) four normal statements. These seven sentences were given as distractors and control cases for the following three PPCD's:

(7) Pelle har inte insett att Kina har invaderat Vietnam för Kina har faktiskt inte invaderat Vietnam 'P. has not realized that China has invaded Vietnam for China has in fact not invaded Vietnam'[2])

(8) Dom säger att kejsaren av Tanzania är mördad men han kan inte vara mördad för Tanzania är en republik 'They say that the

Emperor of Tanzania has been murdered but he cannot be murdered for T. is a republic'

(9) Det är inte tråkigt att Pelle förlorade tävlingen för han vann 'It is not a pity that P. lost the contest for he won'

The subjects turned out to have a good understanding of what 'contradictory' meant in the clear cases: in all, there were only 3 'wrong' answers for those sentences out of a total of 222. The PPCD's on the other hand were much more divided, as can be seen from the following table:

Sentence No.	Number of Ss who marked the sentence as contradictory	Percentage
(7)	7	19
(8)	7	19
(9)	24	65

The following table shows, for each subset of (7–9), who many persons indicated all and only members of that subset as contradictory:

Subset	Number of Ss
(7)	0
(8)	3
(9)	16
(7), (8)	0
(8), (9)	1
(7), (9)	4
All	3
None	10

The conclusions to be drawn from these results seemed to be that reactions vary not only between different people but also between different PPCDs for a single subject. In other words, neither the Fregeans nor their critics can claim total support of the lay opinion.

For several reasons, I decided to make a second test. To start with, I wanted to see if minor changes in the sentences would influence the responses. Also, objections had been raised against at least one of the test sentences, viz. (8). It was claimed that this sentence was not a real PPCD since the pronoun *han* 'he' which occurs in the negated clause is not a definite description. Therefore, I made up a new questionnaire and gave it to a group of 23 beginner students of linguistics. In the new questionnaire the following sentence was introduced instead of sentence (8) (cf. (6) above):

(10) Biskopen i Jönköping viger inte kvinnliga präster eftersom det inte finns någon biskop i Jönköping 'The Bishop of J. does not consecrate female clergymen as there is no bishop of J.'

One of the features that distinguished (7) and (9) was that the former contained the word *faktiskt* 'in fact' in the cancelling clause. It was conjectured that the more emphatic the denial of the presupposition, the more acceptable the whole PPCD would be. To test this hypothesis, the word *faktiskt* was deleted in (7) and added in (9), yielding (11–12):

(11) Pelle har inte insett att Kina har invaderat Vietnam för Kina har inte invaderat Vietnam

(12) Det är inte tråkigt att Pelle förlorade tävlingen för han vann faktiskt

I also added a paradigm example of the cancelling of a Gricean implicature, viz. the following:

(13) Pelle försökte öppna dörren och den gick upp[3]

As for the results of the second test, the clear cases were by and large 'correctly' marked (4 'wrong' answers out of 115). The Gricean sentence (13) was judged to be non-contradictory by 22 persons out of 23. For the PPCD cases, the following results were obtained:

Sentence No.	'Contradictory' responses, number	'Contradictory' responses, percentage
(10)	11	48
(11)	11	48
(12)	13	57

The following points can be noted:

(i) The hypothesis that the addition or deletion of a word like *faktiskt* can influence the responses seems to have been confirmed – the addition of the word in (12) makes the percentage go down from 65 to 57 (probably not significant) whereas the deletion of it in (11) makes the percentage jump rather dramatically from 19 to 48.

(ii) The 'Wilsonian' sentence (10), somewhat astonishingly, turned out to have a much larger number of negative responses than the sentence it substituted for, (8).

(iii) In general, the second test reinforces the picture obtained by the first test: neither the pro-Fregeans nor the anti-Fregeans can claim universal support for their intuitions. Indeed, the fact that percentages jump up and down between different sentences and in particular between pairs of sentences which differ only in the presence of a sentence adverb strongly suggests that this is an area of indeterminacy or vagueness. We shall now see that this is not the first time such a claim has been made.

2. A scholar who is often identified with the Fregean account is P. F. Strawson. The work of Strawson on presupposition which is most frequently quoted is Strawson 1950, where he proposes a Fregean analysis as an alternative to Russell's theory of definite descriptions. However, in Strawson 1964, he gives a considerably modified account. Discussing different possible views on the question what happens when an utterance 'suffers from radical reference-failure' ('are we to say that what we have here is just one special case of false statement or are we to say that our statement suffers from a deficiency so radical as to deprive it of the chance of being either true or false?'), he says:

> I do not think there is any question of demonstrating that one party is quite right and the other wrong. What we have here is the familiar philosophical situation of one party being attracted by one simplified, theoretical – or 'straightened out' – concept of truth and falsity, and the other by another. It might be asked: How does ordinary usage speak on the point? And this, as always, is a question which it is instructive to ask. But ordinary usage does not deliver a clear verdict for one party or the other. Why should it? The interests which ordinary usage reflects are too complicated and various for it to provide overwhelming support for either way of *simplifying* the picture. The fact that ordinary usage does not deliver a clear verdict does not mean, of course, that there can be no other way of demonstrating, at least, that one view is quite wrong. It might be shown, for example, to be inconsistent, or incoherent in some other way. But this is not the case with either of these views. Each would have a certain amount of explaining and adjusting to do, but each could perfectly consistently be carried through. More important, each is *reasonable*. Instead of trying to demonstrate that one is quite right and the other quite wrong, it is more instructive to see how both are reasonable, how both represent different ways of being impressed by the facts.

Allwood, Kempson, and Wilson should be commended for having shown most convincingly and forcibly how the non-Fregean view is reasonable. They have not, however, been able to show why one cannot take the line Strawson chooses in the quotation above. In addition, they manage to give the impression that the difference between their accounts and Strawson's is greater than it is by either concentrating on his earlier work and ignore Strawson 1964 or by misrepresenting this paper.

Thus, Wilson (1975, 19) says of Strawson's 'special case of false statement' analysis:

> The analysis which he discusses is one according to which both the positive *and* the negative of the sentence in question entail what on a presuppositional analysis would be called the presupposition, and on which if the entialment is false it follows that both the related positive and the related negative statement are false.

However, the following quotation from Strawson 1964, 95 indicates that he allows for the possibility that a negated sentence which contains a definite description which does not refer to anything can be true. Discussing statements containing two referring expressions, one 'guilty' of reference-failure and one not 'guilty', he says: '. . . we can naturally enough declare it false or untrue, and naturally enough affirm its *negation* as true, on the strength of the reference-failure of the guilty referring expression.'

Kempson (1975) first describes Strawson as an adherent of the view that 'if there is not King of France, then the statement *The King of France* is neither true nor false'. Then, without mentioning that Strawson has modified his view, she says (p. 85) that 'even Strawson draws attention' to some counterexamples to this view and that (p. 87) 'he attempts to defend his position by analysing the concept of truth and truth-value assignment in terms of "topic", where the topic of the statement is what the statement is about'. This gives the impression that Strawson uses the concept of topic to attempt to save his earlier theory. But the last sentence of Strawson 1964 shows that this is not the case:

> Let me remark that I do not claim to have done more than mention one factor which may sometimes bear on the fact that a truth-value gap theory for the case of radical reference failure is apt to seem more intuitively attractive in some instances than it does in others.[4]

On the other hand, Strawson, who mentions Russell as 'the patron of the . . . "special case of false statement" party' 'in virtue of his Theory of Descriptions and his view on ordinary proper names', might also be accused of exaggerating the differences between himself and others. In fact, when reading the following passage from Russell's 1957 response to Strawson 1950, one may wonder if any difference at all exists between these two philosophers:

Strawson objects to my saying that "the King of France is wise" is false if there is no King of France. He admits that the sentence is significant and not true, but not that it is false. This is a question of verbal convenience. He considers that the word "false" has an unalterable meaning which it would be sinful to regard adjustable, though he prudently avoids telling us what this meaning is. For my part, I find it more convenient to define the word "false" so that every significant sentence is either true or false. This is a purely verbal question; and although I have no wish to claim the support of common usage, I do not think that he can claim it either. Suppose, for example, that in some country there was a law that no person could hold public office if he considered it false that the Ruler of the Universe is wise. I think an avowed atheist who took advantage of Mr. Strawson's doctrine to say that he did not hold this proposition false, would be regarded as a somewhat shifty character.

3. I want to defend here a view which is quite close to that argued for in Strawson 1964. Utterances where what has been referred to as a logical presupposition is not fulfilled are often felt to be deviant – there seems to be little controversy about that. I want to claim with Strawson that there are at least two ways in which such a deviancy can be interpreted. Personally, I would say that the main possibilities are (a) that a statement has been made which is false and (b) that no statement has been made at all.

The first alternative would be to say that something false has been said. As for the second alternative, I would personally prefer the formulation that nothing has been said at all, i.e. that no statement or proposition has been expressed. I think it is hard to disagree with the claim that at least some utterances of declarative sentences do not express any statement. To take an extreme example, suppose I have constructed a computer program which generates random sentences and that I am reading aloud the sentences that it generates, and that one of the sentences is *He is crazy*. Having read this sentence, I have uttered a declarative sentence, but have I said anything true or false?

Both Kempson and Wilson speak of truth-values, truth-conditions entailments etc. of sentences. They admit that one might object that statements rather than sentences carry truth-values; they do not, however, consider this objection to be too serious since it can

be side-stepped if we agree with Lemmon (1966) . . . that sentences do have a truth value relative to some context of utterance. Thus deictic and all indexical sentences will have a truth value relative to a person (the speaker), a place and a time. (Kempson 1965, 38; cf. also Wilson 1965, 3–4.

In other words: Even if a sentence is not a truth-value bearer, there is a function from pairs of sentences and contexts to truth-value; hence we can treat sentences as if they were truth-value bearers. But this presupposes that every context determines a truth-value for every sentence, and that is not the case, as we have just seen.

It is even possible to find cases where one and the same sentence can be regarded both as true and as false depending on how we interpret the situation. The sentence *John has stopped beating his wife* is often said to presuppose that John has at some time beaten his wife. Now, we could of course construct a PPCD of the following kind:

– John has not stopped beating his wife; in fact, he has always been kind to her.

Here, the sentence *John has not stopped beating his wife* would naturally be interpreted as true, according to the analysis of Allwood, Kempson, and Wilson. But consider now the following exchange:

– John has not stopped beating his wife.
– You're lying: he never beat her.

In this situation, where the first utterance is taken as an accusation to the effect that John is beating his wife, it is on the contrary natural to judge it as false. Consider another example of the same kind:

– Why didn't you show up yesterday?
– My car was not working.
– Your're lying – you have no car.

The reason that *My car was not working* is seen here as expressing something false is of course that it is a negative statement which is not naturally understood as a denial of a previous claim but is rather simply an assertion that a certain state of affairs (that the car was out of order) obtained.

In my opinion, observations like these give further support to the view that there may be indeterminacies in the assignment of truth-values to sentences.

NOTES

[1] Allwood acknowledges that there may be a difference between *know* on the one hand and other factive verbs on the other.

[2] The test was given about a week prior to the Chinese invasion of Vietnam.

[3] The sentence means 'Pelle tried to open the door and it opened'. The verb *try* has been said to conversationally implicate that the action does not succeed; this implicature is cancelled by the last clause of the example.

[4] There is a rather subtle difference between two possible views: (a) that only NPs in topic position are connected with presuppositions, (b) that the fact that an NP with reference failure is in topic position makes it easier to choose the truth-value gap alternative. I think that Strawson in fact wants to argue for (b). Kempson interprets him as opting for (a). In an earlier paper, Dahl 1974, I quoted Strawson as holding that a statement is false 'only if it contains false information *about its topic*'. Thus, I also seem guilty of having misinterpreted him, although I did point to the fact that intuitions vary about these cases and to the possibility of there being a vagueness in the concepts of 'true' and 'false'.

REFERENCES

Allwood, J.: 1972, 'Negation and the strength of presuppositions or There is more to speaking than words,' *Logical Grammar Reports* **2.** (Revised version in Dahl, Ö. (eds.), *Logic, Pragmatics, and Grammar*, 1975, Dept. of Linguistics, Univ. of Göteborg.)

Dahl, Ö.: 1974, 'Topic-comment structure revisited,' in Dahl, Ö., (ed.), *Topic and Comment, Contextual Boundness and Focus*, Hamburg: Helmut Buske.

Kempson, R.: 1975, *Presupposition and The Delimitation of Semantics*, Cambridge: Univ. Press.

Russell, B.: 1957, 'Mr. Strawson on referring,' *Mind* **66**, 385–389.

Strawson. P.: 1950, 'On referring,' *Mind* **59**, 320–344.

Strawson, P.: 1964, 'Identifying reference and truth values,' *Theoria* **30**, 96–118.

Wilson, D.: 1975, *Presupposition and Non-Truth-Conditional Semantics*, London: Academic Press.

ANGELIKA KRATZER

BLURRED CONDITIONALS*

1. What is the meaning of *if . . . then* clauses? More than 2000 year ago, Philo argued for what we now call *material implication*. And Chrysippos fought for what we now call *strict implication*. In modern times, G. Frege argued for material implication again. And so did C. I. Lewis for strict implication. Philo and Chrysippos, Frege and Lewis defended their ideas, found followers and died.

Why could this happen? Do people differ in their interpretations of sentences in such a way that they can't be reconciled? I'd better be fair to Frege. He didn't aim at giving an analysis to *if . . . then* clauses in natural language. Consider his remarks concerning material implication: [1]

> The thought expressed by the compound sentence
>
> "If I own a cock which has laid eggs today, then the Cologne cathedral will collapse tomorrow morning."
>
> is also true. Someone will perhaps say: "But here the antecedent has no inner connection at all with the consequent." In my account, however, I required no such connection and I ask that "If *B*, then *A*" should be understood solely in terms of what I have said and expressed in the form "not ((not *A*) and *B*)". It must be admitted that this conception of a hypothetical compound thought will at first be thought strange. But my account is not designed to keep in step with ordinary linguistic usage, which is generally too blurred and variable for the purposes of logic.

But then, do scientists and ordinary people differ in their interpretations of sentences in a crucial way? Do our semantic rules change fundamentally as soon as we talk as scientists?

In 1689, John Wallis showed how hypothetical judgements can be reduced to categorical ones. And what he says about categorical judgements might lead one to the conclusion that – as far as conditionals are concerned – the differences between Philo and Chrysippos, and Frege and Lewis, shouldn't bother us more than the simple fact that a word like *everybody* may sometimes be used for referring to a small group of people and at other times for talking about mankind as a whole.

2. Like Chrysippos, John Wallis believed that only those conditionals are

W. Klein and W. Levelt (eds.), Crossing the Boundaries in Linguistics, 201–209.

true which have the right kind of connection between their antecedent and consequent. Referring to conditionals and other compound propositions (*propositiones compositae*), he writes: [2]

Veraeque aut falsae censendae sunt prout connexio illa rite aut perperam facta est; quaecumque fuerit veritas aut falsitas, partium separatim consideratarum.

(They have to be judged true or false according to whether that connection is correctly or falsely made, whatever the truth or falsehood of their constituents may be if considered in isolation.)

In this definition, there is one word which is particularily vague and difficult to understand: *Connexio* (*connection*).

In stepwise fashion, Wallis tries to get more explicit about it. A conditional that he takes to be true is expressed by the following sentence:

Si Sol oritur, dies est.

(If the sun rises, it is day.)

We are told that in this conditional, there is the right connection between antecedent and consequent. A conditional that lacks this connection is expressed by the following example:

Si Alexander sit Homo, tum Bucephalus est Equus.

(If Alexander is a man, then Bucephalus is a horse.)

Although antecedent and consequent of this conditional are both true, it is still false according to John Wallis:

Non enim inde sequitur Bucephalum esse Equum, si Alexander sit Homo.

(The reason is that it does not follow that Bucephalus is a horse if Alexander is a man.)

Here, John Wallis shifted whatever was blurred in the meaning of *Connexio* on to another word: *sequitur* (*follows*). For Wallis, the word *sequitur* doesn't mean the same as *follows logically*. Whenever he wants to talk about logical consequence – for example when he discusses the validity of inferences – he puts the adverb *necessario* (*necessarily*) in front of the verb *sequitur*.

We find *sequitur* with still other adverbs in the Institutio Logicae. For example, when causal dependence is discussed. For Wallis, a causal dependence between two propositions is based on a relation of natural or essential consequence between those two propositions, that is on a relation of *sequitur naturaliter* or *sequitur eßentialiter*. He illustrates this with the following sentence:

Quia Sol oritur, dies est.
(Since the sun rises, it is day.)

The proposition expressed by this sentence is true if and only if it follows 'naturally' or 'essentially' that it is day from the fact that the sun rises. Wallis considers this causal relation to be something 'more' than the pure consequence relation (*nuda consequentia*) which is required for conditionals. What this eventually amounts to will never become quite clear. Wallis however undertakes further efforts to elucidate the issue. He asks himself: What is the denial of a conditional? What is the denial of the proposition expressed by the following sentence?

Alexander, si fortis sit, vincet.
(If Alexander is brave, he will be victorious.)

The answer is: A conditional is denied by denying the connection (*copulam negando*), that is by denying the consequence relation between antecedent and consequent (*Consequentis ab Antecedente sequelam*). The denial of the above sentence should then be equivalent to

Non sequitur enim, eum certo victurum esse, si fortis sit.
(It does not follow that he is certain to be victorious if he is brave.)

This sentence is in turn equivalent to

Fieri potest, ut non vincet, etiamsi fortis sit.
(It is possible that he will not be victorious, even if he is brave.)

This suggests that John Wallis considers conditionals to be implicitely modalized. In possible worlds terminology, the proposition expressed by the above sentence would be true in a world if and only if there is an (accessible) possible world such that Alexander is brave but yet won't be victorious. This is actually quite close to Wallis' final step in the reduction. For the undenied 'Alexander' – sentence, this reduction would look as follows:

Every case where Alexander is brave is a case where he will be victorious.

Wallis' original example is:

Si sol splendet, dies est.
(If the sun shines, it is day.)

which is reduced to the categorical statement:

Omnis casus quo sol splendet est casus quo dies est.
(Every case where the sun shines is a case where it is day.)

There is still a lot of vagueness in this reduction. What are 'all' cases? All imaginable cases or all cases of a certain kind? Let us consider now what John Wallis himself says about the interpretation of quantifiers like *all, every, none*, etc.:[3]

Et quidem ipsae Universalitatis (utcumque Hyperbolice prolatae) saepenumero nihil aliud significant, quam quos *Universalibus suppares* modo diximus. Utputa cum in communi colloquio quotidie dicitur, *Hoc omnibus notum est, Nemo hoc ignorat, Nemo inficiabitur*, etc. (Gallis familiare illud) *Tout le mond*, (ubi forte *tres* aut *decem* sunt ille *totus mundus*), *Nil tale unquam contigit, In hoc conveniunt Omnes*, non aliud intellegendum erit quam *Plerique* aut *Paucissimi*.

This means roughly the following:

In colloquial speech, words like *all, every* or *whole* do not always express real universality but only quasi-universality. Wallis gives the French example *tout le monde* (*tout le mond* in the original). This expression may sometimes refer to only three or ten persons which constitute the whole world in this particular context. We find here the roots of what was baptized a *universe of discourse* by George Boole. The following passage is taken from the *Laws of Thought*:[4]

In every discourse, whether of the mind conversing with its own thoughts, or of the individual in his intercourse with others, there is an assumed or expressed limit within which the subjects of its operation are confined. The most unfettered discourse is that in which the words we use are understood in the widest possible application, and for them the limits of discourse are coextensive with those of the universe itself. But more usually we confine ourselves to a less spacious field. Sometimes, in discoursing of men we imply (without expressing the limitation) that it is of men only under certain circumstances and conditions that we speak, as of civilized men, or of men in the vigour of life, or of men under some other condition or relation. Now, whatever may be the extent of the field within which all the objects of our discourse are found, that field may properly be termed the universe of discourse.

A lot of contemporary work in semantics deals with the fact that the interpretation of many expressions of natural language depend on a parameter that has to be fixed by the utterance context. It is part of our knowledge of the meaning of these expressions that we know which parameters have to be fixed: the speaker for *me*, the listener for *you*, the place of the utterance for *here* and so on. Very often in our conversations, these parameters aren't fixed in a determinate way. As a result, what we say is vague.

What Wallis and Boole observed, is that quantifiers are context-dependent expressions, too, and that the relevant parameter is a universe of discourse.

Given Wallis' analysis of conditionals, this means that they should be context-dependent in much the same way as quantifiers are and that their interpretation should depend on a universe of 'cases' which may vary from situation to situation. The difference between Philo and Frege on one side and between Chrysippos and Lewis on the other side may then be seen not as a difference in interpreting conditionals but rather as a difference in fixing the open parameter.

In modern terms, Wallis' analysis amounts roughly to taking conditionals to be variably modalized material implications. The logical form of *if . . . then* clauses would then be as follows:

$$Necessarily\ (A \supset C)$$

The proposition expressed by an utterance of a sentence of this form would be true in the actual world if and only if the proposition expressed by C is true in all those 'accessible' worlds in which the proposition expressed by A is true. If all possible worlds are accessible from the actual world, then the corresponding conditional is strict implication. In the degenerate case (rejected by Wallis) where no other world but itself is accessible to the actual world, the resulting conditional is material implication. And there are all sorts of implications inbetween – possible candidates for providing a more or less strong connection between antecedent and consequent.

We may wonder whether this analysis of conditionals is plausible according to modern standards. In the following section, I'll give a short illustration of the kinds of objections it would meet today.

3. There is still quite a number of people defending material implication as the right interpretation for indicative *if . . . then* clauses. For them, no context-dependency affects their truth-conditions and their logical form is simply

$$A \supset C.$$ [5]

No implicit modalization has to account for a connection between antecedent and consequent. That sentences like Frege's 'cock'-sentence and Wallis' 'Bucephalus'-sentence sound strange is attributed to independently motivated pragmatic principles. It would simply be inappropriate to utter these sentences, although what is said by uttering them is true. There is some discussion about what these independently motivated principles are. One might be sceptical about them as Lewis is in [12]. My own qualms, however, concern a different point: There are some types of *if . . . then* -clauses (including indicative ones) that can't possibly be formalized by means of material implication.

Consider the following sentences:

(1) If John has stolen the earrings, he must go to jail (in view of what the law provides).

(2) If John has stolen the earrings, he has probably sold them to a friend.

(3) If John had stolen the earrings, the dog wouldn't have barked.

Formalizing sentences (1) to (3) as

$A \supset (\textit{necessarily } C)$
$A \supset (\textit{probably } C)$
$A \supset (\textit{would } C)$

respectively would lead to the absurdity that the corresponding conditionals would all be true just in case John hasn't stolen the earrings. I can't see any pragmatic principles that could save the analysis.

A formalization à la Wallis doesn't fare much better. We would take the modals to have wide scope over the whole sentence, that is we would have something like the following:

$$\left.\begin{array}{l}\textit{Necessarily}\\ \textit{Probably}\\ \textit{Would}\end{array}\right\} \quad (A \supset C)$$

We would assume that, accidentally, the modals crop up in the consequent, if conditionals are explicitely modalized. And to these modals we would give an interpretation roughly along the following lines:

> The proposition expressed by an utterance of a sentence of the form
> *(in view of what the Law provides) necessarily A*
> is true in a world *w* if and only if the proposition expressed by *A* is true in all worlds compatible with what the Law provides in *w*.
>
> The proposition expressed by an utterance of a sentence of the form
> *probably A*
> is true in a world *w* if and only if the proposition expressed by

A is true in all those worlds that are compatible with what is considered to be the normal course of events in *w*.

The proposition expressed by an utterance of a sentence of the form
would A
is true in a world *w* if and only if the proposition expressed by *A* is true in all those worlds which are compatible with a certain set of 'relevant' facts of *w*.

These suggestions lead to many problems.

As for sentence (1), interpreting it as a modalized material implication, leads to the well-known paradoxes of deontic logic.[6] If John breaks the Law in stealing the earrings, then the analysis predicts that the conditional expressed by (1) should be true vacuously.

Similar paradoxes arise for (2), in case John's stealing the earrings is not compatible with what we consider to be the normal course of events.[7] And as for (3), there is the difficulty of being more specific about these 'relevant' facts. This is basically Goodman's problem of cotenable extra premises which he had to leave unsolved.[8]

There is another difficulty concerning all three types of sentences: For modalized material implications, the three inference patterns of 'strengthening the antecedent', 'transitivity' and 'contraposition' are predicted to hold. Yet it has often been pointed out that these inference patterns are not valid for deontic conditionals, probability conditionals and counterfactuals.[9] As an illustration of 'strengthening the antecedent' consider the following examples:

(1′) If John has stolen the earrings and has shot himself straightaway, he must go to jail (in view of what the Law provides).

(2′) If John has stolen the earrings and has destroyed them straightaway, he has probably sold them to a friend.

(3′) If John had stolen the earrings and had teased the dog, the dog wouldn't have barked.

Given that the propositions expressed by (1), (2) or (3) are true we can't infer that the propositions expressed by (1′), (2′) and (3′) respectively are true as well.

Now this means that anyone who insists on interpreting 'ordinary' indicative *if . . . then*-clauses in terms of modalized (or bare) material implications, would have to concede that sentences like (1), (2) or (3) would have to be interpreted in a completely different fashion. This is an undesirable conclusion, since *if . . . then* doesn't seem to be ambiguous. Furthermore, there is still a non-trivial common core of inference patterns that are valid for both types of conditionals.[10] Here is an example:

If *A*, then *B*
If *A*, then *C*
———
∴ If *A* and *B*, then *C*

If *A* is the case, then *B* ought to be the case
If *A* is the case, then *C* ought to be the case
———
∴ If *A* and *B* are the case, then *C* ought to be the case

If *A*, then probably *B*
If *A*, then probably *C*
———
∴ If *A* and *B*, then probably *C*

If *A* were to be the case, then *B* would be the case
If *A* were to be the case, then *C* would be the case
———
∴ If *A* and *B* were to be the case, then *C* would be the case

I think that these considerations suggest that we should look for a uniform analysis of conditionals that is flexible enough to allow for differences, but that is also restrictive enough to characterize the common core. This is what I attempted in [10] and some earlier papers. The analysis given there is indebted to Wallis for stressing context-dependency and the intrinsic connection between modals and conditionals. And I think it saves enough of his insights to let the four old men sleep in peace.

NOTES

* This paper is a radical revision of an earlier version that I wrote while being a researcher in the Sonderforschungsbereich 99 at the University of Constance, sponsored by the German Science Foundation.

1 Frege [5], page 84. The English translation is taken from R. Stoothoff (with minor changes), *Mind* **62**, 1963.

2 This quote as well as the following ones (until further notice) is from Wallis [13], pages 139ff. The translation is my own.

3 Wallis [13], page 126.

4 Boole [2], page 42.

5 See Grice [7] or Jackson [9].

6 See Hansson [8], van Fraassen [4].

7 See also Lewis' triviality results in [12] for an objection of a more general kind.

8 Goodman [6].

9 See Lewis [11], Adams [1].

10 See Burgess [3].

BIBLIOGRAPHY

[1] Adams, E. A.: 1975, *The Logic of Conditionals*, Dordrecht, Reidel.

[2] Boole, G.: *An Investigation of the Laws of Thought*, New York, Dover Publications, reprint of the 1854 edition.

[3] Burgess, J.: 1979, *Quick Completeness Proofs for some Logics of Conditionals*, Manuscript, Princeton University.

[4] van Fraassen, B.: 1972, 'The logic of conditional obligation', *Journal of Philosophical Logic* 1, 417–438.

[5] Frege, G.: 1966, *Logische Untersuchungen*, G. Patzig (ed.), Göttingen, Vandenhoeck and Rupprecht.

[6] Goodman, N.: 1947, 'The problem of counterfactual conditionals', *The Journal of Philosophy* 44.

[7] Grice, H. P.: *The William James Lectures*, unpublished.

[8] Hansson, B.: 1969, 'An analysis of some deontic logics', *Nôus* 3.

[9] Jackson, F.: 1979, 'On assertion and indicative conditionals', *The Philosophical Review* 88.

[10] Kratzer, A.: 1981, 'The notional category of modality', in H. J. Eikmeyer and H. Rieser (eds.): *Words, Worlds and Contexts. New Approaches in Word Semantics*, Berlin–New York, de Gruyter.

[11] Lewis, D.: 1973, *Counterfactuals*, Oxford, Blackwell.

[12] Lewis, D.: 1976, 'Probabilities of conditionals and conditional probability', *The Philosophical Review* 85.

[13] Wallis, J.: 1699, *Opera Quaedam Miscellanea*, Oxford. Reprinted in Wallis, J., *Opera Mathematica*, Vol. III, Hildesheim and New York, Olms, 1972.

HELMUT SCHNELLE

SEMANTICS AND PRAGMATICS IN PSYCHO-PHYSIOLOGICAL CONTEXT

0. INTRODUCTION

For many theoretical linguists and applied logicians, model theoretic semantics à la Montague, Cresswell a. o. seems to represent the most advanced stage of the theory of semantics and pragmatics. But it should be clear that this theory remains in the context of realistic semantic theories, as v. Kutschera has called them. Such theories "interpret meaning as a conventional relationship between signs and concrete or conceptual entities which exist independently of the linguistic signs" (v. Kutschera, 1975, p. 19). These theories may still be called realistic theories even if they no longer assume, as in the classical position, that the meaning of a linguistic expression does not depend on conditions of use. In fact, modern model theoretic analyses can account for the variations dependent on conditions of use. The pragmatic account of the context is, however, "realistically" semanticized.

Recently, M. Bierwisch has made the interesting proposal to reinterpret Montague's semantics in a psychologistic context (see Bierwisch 1980). By the reinterpretation proposed, meaning is not a relationship between signs and entities of independent existence, but primarily a relationship between signs and mental entities in the speakers of language. Bierwisch writes: "My proposal is now, to restrict D the domain of possible extensions in such a way that it becomes the structure of the internal, cognitive experience of a person p. In other words, D is to be construed as the formal structure of (a certain aspect of) the mental states of p." In following this course, "possible worlds turn out to be what they (unavowedly) have been all along: cognitive projections of real persons." (ibid.)

Bierwisch's proposal involves a number of problems which require detailed discussion. First, it must not be forgotten that realistic semantics of logical analysis has been introduced in the context of antipsychologistic critiques of modern logic. Are the arguments advanced by logicians and philosophers no longer relevant? Second: Embarking on psychological semantics seems to require a much more radical revision of Montague's approach – and other model theoretic approaches – than Bierwisch seems to assume. Third: A revision of Montague semantics in psycho-physiological context can only

W. Klein and W. Levelt (eds.), Crossing the Boundaries in Linguistics, 211–220.

involve part of the required description. Let me now discuss these problems in detail.

1. THREE ASPECTS OF LANGUAGES

I believe that the arguments for a strictly non-psychologistic conception of logic so conclusively advanced by Frege, Husserl and all modern logicians following them, do not hold for linguistics, contrary to what many structural linguists believed. Logic can and should indeed be confined to the analysis of the *conditions for correct reasoning* and not be extended to the psychology of actual reasoning. Linguistics, on the other hand, must analyze the actual aspects of language use. In a sense, logic can be considered to be an explication of some fundamental concepts, such as the concepts of truth, consistency, completeness of conceptual analysis etc. They are idealized concepts which are norms for our actual reasoning.

Languages, however, are not determined by such idealizations. We could at most postulate structured processes underlying language use. Therefore, linguistics cannot be confined to the analysis of structural conditions only. Instead, languages can and should be studied in three different domains: First, as systems of abstract expressions (words or morphemes, sentences, texts) and their relations to realistic meanings, second, as systems of conventionally regulated intentional acts and third, as psycho-physical processes. Often the studies of languages are restricted to one of these domains. For instance, the grammatical studies of languages (whether synchronic or diachronic) are confined to the studies of the *systems of expressions*, i.e. to the studies of words or morphemes, sentences and texts as well as their *phonological and morpho-syntactic forms* and *their meanings* understood as entities of some sort. Current theories of grammars, such as transformational generative grammars, Montague grammars etc. must be understood to be elaborations of this aspect.

On the other hand, there is a long tradition considering languages to be specific and essential kinds of human *faculties for performing intentional acts* connected with uttering or thinking in words, sentences or texts. It is the distinctive character of these acts that they are *regulated by convention*. Current speech act theory is to a large part an elaboration of this aspect.

In contrast to these grammatical and act-theoretic views of languages, theoreticians of the last century (Steinthal, Paul, Wundt) emphasized that languages are central parts of the psycho-physical structure of human beings and that words and sentences and their grammatical properties are merely abstractions from the actually existing psycho-physical processes. A particularly important substructure is the articulatory and auditory apparatus producing sound signals in the transmission channel (vibrations in the air). Behaviorism of our century assumed that language description could be based on this substructure only and that semantics consisted in finding the regular correlations of sound signals to the observable contexts of use. This restriction which Behaviorism imposed on the earlier program proved to be unsuccessful. In principle, we are back at the earlier positions. Methodologically however, the situation has much evolved, since cybernetics has provided powerful and precise descriptive means which surpass by far the older associativism. Linguistic theories in the context of computational linguistics and artificial intelligence research are current elaborations of this third domain of language studies.

Though it is certainly possible to restrict theoretical description to one of the three domains mentioned (the grammatical aspect, the act-theoretic aspect, and the psycho-physical aspect) there cannot be any doubt that our ultimate aim must be an appropriate analysis of each of the three aspects in their mutual interrelation.

Whereas the grammatical and act-theoretic aspects have been vigorously developed during this century, psycho-physiological accounts have found much less attention. Many linguists feel presently that this field of research should attract more research activity. We need an account of the psycho-physiological counterparts of grammatical structure and speech acts in the speaking and understanding organism.

However, many linguists still believe that an adequate description of these psycho-physiological counterparts is much too complicated and that we lack most of the empirical facts from psychology or physiology. They think that in the present situation their descriptions of grammatical structure and of speech acts provide for the general conditions on the psycho-physiological counterparts which furthermore imply some psychologically and perhaps physiologically relevant features of these counterparts. One such feature is the generative capacity which the still unknown processes must have. They think that providing general conditions on processes is enough.

With M. Bierwisch, I think that this attitude is much too conservative at the present stage of science. I admit that we could not hope to obtain adequate description of the psycho-physical aspects of language right away but I would require to formulate precise models that could be put into correspondence with the physiological and psychological facts that are available right now. Our present accounts of grammatical structures and speech act systems could not serve *that* purpose.

2. SEMANTICS PSYCHOLOGIZED

When we attempt to set up a psychological and physiological counterpart to semantics and pragmatics, it may seem rational to start by an examination of the most advanced system of semantic and pragmatic analysis, model theoretic semantics, such as the one proposed by Montague. But, is it possible to keep the formal body of the approach intact and merely reinterprete the meaning relation, as proposed by Bierwisch? Should the descriptive structure be the same in abstract semantics as in its psychological counterpart?

I think that this is not the case. An examination of the context of psychological and physiological analysis shows that even very basic assumptions in Montague semantics should undergo revision and that its pragmatics should be completely substituted by the more natural description possible in the new context.

The essentially new aspect of a psycho-physiological context of analysis, as compared with an "objective", realistic one, consists in the fact that language and the possible worlds do not exhaust everything there is. On the contrary, they are only determinants of parts of the persons making use of language and their possible worlds conceptions when they speak or interpret incoming signals. Let us see how this new context should influence a reorganization of Montague's semantics and pragmatics.

The first reorganization should concern the very basis of Montague's semantics, the status of individuals and properties. Formally, every possible referential entity in Montague's system is a set-theoretical construct out of the entities of the basic sets

A,	the set of individuals,
$\{0, 1\}$,	the set of truth values,
I,	the set of possible world indices,
J,	the set of pragmatic indices (specifying speakers, hearers etc.)
T,	the set of time moments.

(The set of time moments is considered to be a strict simple order relative to an axiomatic time order relation $<$). The entities in this list are absolutely basic and atomic semantic entities in Montague's framework.

Could these entities keep their status in a psycho-physiological reinterpretation? I think not. If the individuals were construed as the ordinary, concrete individuals a given person knows or could conceive of, they should at least have a counterpart which we might call the possible perceptual appearances of the individual for the given person. These perceptual appearances are certainly constructs out of basic perceptual appearances such as coloured spots, sounds, smells etc.

It was a persistent problem of empiricist philosophers, from Locke to Quine, to determine the "roots of reference", i.e. the way individuals and entities in general are constituted in the development of experience or in each act of experience. Secondary qualities such as those mentioned played a crucial part in this constitution, though it also turned out that dispositional qualities and theoretical qualities seem to have their share without being constitutable from secondary qualities.

The processes of constitution analyzed in empiricist philosophy have their counterpart in a psycho-physiological analysis of semantics. After all, the organism receives external signals from its environment, which are analyzed in the processes of perception. It is on the basis of these processes that individuals in the internal representational world can be identified in actual situation. From the point of view of perception, individuals are far from being basic entities in the hierarchy of constructs. Their appearances at least are constructional results out of qualities.

Since the appearances of the individuals must be constructed out of qualities, one may well inquire whether it might not be appropriate to construct the individuals generally from qualities. Attempts at semantic systems based on qualities as basic entities should provide for a more adequate starting point for psycho-physiologically reinterpretation than the classical model theoretic one used by Montague. The discussion of further details of such a logical framework lie beyond the scope of this article.

Instead, let me briefly indicate a physiological reconstruction of the appearances of individuals. Let the organism have peripheral neurones: the peripheral input neurones of visual, auditory and somaesthetic periphery and the peripheral output neurones or motoneurones causing the activity of muscles. The firing of these neurones over some duration is a certain firing pattern; the class of possible firing patterns is easily determined on the basis of the elementary relations of simultaneous firing and sequential order in firing. We shall distinguish input patterns and output patterns. A possible *perceptual feature* is a recursively enumerable subset of the set of input patterns. A *possible action feature* is a recursively enumerable subset of output patterns.[1]

For some set of perceptual features the organism has an effective procedure of some kind (processor or network) such that the procedure produces an internal signal shortly after the perceptual periphery has a firing pattern that is an element of the corresponding perceptual feature. The set of perceptual features for which the organism has at some given time an effective procedure as described will be called the *set of the perceptual features of the organism*.

Correspondingly: For some set of activity features the organism has an effective procedure of some kind (processor or network) such that the procedure produces an output firing pattern shortly after a corresponding internal signal has been activated. The set of activity features for which the organism has at some time an effective procedure of this type will be called *the set of the activity features*.

We may now come to a reinterpretation of abstract or objective semantic bases of a language of concrete objects in terms of psycho-physiology. In abstract semantics individuals are basic; in psycho-physiological semantics appearances of individuals – or more exactly: known or assumed-to-be-known individuals – are perceptual features. But not only individuals turn out to be perceptual features, so do (concrete) properties and relations. Actions on the other hand correspond to a pair of a perceptual feature and an activity feature. Actions get clearly differentiated from properties! The perceptual feature in the pair determines the action as it is perceived if somebody else executes the action and the activity feature determines the action as it is executed by the organism itself.[2]

3. PRAGMATICS PSYCHOLOGIZED

More radical revision even is required with respect to pragmatic analysis. Montague's pragmatics is a semantisation of pragmatics: Certain entities of the semantic basis can play the role of contextual indices. In this way the basic assumptions of realistic semantics, which correlate language with the world or the atomic or complex entities in the world need not be revised. But the price to be paid for this strictly semantical approach is a completely unnatural account if judged in psychological context.

Consider the sentence

(1) Come here

In analyzing an utterance of (1) made by speaker s at time t to hearer h – i.e. at index (s, h, t) – we should say that the speaker requests the hearer to come near to him in the actual world at the time of the utterance. If this semantic structure is applied to the index one obtains the utterance meaning that *s* requests *h* to come near to *s* at *t*.

Now, if Jack says (1) to me on Oct. 1, 1980 at exactly 2 p.m., do I understand that the meaning of his utterance is

> Jack requests Helmut Schnelle to come near to Jack on Oct. 1, 1980, 2 p.m.?

What if I don't know that he is Jack or that it is now 2 p.m.? Didn't I get the utterance meaning in this case?

There seems to be something wrong with this account, in particular with the account of deixis. Indeed, if we psychologize the description appropriately we could render it much smoother. I would say that what I understand is rather something I would paraphrase – even in internal speech – as follows:

> You (who are right now speaking to me) ask me to come near to you right now.

The point is that an interpretation of "I" and "now" is quite easy in psychological context. *Within* the interpreting processor, "I" always refers to the processor and "now" always refers to the actual moment of processing or some interval containing that moment. If the processor has a procedure realizing the perceptual features "that somebody who is speaking to me", "you" is equally easily interpreted, as referring to this feature complex actually present.

It is quite clear that the processor needs in addition some translators, one for immediate use, the other for memory. The translator for immediate use is applied as follows: If somebody speaks to me and his sentences contain "I", this term will have to be translated internally, unless occurring in a citation, into "you" if he speaks to me or into "he" ("she", or "it") if not. In immediate use, we do not need to translate the meaning into a reading rendered by deixis free terms. Language is always relativized to the origo of speech, as Bühler called it, the origo marked by I-here-now. When logical analysis is, as it were, like a classical geometry without a system of coordinates, pragmatical analysis is like analytical geometry with shifting coordinates. But not only the origo is always marked; in each situation certain "points" are marked by their prominent and specified status, such as the person speaking to me. It is natural, that our language contains terms referring to this actual – though shifting – data.

However, if what is said to me must be stored in memory, it is to be marked in a way that is independent from the situation in which it occurred.

In memorizing what somebody said to me, I shall tag the sentence or some paraphrase to be stored by the name by which I identify the speaker: "XY said to me: . . . ". The "I" and "you" occurring in the sentence itself need not be translated. S, the translator for memory, may perhaps only be a tagging device. This resembles an index as used by Montague; his device may considered to be adequate for memorizing use but not for immediate use.

Even less adequate than personal deixis is temporal deixis in Montague grammars. Again the origo of speech is not taken into account. In a processing or operating system the moment of action is always present and does not need additional specification. The present moment and the immediate past are always vivid and given in the system. These will be called the immediate time aspects. Children have this conceptual pair available even before they start to learn language. Being active and goal oriented organisms they furthermore have available whether the goal of their presently executed act is or is not yet reached -- such that the act is in the achieved or perfective state. The basic elements of aspect are therefore also available and will be reckoned among the immediate time aspects. On the other hand, it should be obvious that children at a very early age will not have available a fully ordered time concept. Therefore, a psychological reinterpretation of Montague's framework must eliminate his temporal analysis.

As I have discussed on several occasions (Schnelle, 1979; 1980a, 1980b, 1980c) reference to objective time is natural only for sentences containing words or phrases explicitly referring to time moments or time intervals. The meaning of the other sentences should be specified in terms of simpler notions of time. We should assume several notional levels capturing

1. immediate time aspects,
2. episodic time order,
3. subjective time measure,
4. objective time measure,
5. objective time order.

I shall not go into the details of this analysis since these have been presented extensively elsewhere. The essential aspect is, however, in pragmatics as in semantics, that the availability of the processor as a referential basis allows and requires interpretations which are much more adequate and flexible than the objective semantics of logical analysis.

4. CONCLUSION

In arguing for a development of psycho-physiological counterpart theories for grammatical and speech act analyses, I do not want to imply that these could be replaced by such analyses. In view of the division of labour different methods are appropriate for different problem areas in linguistics. More abstract methods of grammatical analyses are certainly appropriate for furthering detailed analysis that provides for an even more refined analyses of centuries of research. However, care will be particularly needed in semantics and semanticized pragmatics. It may be doubtful whether progress in this field should really be sought in the context of realistic semantics without regard to the procedural contexts of analysis. These doubts cannot be substantiated, however, unless clearer insight into psycho-physiologically adequate counterparts of semantics and pragmatics have been obtained.

NOTES

[1] The analysis proposed resembles closely the analysis in Kleene 1956, pp. 6/7. Kleene calls an event what I have called a possible perceptual feature, though I do not require that the firing patterns are ordered like the rows and columns of a matrix. Regular events as defined by Kleene are a subset of the class of recursive events, namely those events that can be detected by a finite and fixed nerve net. As has been shown later, growing nerve nets or nerve nets containing some infinite regular nerve nets functioning like push-down stores can identify arbitrary recursive events, i.e. arbitrary perceptual features.

[2] Since the activity executed by the organism itself requires controlling perceptions, we should have been more precise by taking the second member in the pair to be again a pair consisting of an activity feature and a perceptual feature controlling the activity.

REFERENCES

Bierwisch, M.: 1980, 'Utterance meaning and mental states', in F. Klix (ed.), *Memory and Cognition*, Berlin.

Kleene, S. C.: 1956, 'Representation of events in nerve nets and finite automata', in C. E. Shannon, J. McCarthy (eds.) *Automata Studies*, Princeton: Princeton Univ. Press, pp. 3–42.

Kutschera, F. von: 1975, *Philosophy of Language*, Dordrecht: Reidel.

Schnelle, H.: 1979, 'Circumstance sentences', in A. Margalit (ed.), *Meaning and Use*, Dordrecht: Reidel, pp. 93–115.

Schnelle, H.: 1980a, 'Pre-tense', in C. Rohrer (ed.), *Time, Tense, and Quantifiers*, Tübingen: Niemeyer, pp. 329–354.

Schnelle, H.: 1980b, 'Phenomenological analysis of language and its application to time and tense', in J. Parret et al. (eds.) *Possibilities and Limitations of Pragmatics*, Amsterdam: J. Benjamins.

Schnelle, H. 1980c, 'Introspection and the description of language use', in F. Coulmas (ed.) *Native Speaker Festschrift*, The Hague: Mouton.

WILLEM LEVELT AND BEN MAASSEN

LEXICAL SEARCH AND ORDER OF MENTION IN SENTENCE PRODUCTION

Wörter müssen nur aktualisiert,
Sätze müssen erzeugt werden.
Manfred Bierwisch (1979, p. 38)

INTRODUCTION

In the process of speaking conceptual content is expressed in linguistic form. This requires the speaker to make a variety of conceptual as well as linguistic decisions, and it is still a mystery how these decisions interact in the generation of fluent speech. Among the conceptual decisions taken are ones of content selection and linear order. Content selection is a matter of deciding what should be expressed, given the speaker's intentions and given mutual knowledge in the speaker-listener context. It will involve retrieval of information from memory or from the on-going scene in which the speaker is present. However, at the same time it is largely impossible for a speaker to give simultaneous expression to two or more units of information (let us call them "thoughts"). For linguistic expression these need be strictly ordered. The ordering of this information for expression we will call "linearization". Some major determinants of linearization are, once again, mutual knowledge but also "economy" for working memory: speakers appear to order thoughts for expression such that load on working memory during speaking is minimized (cf. Levelt, 1979 a, b, 1981). These are essentially non-linguistic determinants, however, and one may ask whether *linguistic* factors also exert an influence on ordering in expression. Among the linguistic decisions to be taken by the speaker are those Garrett (1975) calls "functional" and "positional" decisions. Functional decisions involve, in particular, lexical choice: words are selected for the expression of thoughts by a process of *lexical search*. Kempen and Hoenkamp (1979) and Kempen and Huybers (1980) argue convincingly that this search is, in the first instance, a search for "lemmas" which are still unspecified for phonetic or articulatory form. Positional decisions, on the other hand, have to do with the realization of appropriate *syntactic frames* and grammatical formatives. Do lexical and syntactic decisions affect the process of linearization, or should linearization be understood as a relatively

W. Klein and W. Levelt (eds.), Crossing the Boundaries in Linguistics, 221–252.

autonomous conceptual process, one which feeds forward onto linguistic decision making but does not receive feedback from that level? Or, in other words: are linearization and linguistic formulation embedded in a heterarchical organization, where every component can "talk" to the other, or is speaking rather a more hierarchical process in which not all components can directly interact? A theory of the latter kind is stronger than one of the former, and should receive our favor.

Earlier work on linearization (Levelt, 1979 a, b, 1981) has not shown any feedback from the linguistic to the conceptual level in speaking. However, this was not especially the aim of that research. Rather, it was investigated how thoughts would be expressed from sentence to sentence in discourse. In order to give the idea of feedback from the linguistic level a fair test, experiments are needed in which lexical search and syntactic "framing" might affect information ordering decisions.

Let us make this more concrete by considering an example. An observer is asked to describe the events he will see and is shown a circle and a triangle on a screen. The circle is to the left of the triangle. At a certain moment, the circle moves upward a bit, and somewhat later the triangle makes a similar vertical movement. If the interval between these two events is large, the observer will probably say something like: "The circle is rising . . . The triangle is rising". At shorter intervals, one may expect sentence coordination: "The circle is rising and the triangle is rising", and at still shorter intervals NP-coordination may result: "The circle and triangle are rising". If such variations in formulation in fact result one could partly account for them in terms of the ordering of percepts: it is natural and appropriate to express the order of events by a corresponding order of phrases. Moreover, if the two events are perceived as parts of a single simultaneous event (when the time interval between them is null), NP-coordination would be especially appropriate to express this. In short, and hardly surprisingly, conceptual factors affect linguistic choice. Event order is a major determinant of conceptual coding, which in turn governs linguistic order. The issue we want to address in this paper is whether order of mention can also be affected by non-conceptual linguistic decisions, i.e. by functional and positional operations. In the present context, this would mean that order of mention of two events is affected by factors such as syntactic framing and lexical search.

Let us first consider possible effects of *positional* decisions. A simple example can help clarify this. Suppose we give the observer the instructions to describe what he sees using a fixed syntactic frame: "X rose before Y rose". If the circle goes up first, that event has to be mentioned in first position.

If, however, the fixed frame is "Before X rose, Y rose", the circle's rising has to be mentioned in second position. Choice of syntactic frame thus affects order of mention. One might argue that this is a trivial case because in normal speech such frames are not given beforehand, but selected by the speaker to give appropriate expression to relevant content. Though this may be the rule, there are well-documented exceptions. Bühler (1908) describes how the subjects in his experiments chose a syntactic frame before filling in the content-words: "When we want to express a difficult thought, we first select the syntactic form for it, we first become conscious of the operational plan, and it is this plan which then controls the wording" (p. 86). And in 1934 he writes that "an empty syntactic schema preceded the actual formulation of an answer" (p. 253). If "*X* before *Y*" or "Before *X, Y*" are examples of such syntactic schema's, they may well determine the order of mention of events. Kempen (1977) gives examples of everyday situations in which syntactic frames clearly have priority in expression. In the repetitive speech of a radio sports reporter, for instance, the on-going events are cast in pre-established syntactic frames. Levelt and Kelter (1981) show that the syntactic form of a question can affect the frame of the answer, without any "conceptual intervention".

So, it would be wrong, a-priori, to reject the hypothesis that positional decisions may affect order of mention in everyday speech. This issue, we think, is an open one, and deserves careful experimentation.

The present study, however, is limited to the possible influence of *functional* linguistic decisions on order of mention. More specifically, it addresses the question whether *lexical search* affects this order. Let us consider again the circle-and-triangle situation. If the two figures move upwards simultaneously, perceived order of events can no longer be a determinant of order of mention. Still, in this case there may be other conceptual or perceptual influences on this. The leftmost figure, for instance, may be mentioned first (this was in fact the subjects' dominant tendency in our preliminary experiments). But if the objects' positions in the array are controlled for as well, will difficulty of lexical search demonstrably affect order of mention? If it is made difficult for a subject to find the name for the triangular object he perceives, will he tend to mention its rising in second position? Or is the decision about order of mention taken at another – earlier – level at which difficulty in naming plays no role? In that case difficulty in lexicalizing may affect speech latency if the difficult word is early in the sentence, but should not affect its position in the sentence.

EXPERIMENT 1. USING ALLONYMS

Let us start with the question how one might influence the ease of actualizing words during sentence production. Our first effort in this direction was as simple as it was artifical: We asked subjects to give event descriptions of the sort mentioned above. But instead of always calling a triangle "triangle", a subject was required to use a new name for it periodically during the experiment: for one block of trials it was to be called "tent", then "roof" for the next block, etc. Using such allonyms might make it more difficult for a subject to name this figure, and we wanted to learn if this would affect order of mention, provided the name of the other figure (e.g. "circle") was kept the same. Lindsley (1976) showed that using allonyms increased speech latencies in a task where subjects had to describe static pictures of events.

We were also interested here in possible effects of distance in a sentence between the two names, and of their positions in the sentence. The possible role of distance – grammatical as well as measured by separation in words – is best illustrated by means of examples of NP-coordination versus sentence coordination.

(1) Circle and triangle go up
(2) Circle goes up and triangle goes up

The two figure names in sentence (1) fall within a single NP and are closer than in sentence (2), where they occupy different clauses. An effect of naming difficulty on order of mention seems more likely in the former than in the latter case, since the search for the two names, as parts of the same phrase and in close succession, will almost surely overlap in time. The one found first thus has a good chance of appearing in first position. In the case of sentence coordination, on the other hand, a subject might begin to utter the first clause before having initiated retrieval of the second figure name here; there would be less occasion for a "race" between the two lexical search processes.

A further issue is that in both NP- and S-coordination constructions discussed so far, circle and triangle are "on a par": with equivalent simultaneous motion, the informational force of a sentence is hardly affected if the figure names change place. This is quite different if a sentence such as (3) is used

(3) Circle, which is next to triangle, goes up.

If a speaker uses this sentence, he is describing just one of the two events, using the other figure and event as a reference point. If the speaker is free to choose which event he will focus on, we can ask whether his decision will depend on naming ease. If indeed the event involving the easy name is chosen, one would have some evidence for feedback from lexical search to conceptual focussing (which, in its turn, determines order of mention in the sentence), i.e. to a very early stage in speech planning.

Finally, we were interested in possible effects of naming difficulty on latency to begin speaking. Sentences (1) to (3) begin with a figure name. One might expect that a difficult name would increase speaking latency if it appears in sentence-initial position. But what if the first name to be mentioned only comes somewhat later on in the sentence? To get an impression, we used a fourth sentence type, otherwise analogous to sentence (3):

(4) Up goes circle, which is next to triangle

Here the direction of movement is topicalized, which has the effect of moving the figure name away from initial position. Since this sentence starts with the movement predication, one can ask whether the formulation of the sentence is complicated by lexical difficulty, or whether such an effect is limited to sentence-initial constituents. The latter finding would suggest that a subject can start speaking before any figure name has been found by lexical search.

In summary, we designed an experiment in which subjects had to describe two simultaneously moving figures by means of a fixed syntactic frame. These frames were Dutch equivalents of the forms (1)–(4). To vary naming difficulty, we instructed a subject to use an allonym, e.g., "roof" for triangle, and changed the allonym to be used from one set of trials to the next. As dependent variables, we took the order of mention of the two figures in the given fixed syntactic construction, and latency to begin saying the sentence after stimulus onset.

Method

The experiment was run under the control of a PDP 11/55 computer. The graphics used were presented on an electronic display (Vector General) interfaced to the computer. They consisted of three geometric figures, some of which moved in upward or downward direction. The time course for one trial was as follows. First, a small cross appeared in the middle of the screen which served as a warning signal and fixation point. After one second, three figures appeared, positioned in triangular form around the cross (see Figure 1).

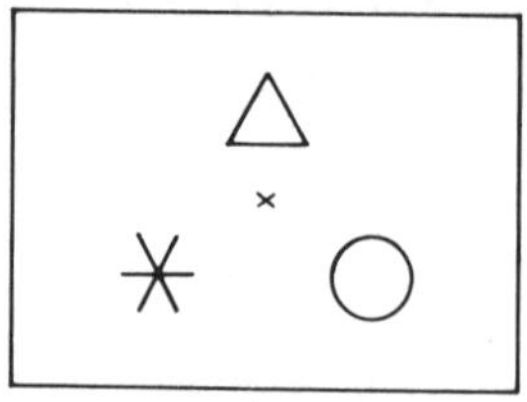

Fig. 1. A stimulus picture of Experiment 1; in Experiments 2 and 3 similar pictures were presented (only figures differed).

Immediately following this appearance, one or two of the figures began a phi-movement. A vertical displacement was carried out in three steps with between-step intervals of 60 ms, amounting to a shift of 2 cm (2 degrees of visual angle). Following this event, the figures remained in their final positions for 820 ms. The picture then disappeared. So the total event, including warning signal, had a duration of exactly two seconds. Response latency was defined as the time between appearance of the picture and onset of the utterance. By pressing a push-button, the subject could initiate the following trial.

The experiment was divided into blocks of trials so we could instruct subjects to change syntactic frames and allonyms used. Each block consisted of 36 trials, preceded by 3 practice trials. On 24 trials two of the figures moved – simultaneous and in the same direction, both upward or both downward – so that all four syntactic frames (see below) were appropriate. One of the moving figures was always chosen out of the set cross, star and diamond which were described with their normal names in Dutch, namely "kruis", "ster" and "ruit", respectively. The other moving figure was chosen equally often from one of two pairs: square and circle or pentagon and triangle. In each block, the figures of one pair were named with allonyms and those of the other pair with their normal, geometric names. Half of the descriptions contained two normal names, and the other half one normal name and one allonym. The normal Dutch name for square is "vierkant", the allonyms used were "doos" (box) and "blok" (block); for circle the normal name is "cirkel" and the allonyms used were "munt" (coin) and "schijf" (disk); pentagon is normally called "vijfhoek", while the allonyms were "mijter" (mitre) and "vlieger" (kite); for triangle the normal name is "driehoek", the allonyms used "tent" (tent) and "dak" (roof). The positions of the two moving figures were completely counterbalanced. Apart from 24 experimental trials each block also contained 12 distraction trials. Of these there were 3 trials where no figure moved and where the subject should remain quiet, and 9 in which only one figure moved, chosen equally often from the three groups. The order of trials within a block was randomized.

The four syntactic frames we required subjects to use for the events where two figures, *x* and *y*, moved were the following four:

(1) NPC: noun phrase conjunction
"*x* en *y* gaan omhoog/omlaag"
(*x* and *y* go up/down)

(2) SC: sentence conjunction
"*x* gaat omhoog/omlaag en *y* gaat omhoog/omlaag"
(*x* goes up/down and *y* goes up/down)

(3) SS: subject first, subordinate clause
"*x*, die naast/boven/onder *y* staat, gaat omhoog/omlaag"
(*x*, that next to/above/below *y* is, goes up/down)

(4) VS: verb first, subordinate clause
"omhoog/omlaag gaat *x*, die naast/boven/onder *y* staat"
(up/down goes *x*, that next to/above/below *y* is)

The syntactic frame for the description of a single moving figure was "*x* gaat omhoog/omlaag" (*x* goes up/down) throughout the experiment. Each subject received one block for each of the four syntactic frames; the order of the syntactic frames was varied over subjects according to a Latin Square design. The use of allonyms also changed per block. Half of the subjects first had to use "doos" and "munt", then "vlieger" and "dak", then "mijter" and "tent" and finally "blok" and "schijf". For the other half of the subjects the order was: "mijter" and "tent", "blok" and "schijf", "doos" and "munt", and finally "vlieger" and "dak".

Apart from three practice trials at the beginning of each block, there was also one practice block at the beginning of the experiment. Though the form of descriptions was left free in this block, most of the times syntactic frames (1) and (2) were chosen.

Procedure

The subject was seated in a sound proof booth 50 cm from the stimulus display. He or she was instructed to give the verbal description for an item as soon as possible after seeing figures move. Latency to speech was measured by a voice-operated relay and real-time clock interfaced to the computer. All test sessions were also tape-recorded.

The experimenter monitored what the subject said and viewed the correct description and latency recorded typed out on a teletype. With this information at hand, he could decide if the utterance produced was correct and the measurement for the latency reasonable, e.g. not a result of other noise than speech on part of the subject. When an error occurred, the experimenter pressed an error-button with the effect of presenting the picture again at the end of the current block. If the description given and the latency measured were both unproblematic, the experimenter pressed one of two buttons, indicating which of the two moving figures was mentioned first in the utterance. Codes for the figures and latencies recorded were stored in the computer for later analysis.

Twenty-one high school and university students living in Nijmegen participated in the experiment. Each subject received 7 guilders for the 45 minutes needed for the experiment.

Results

For each subject, we calculated mean latency, mean variance of latencies – not including the variance between conditions – and percentages of error made, not including "technical" errors. The means and standard deviations of these three measures over subjects were also calculated. Data from subjects who had a value in one of the three distributions that was more than two standard deviations from the overall mean were discarded and new means and standard deviations were calculated. This was repeated iteratively until no subjects with such extreme values remained. In this way data from five subjects were excluded from further analysis. These five each had extremely high (as defined above) error rates, namely at least 24%, vis-à-vis 12% for the remaining subjects. The variance of 3 of the 5 subjects and the mean of one of these 3 also exceeded the means of the remaining subjects for at least 2 standard deviations. For those five subjects the mean latency was 250 ms above the mean of the remaining 16.

The central question in the experiment was whether naming difficulty would influence the order of mention. This does appear to have been the case: of the utterances containing an allonym, 70.5% had that allonym in first position. So, contrary to our expectations, there was a tendency to start with what we considered the *difficult* name; this was a highly significant result

($t = 6.994$, df = 15, $p < .001$). Furthermore, this tendency was independent of the syntactic frame of the utterance.

An analysis of variance was performed on the (arcsine-transformed) proportions of utterances containing an allonym, that had the normal or easy name (E) in first position and the allonym or difficult name (D) in second position (the ED-utterances). Independent variables were Subjects, Syntactic Frames and Figure-Pairs (the actual pairs of figures that were presented); Subjects and Figure-Pairs were taken to be random factors. The factor Figure-Pairs is highly significant ($F_{11,165} = 6.794$, $p < .001$). When square and circle had to be named with allonyms, they occurred in first position more often than is the case with pentagon and triangle (76% vs 65%). Subjects also varied among themselves in positioning the allonym first ($F_{15,165} = 2.464$, $p < .01$), but no subject used it less often than the normal name in first position. Syntactic frames, our main control variable, was not significant at all. The percentages of utterances with allonym in first position were 72.3% for frame NPC, 71.4% for SC, for SS 68.0% and for VS 70.4%.

Our second dependent variable was speech onset latency. In Figure 2 are plotted the mean latencies of utterances with two normal, easy names (EE: easy easy), the means of the utterances with a normal name in first and an allonym in second position (ED: easy difficult) and the means of those utterances with an allonym first and a normal name second (DE: difficult easy). The total mean latencies (e) as well as the means for each of the four syntactic frames separately (a–d) are plotted.

When an utterance contains an allonym, then starting with that allonym gives a shorter latency than starting with the other, normal figure name. In a least squares analysis of variance with the factors Subjects, Syntactic Frames and Order of Mention (ED vs. DE, now introduced as independent variable), performed on the latencies of the utterances containing an allonym, this difference is significant ($F_{1,15} = 8.485$, $p = .01$). Also significant was the difference between Syntactic Frames ($F_{3,45} = 14.457$, $p < .001$). Although the interaction between Syntactic Frames and Order of Mention is not significant ($F_{3,45} = 1.062$, $p > .25$), there is nevertheless an effect of Syntactic Frame on the latency-difference between ED and DE utterances. Separate t-tests for comparing ED and DE give a significant result only for those syntactic frames in which the naming variation occurs in the first word of the utterance: for frame NPC ($t = 3.045$, df = 45, $p < .01$), for SC ($t = 2.112$, df = 45, $p < .025$) and for SS ($t = 1.783$, df = 45, $p < .05$). For frame VS where the name occurs later in the utterance, $t = -.137$, df = 45, $p > .25$.

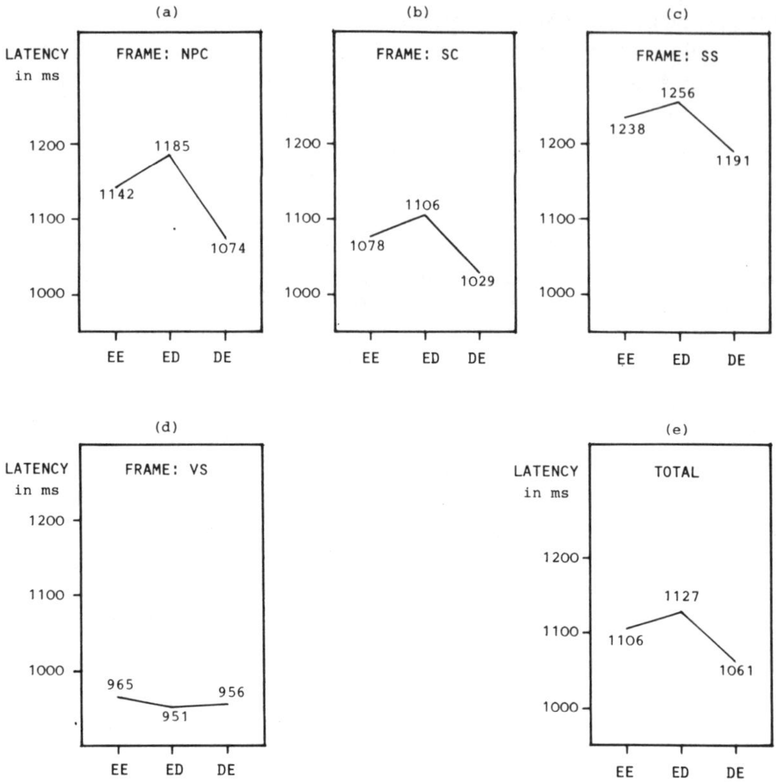

Fig. 2. Mean latencies of utterances with two normal ("easy") names (EE), normal name in first and allonym ("difficult" name) in second position (ED) and allonym in first and normal name in second position (DE). In (a) this is plotted for syntactic frame NPC, in (b) for frame SC, in (c) for SS and in (d) for VS; (e) gives the total means.

Discussion of the results

The main finding of this experiment is that use of allonyms did affect order of mention, but in a way opposite to our expectations; in 70.5% of the cases the allonym was mentioned in *first* position. There is no indication that using the allonym was more difficult for the subject. On the contrary, there is reason to believe that it was easier: from Figure 2 it appears that when the allonym is in first position, the latency to speech is shorter. This effect is absent only (this time in line with our expectations) for the fourth syntactic frame, where the first figure name mentioned does not come in sentence initial position. The shorter speech latencies for the other three frames with the allonym in sentence-initial position are just the reverse of Lindsley's (1976) findings, who found an increase of speech latency in such cases. How could it be that allonyms are relatively easy in our case? Presumably, the subject develops a special strategy to cope with the experiment's requirements. The strategy could be this: (1) keep the trouble figure (i.e., the figure with the assigned allonym) in the perceptual focus of attention (2) at each trial keep the allonym available in short term memory (3) use a focus- first order of mention. This procedure would be both approriate and effort reducing. It is appropriate in that an event which is emphasized by the experimental instructions receives priority of mention; it is effort-reducing in that STM is relieved at the earliest possible moment, from the beginning of the sentence. Retrieval from STM is moreover rapid, so that the speech latency can be quite short.

There is some evidence that this strategy is in fact used. Firstly, that subjects mark "trouble figures", independent of their names appears, on the one hand, from the fact that the order of mention effect is the same for all syntactic frames. Order of mention is not more affected if the two names are closely together in the same NP; the subject moreover tends to select the trouble figure's movement for his event description in the third and fourth frame. That indicates, that the figure is focussed upon in an early stage of speech planning, before the lexical decision is made. On the other hand, there is evidence that trouble figures tend to appear in first position even in case they have *no* allonyms. More precisely, if a figure that has been an experimental figure with allonyms in an earlier block of trials has its "normal" name in a succeeding block of trials, it still tends to be mentioned in first position. For the blocks in which no allonyms are assigned, i.e. where both figure names are "normal", we find that in a significant ($p < .05$, t-test) 55.7% of the trials that figure is mentioned first which is a "trouble figure" in other blocks. The attentional set of focus on particular figures seems to extend somewhat over blocks of trials. Secondly, the second part of the strategy cannot work for these latter cases. Naming the trouble figure first cannot be done by releasing the allonym from STM, since there is no allonym in these cases. We would therefore *not* expect shorter speech latency if the trouble figure is mentioned in sentence initial position. We found this to be the case; the mean latency was even slightly longer (1116 vs. 1094 ms).

The most likely, but surely post-hoc, explanation for the findings in this experiment is that the instructions induce the subject to focus perceptually on the experimental figure. It should be noticed that such a strategy was excluded in Lindsley's case, since Lindsley simultaneously introduced allonyms for *all* the objects in his pictures. Perceptually focussing just one or two particular objects would not have been a helpful strategy for his subjects. Since focussing is, clearly, a non-linguistic determinant of order of mention our experimental procedure is, in retrospect, unfit to test possible effects of lexicalization difficulty on order of mention.

How else could we affect lexical difficulty? It should be a procedure which cannot induce the subject to focus beforehand on a particular figure. Moreover, we would like to use "normal" names only and not focus subject's attention on a particular name, so that subjects would not be able to give precedence to one name by using special STM-strategies.

The next experiment makes use of already existing differences in figure naming difficulty. It is known that some words are harder to retrieve than others, and this may also be true for names of geometrical figures. If, for instance, "circle" is relatively easy to retrieve and "diamond" relatively hard, then we can ask if there is a preferred order of mention, i.e. "circle"-first, for particular syntactic frames. In such an experiment, the subject is fully unconscious of the experimental variable; there is no reason to expect focussing on particular figures, nor on particular figure names.

As we suggested earlier, the theory we would prefer is one where lexical search does *not* affect order of mention, i.e. where linearization and functional decisions have a hierarchical one-way rather than a heterarchical two-way relation. A hierarchical theory here predicts that lexical difficulty will not affect order of mention. But a negative result might only mean that the method of measurement is too insensitive. Two precautions were taken to preclude this type of interpretation. First, we used stimuli and syntactic frames which *did* give rise to order of mention effects in the previous experiment. Secondly, we measured speech latencies to ascertain that variation in lexical difficulty was still affecting the sentence production process.

EXPERIMENT 2. USING NORMAL NAMES: HARD AND EASY ONES

This experiment consisted of two parts. The preliminary part was to determine naming latencies for different geometrical figures, in order to objectively choose relatively "hard" and "easy" names. This preliminary experiment in turn consisted of two parts. It is important to ascertain that differences in naming latency are not due to differences in perceptual recognizability of figures, but only to naming a figure once recognized. So, apart from measurements of naming latency, the preliminary experiment included measurements of recognition latencies. Figures which differed in naming latency but were equal in recognition latency were then used in the main experiment. There, we again determined order of mention and speech latency for two-event descriptions.

Preliminary Experiment

Method

Ten different figures were used: square, diamond, pentagon, cross, rectangle, triangle, star, ellipse, circle, and sickle or (half) moon. These were presented one-by-one in blocks of 60 trials. The time course of one trial was as follows: first, a small cross appeared in the middle of the visual display, accompanied one second later by a figure which appeared above it and the subject reacted as quickly as possible. The figure remained present for one second, then the picture disappeared. Again, the experiment was self-paced; the subject initiated the next trial by pushing a button. The order of trials within blocks was fully randomized with the restriction that no figure could occur more than two times in succession.

In the naming part of the preliminary experiment subjects had to name the figures shown as quickly as possible and the latency of this response, the time between appearance of the figure and onset of the description, was measured. When an error occurred, the picture was presented again at the end of the block. Before the naming blocks were presented, subjects received 30 practice trials; they rapidly and spontaneously used only the names mentioned in Table 1. Each subject received four naming blocks, naming each figure a total of 24 times.

The recognition task was done with the same subjects. The same blocks of pictures were presented (in a different order), but now, instead of naming the figures, subjects were asked to press a "yes"-button if the presented figure was the target-figure for that block (a figure specified as such by instruction) and a "no"-button if it was one of the other nine figures. To keep the situation comparable with the naming condition, the same blocks of trials were presented; thus, the ratio of number of "yes" to number of "no"-responses was 1 to 9. The "yes" and "no"-buttons were pressed with right and left index fingers respectively.

Every subject was given four recognition blocks with four different target figures. Each of the ten figures was target figure once in each of the four serial positions of recognition blocks (blocks that did not fit this design were left out in final analysis). Half of the subjects did the naming task first, and half the recognition task. Position by blocks within the recognition task was counterbalanced over figures.

The experimental setting was the same as in Experiment 1. There were 14 subjects, selected from the same pool as in the previous experiment, but with no overlap. A 15th subject was given 10 recognition blocks only, one for each figure.

Results

Distributions of percentages of errors, mean latencies and mean variances of latencies were determined in the same way as in Experiment 1. One subject was eliminated because of a computer breakdown during his session. Another was dropped for having an extremeley high mean variance and generally slow mean latency of responses in the naming task.

In Table 1 schematic drawings of the ten figures and their Dutch names are presented together with mean naming-latency (RT_{nam}), recognition latencies (RT_{yes} – the mean latency of yes-responses) and the difference between these two ($RT_{nam} - RT_{yes}$). An analysis of variance was carried out on both naming latencies and recognition latencies. In the analysis of the naming latencies the factor Figures was significant ($F_{9,99} = 7.71$, $p < .01$). In the analysis of the recognition latencies, the factor Figures was *not* significant ($F < 1$), only the interaction between Serial Position and Figures ($F_{36,247} = 3.85$, $p > .001$). So, unlike naming-latencies, recognition latencies are not significantly different for the ten figures.

We took the differences between the naming latencies and the recognition latencies, shown in the last column of Table 1, to reflect the time needed for retrieving the figure names. By inspection of these differences, two sets of three figures each, were selected, a difficult set, whose names were relatively hard to retrieve (square, diamond and pentagon) and a set of figures with easily retrieved names (triangle, circle and moon). The difficult figures had a mean naming latency of 769 ms and a mean recognition latency of 511 ms. For the easy figures these values were 686 ms and 506 ms respectively. In an analysis of variance on naming-latencies of these six figures, with easy and difficult groups introduced as a "lexicalization factor", the difference between these groups was significant ($F'_{1,7} = 19.00$, $p < .01$); Figures within groups was not significant ($F_{4,44} = 2.35$, $p > .05$). In the same analysis on

FIGURE	DUTCH NAME	RT_{nam}	RT_{yes}	$RT_{nam} - RT_{yes}$
	"vijfhoek"	765	499	266
	"vierkant"	772	510	262
	"ruit"	770	524	246
	"ster"	707	473	234
	"kruis"	732	499	233
	"rechthoek"	730	497	233
	"ellips"	703	478	225
	"driehoek"	710	526	184
	"maan"	656	477	179
	"cirkel"	691	516	175

TABLE I.
The presented figures and their Dutch names of the preliminary part of Experiment 2, together with mean naming latency (RT_{nam}), recognition latency, i.e. mean latency of yes-responses (RT_{yes}) and the difference between the two ($RT_{nam} - RT_{yes}$), all in ms. The underlined figures are those selected for further experimentation.

recognition latencies neither effect has significance ($F < 1$ for each).

From these data it was now possible to construct the main experiment. As a main experimental variable, it contrasted the three figures with "easy" names (triangle, circle and moon) with the three with "hard" ones (square, diamond and pentagon).

Main Experiment

Method

The pictures presented on any trial consisted of three figures, positioned in triangular form around a small cross used as a fixation point. In most cases two of the three figures made a phi-movement in upward or downward direction. The time course of one presentation was the same as in Experiment 1.

The experiment again was divided into blocks of trials. Each block consisted of 30 trials: 3 practice trials, 18 experimental trials and 9 distraction trials. In the experimental trials two figures moved, both upwards or both downwards, one chosen from the easy set (triangle, circle and moon) and one from the difficult set (square, diamond and pentagon). The third figure, which remained motionless, was chosen randomly from the six figures, but was as often a difficult figure as an easy one. The six possible position combinations in the pattern for the easy and difficult moving figures were used equally often. Of the distraction trials, in three cases no figure moved; the subjects were here to say either nothing or "nothing". In the remaining six distraction trials only a single figure moved, one trial for each; these diaplays were to be described with the frame "*x* gaat omhoog/omlaag" ("*x* goes up/down").

Since latency differences as a function of lexical difficulty were not found in Experiment 1 for construction (4), it was omitted here. Only syntactic frames (1) NPC ("*x* and *y* gaan omhoog/omlaag"), (2) SC ("*x* gaat omhoog/omlaag en *y* gaat omhoog/omlaag") and (3) SS ("*x*, die naast/boven/onder *y* staat, gaat omhoog/omlaag") were used. Syntactic frames were varied between blocks, with each subject receiving each frame type in two blocks, in a counterbalanced order (ABCCBA). The order in the first ABC run, and thus also in the CBA run, was varied according to a Latin Square design.

The experimental setting and task were the same as in Experiment 1 for both the subjects and the experimenter. There were 21 fresh subjects from the same pool as in the preceding experiments.

Results

Three subjects had mean latencies and mean latency variances that were both at least two standard deviations from the group means of the remaining subjects. Two of these three also had an unusually high percentage of errors (23% vs. 10% for the remaining subjects). And one subject had a mean latency (1710 ms) almost twice the overall mean. These four subjects were all excluded from further analysis performed on the remaining seventeen.

All descriptions of two moving figures contained an easy and a difficult figure name. Contrary to Experiment 1, there was no significant tendency for either of them to appear more often in sentence-initial position: in 51% of the cases the easy name came first and in 49% the difficult name. As in Experiment 1, there was again no effect of syntactic frames on order of mention. In an analysis of variance on the transformed proportions of utterances that started with an easy name, with as main factors Subjects, Version (first vs. second run through the syntactic frames), Syntactic Frames and Figure Pairs, only Figure Pairs ($F_{8,128} = 2.227$, $p = .029$) and Version ($F'_{1,24} = 7.374$, $p = .011$) were significant. Syntactic Frames was not significant ($F < 1$). The proportion of utterances starting with an easy name was 52.8% for frame NPC, 49.2% for frame SC and 51% for frame SS. With respect to figure pairs there was a slight tendency to start with the circle and a bit stronger tendency to start with the pentagon. With respect to Version, there was a non-significant tendency to start with the easy figure (in 53% of the cases) in the first three blocks and with the hard figures in the last three blocks (51.9%).

Thus, the variation in naming difficulty had little effect on order of mention. It did, however, affect the latency to speech.

The upper curve of Figure 3 plots the mean latencies of utterances describing two moving figures and starting with the name for the figure depicted on the *x*-axis. In an analysis of variance of these latencies, Naming Difficulty (that is ED vs. DE utterances) had a highly significant effect ($F_{1,16} = 84.279$, $p < .001$) as did Syntactic Frames ($F_{2,32} = 34.426$, $p < .001$). When figures within groups is added as a random factor in the analysis, Naming Difficulty still is significant ($F'_{1,5} = 12.954$, $p = .016$) as is Syntactic Frames ($F'_{2,19} = 16.792$, $p < .001$). Figures within groups is itself significant ($F_{4,64} = 4.062$, $p < .01$). Clearly, two-event utterances starting with an easy name are initiated faster than those starting with a difficult name. The same holds for utterances describing only one moving figure, which can be taken as an independent measure of meaning latencies for the figures in these sentence contexts. The middle curve of Figure 3 plots these latencies. Analysis of variance was performed on them as with the double name utterances. Again significant were: Naming Difficulty ($F_{1,16} = 38.435$, $p < .001$) and Syntactic Frames ($F_{2,32} = 15.736$, $p < .001$). Again, when Figures within groups is added as

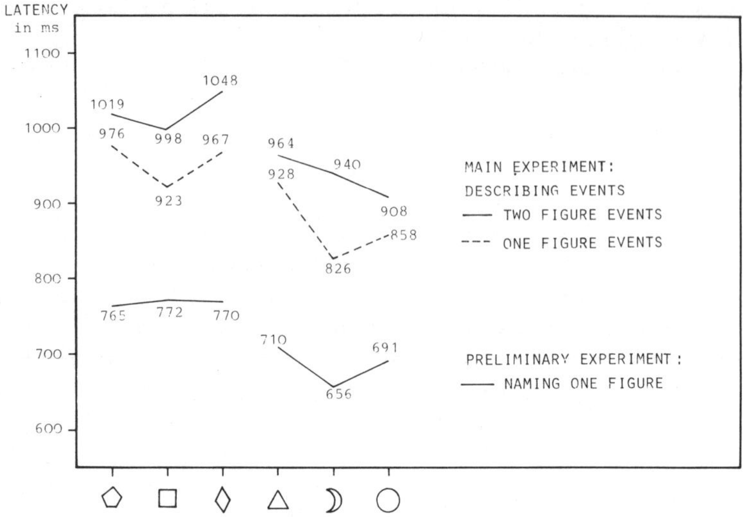

Fig. 3. Mean latencies of Experiment 2. The lower curve represents the naming latencies of the preliminary experiment, the middle and upper curve the latencies of utterances for description of one- and two-figure events. On the abscissa are the figures named in initial position (for the one-event descriptions these are, of course, the only figures mentioned)

random factor, Naming Difficulty nearly reaches significance ($F'_{1,5} = 5.353$, $p = .067$). Syntactic Frames remains significant ($F'_{2,27} = 8.492$, $p < .01$), and Figures within groups ($F_{4,64} = 8.128$, $p < .01$) and the interaction between Syntactic Frames and Figures within groups ($F_{8.128} = 2.432$, $p = .017$) are significant. For comparison the naming latencies of the preliminary experiment are also depicted in the bottom curve of Figure 3.

As in Experiment 1 there were consistent latency differences between syntactic frames; utterances of the form SS took longest to initiate, followed by NPC and SC (see the upper curve in Figure 4). Even the smallest difference, between NPC and SC, is reliable ($t = 2.687$, $df = 32$, $p < .01$ one-tailed).

A rather queer result is represented in the lower curve of Figure 4. For the utterances describing one moving figure, the differences between syntactic frames are exactly the same as for the two figure descriptions. But here it is not the frame of the utterance itself which is meant (this was "*x* goes up/down" throughout the whole experiment), but the syntactic frame of the other utterances of the block in which it is embedded; this is a significant effect ($p < .01$), to which we will return in the discussion.

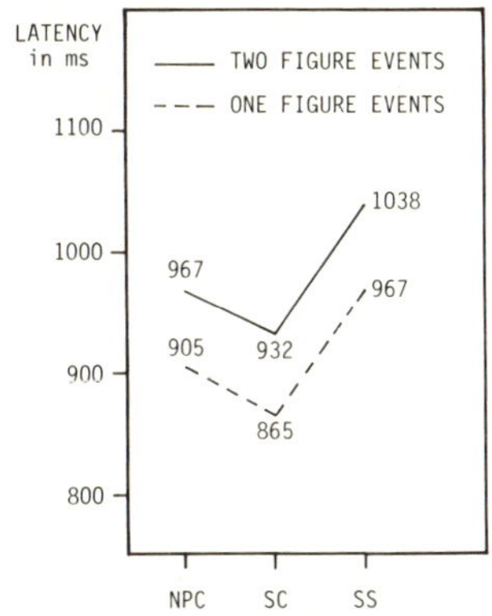

Fig. 4. Mean latencies of Experiment 2, for syntactic frames NPC, SC and SS. The upper curve represents the utterances containing two figure names. The lower curve gives latencies for the single-name utterances which appear in the blocks defined by the two-event syntactic frames NPC, SC and SS.

Discussion of the results

Before discussing the main findings on order of mention it should be noticed that difficulty of naming was indeed an effective variable in the experiment qua latency to speech. For each of the three syntactic frames, speech latency was longer if a difficult name appeared in sentence-initial position. It was on the average 85 ms longer, which is nearly the same as the average 83 ms difference in naming latency found between difficult and easy figures in the preliminary experiment.

It is therefore a remarkable result that no effect was found for order of mention. The easy name appeared in first position in a non-significant 51% of the trials, and there were no significant differences between the three syntactic frames in this respect. From this, the conclusion can be drawn that the speaker decides on the order of mention irrespective of difficulty of lexical search. There is, moreover, inferential evidence that the order of mention decision is taken *before* lexical search occurs. If it took place *after* lexical retrieval one would not expect an effect on speech latency itself since both names would be available before the start of speech. The process, therefore, seems to be that after perceiving the events, the speaker decides on an order of mention, and only then retrieves the figure names: If the first figure to be mentioned happens to have a hard-to-retrieve name, the speech process will be retarded; if it has an easy name the process will be speeded up.

The latencies measured show another interesting variation as well: the three syntactic frames differed significantly in voicing latency. As can be seen from Figure 4, latencies were shortest for the sentence-coordinated frame ("*x* goes up/down and *y* goes up/down"), longer for NP-coordination ("*x* and *y* go up/down") and longest for the subordinated construction ("*x*, which is next to *y*, goes up/down"). This conforms to the pattern of results in Experiment 1. It would, however, be premature to assign much value to these differences. If a speaker found a particular frame more appropriate for describing what he saw, the mean latency for this frame could be expected to be relatively short, and inversely for inappropriate frames. Intuitively, the subordinated construction used here seems quite inappropriate for any of the events to be described, which may explain the greater delay in articulatory latency. This could be called a "congruency"-effect for speaking, and may have nothing to do with the "intrinsic" difficulty of a particular syntactic frame. Neither the present experiment nor the previous one, however, can distinguish between appropriateness and intrinsic difficulty, since by instruction the subjects were not given freedom of choice. Only if the syntactic frame is unrestricted can one assume that a speaker gives an appropriate formulation. Then, any remaining differences in latencies between frames should have to do with "intrinsic" formulation difficulties for different frames. This argues for an experiment in which there is freedom of formulation.

There is a related argument for trying to replicate the present findings under free choice of sentence constructions. Normally, a speaker would generate a syntactic form at the occasion of each event to be described, but here, with blocked presentation, speakers were essentially asked to store the experimental frame in memory and use it for each two-event trial. It is immaterial for the present argument whether this use is a retrieval of the frame for constructing the utterance, or whether the stored frame is to be used as a criterion by the speaker while monitoring his own production (as proposed by Kempen and Huybers, 1980). The evidence we have that the subject has a special attentional set for the block's syntactic frame is that the latencies for single-event descriptions *also* differed between blocks (cf. Figure 4). If a block had a difficult two-event frame (such as the subordinate construction), latencies were generally relatively long, not only those in which that frame itself had to be used (the two-event cases), but also those where the frame was not used (the single-event cases in a block). As was noted above, these differences between blocks on single-event descriptions were also reliable. Thus, we might suppose that, dependent on the frame, short-term memory load varied from block to block, and affected the latencies for all descriptions in a block. The latency differences found between syntactic frames therefore, can be due to the short term memory load they create, rather than to any "intrinsic" difficulty in *generating* those frames.

EXPERIMENT 3. FREE FORMULATION

In this experiment, possible effects of lexicalization difficulty on order of mention were studied under conditions of free formulation. We decided to slightly increase the range of events to be described in order to reduce the likelihood that subjects would *themselves* generate a "stock frame" and hold it in short term memory throughout the experiment. To the set of two-event stimuli, we added, firstly, the possibility that the one figure would go up and the other go down; this would presumably make sentence-coordination (*x* goes up and *y* goes down) more appropriate than forms of NP-coordination. Secondly, we added as "filler'-trials cases where the two moving figures were of identical shape. This would lead (and in fact led) to a variety of other syntactic constructions (such as "two diamonds go up").

Another change in the experiment was made to elaborate our earlier findings indicating that speech latencies are shorter if a description has begun with an easy name. The design of the previous experiment made it impossible to check independently whether lexicalization difficulty has a *general* effect on speech latency. There were always one easy and one difficult name involved in a trial. We thus wanted to learn whether latencies would be shorter if *both* names were easy than if only the first one mentioned was (and similarly whether latencies would be longer if both names were difficult rather than just the first one). For this reason, events were added where both moving figures had easy names, or both had difficult names. In more detail, the experimental design was as follows.

Method

The pictures presented again consisted of three figures positioned in triangular form around a small cross used for fixation, as in Figure 1. In every presentation one or two figures moved. Catch-trials with no moving figures were left out. The time course of a single presentation was the same as in the earlier experiments.

The pictures were presented in blocks of 60: 6 practice trials, 12 trials in which one figure moved, 6 trials in which two identical figures moved and 36 trials in which two different figures moved. Of these latter trials, there were 18 where one easy and one difficult figure moved, that is one figure was chosen from the set triangle, circle and moon and the other from the set pentagon, square and diamond. These items we will call ED or DE, depending on the order used in a subject's description. This replicates the conditions of Experiment 2. In addition, there were 9 trials in which two easy figures moved (condition EE) and 9 where two difficult figures moved (condition DD). The cases with only a single moving figure (condition S) offered an opportunity to compare lexicalization in a sentential context to the pure naming data of Experiment 2; each of the six figures moved alone twice in each block. There are six position-combinations for two different moving figures and three for two identical moving figures. Within a block all position combinations were equally often used as far as "easy" versus "difficult" figures were concerned. For combinations of particular figures a complete balancing over figures was realized over blocks, so that in the end every pair of figures occured in all position combinations equally often. This also holds for direction of movement. In half the trials the two figures moved in opposite directions (one up and one down), in the other half they moved in the same direction (both up or both down). This was also varied within blocks as much as possible in every relevant condition. Each subject received three blocks of trials preceded by about 20 or 30 practice trials.

On each trial, subjects were free to choose the syntactic frame of the description given. In practice, however, they almost exclusively used the frames NPC and SC. In order to code this distinction, the experimenter used a second set of code buttons, apart from those used to indicate with which figure name the utterance started, to indicate syntactic frames (NPC, SC and "other"). The computer program was designed to wait for both button presses and after some practice the experimenter could perform this without noticeable delay for the subjects being tested. Apart from the voice onset latencies, the voice offset latencies were also measured. This made it possible to determine utterance durations.

The setting for the experiment was the same as earlier. There were 23 subjects, again paid volunteers from the same pool, all attending this type of experiment for the first time.

Results

In the same way as in preceding experiments, distributions of mean latencies, mean latency variances and mean percentage of errors were calculated. One subject had a high percentage of errors (24% vs. 8% for subjects not excluded). Three subjects had extremely high latency variances, and one of these three also had an extremely high mean latency. These four were excluded from further analysis, which was thus performed on the remaining 19 subjects.

The main question, whether naming difficulty influences order of mention again has to be answered negatively. Of the utterances containing one easy and one difficult name 52.5% started with the easy and 47.5% with the difficult name. This difference is not significant ($t = 1.611$, $df = 18$, $p > .10$ two-tailed).

Subjects themselves could choose the syntactic form of their utterances. The frames NPC ("*x* and *y* go up/down") and SC ("*x* goes up/down and *y* goes up/down") were chosen almost exclusively. Frame SC was used more frequently (in 61.2% of the cases) than frame NPC (38.8%); this difference is clearly significant ($t = 5.907$, $df = 18$, $p < .001$ two-tailed).

As in the previous experiments, there was no interaction between syntactic frame and order of mention. In an analysis of variance on the (transformed) proportion of utterances containing an easy and a difficult name which started with the easy one, i.e. ED-sentences, only the factor Figure Pairs ($F_{8,144} = 3.203$, $p < .01$) and the interaction between Syntactic Frames and Figure Pairs ($F_{8,144} = 2.263$, $p = .025$) were significant; Syntactic Frames by itself had no effect ($F' < 1$). The significant findings for Figure Pairs and its interaction with Syntactic Frames was due to a tendency to start a description with a moving circle shown, especially in the cases where syntactic frame NPC was chosen. This preference totally accounts for the slight difference between percentages of ED and DE utterances.

As to the second main question, the effect of naming difficulty on onset latency, mean latencies of utterances starting with each of the figures are presented in Figure 5. Utterances beginning with an easy name were initiated significantly faster than utterances starting with a difficult name; the difficulty of the second name spoken in the sentence has no influence (mean latencies of EE versus ED utterances are 998 and 991 ms respectively; for DE and DD utterances these values are 1030 and 1032 ms). In an analysis of variance on the latencies, with as fixed factors Syntactic Frames, Difficulty of First Name (that is, EE and ED vs. DE and DD utterances) and Difficulty of Second Name (EE and DE vs. ED and DD), only difficulty of First Name ($F_{1,18} = 11.357$, $p < .01$), and Syntactic Frames ($F_{1,18} = 13.101$, $p < .01$) were significant. Thus, the difference between easy to name and difficult to name figures was again validated.

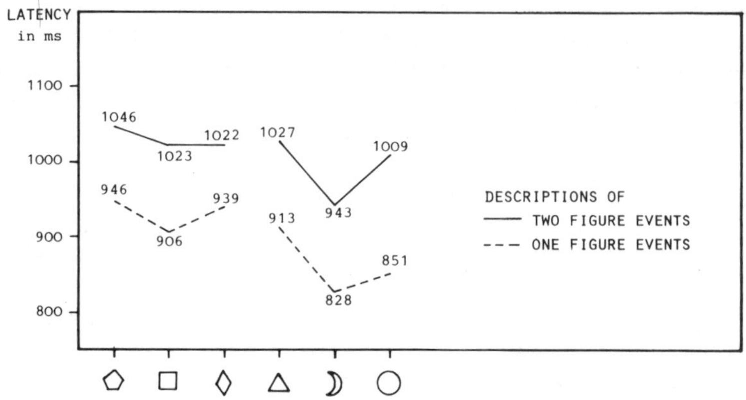

Fig. 5. Mean latencies of the utterances in Experiment 3 with the figure on the abscissa mentioned in initial position. Upper curve (drawn line) is for two-figure events, lower curve (dotted line), is for one-figure events.

The lower curve in Figure 5 shows onset latencies of utterances describing single moving figures. In an analysis of variance on these utterances, Naming Difficulty ($F_{1,18} = 27.281, p < .001$) was also significant. When Figures within groups is added as a random factor, the result remains ($F'_{1,6} = 4.971$, $p = .066$), and Figures within groups ($F_{4,72} = 2.877, p = .028$), is also significant.

Discussion of the results

As in the previous experiment lexicalization difficulty was an effective influence on speech onset latencies: if an easy term appeared in first position speech latency was shorter than if a difficult term appeared first. An additional result was that the ease or difficulty of the second name had no effect on this latency. This suggests that the second name used was not retrieved before the start of speech. We will return to this finding later in the discussion.

Though lexicalization difficulty had a measurable effect on task performance, it did not affect order of mention. The easy term appeared in first position in only 52.5% of the sentences produced. This confirms the findings of the previous experiment, now under conditions of free formulation. The main conclusion from the present experiments, therefore, must be that order of mention is not affected by lexical search. In other words, there is a process hierarchy in the production of speech in which there is no feedback from lexicalization processes to linearization decisions. The present results are not sufficient to make the much stronger claim that order of mention decisions have only feed-forward but no feedback relations to the level of linguistic decisions, i.e. functional and positional decisions in Garrett's model. Still, they are in full agreement with such a state of affairs.

Some of the results in the present experiment may also throw light on other relations between components of the speech production mechanism. The first of these concerns some possible other determinants of linearization. One factor that clearly affects linearization is the spatial arrangement of the two moving figures. There are three possible orientations between them, given the triangular stimulus arrangement (see Figure 1). When the two figures at the base of the triangle moved, then in 55.2% of the cases they were described in the order left-first, right-second. When the top figure moved together with one of the bottom figures, they were described from top to bottom 74.9% of the time when the other figure was on the bottom left, and 78.5% of the time when it was the bottom right figure. So, clearly, there is both a weak tendency to describe from left to right and a strong one to describe from top to bottom. In the description of cases in which one figure moved up and the other one down, subjects had no systematic preference for first mentioning either motion.

A second result concerns the choice of syntactic frames. In the free choice situation, subjects almost exclusively (in more than 99% of the cases) used the NP-coordinated or S-coordinated sentence frame. NP-coordination, however, was less frequent (38.8%) than S-coordination (61.2%). One obvious determinant of this difference is the type of event presented. Descriptions of "disjunctive" events, where the figures move in opposite directions, always take the sentence-coordination form: "x gaat omhoog en y gaat omlaag" ("x goes up and y goes down"). Clearly NP-coordination in these cases (such as "x and y move") was not felt as a convenient description type. For cases where the two movements were in the same direction, on the other hand, S-coordination was used in only 22% of the cases. It is thus clear that S-coordination was preferred for describing "disjunctive" movements and NP-coordination for "conjunctive" movements. One could summarize this by saying that there is a "congruency principle" which gives optimal linguistic expression to a perceptual configuration. Others have obtained similar results under quite different experimental conditions (see e.g. Flores d'Arcais, 1975).

A third set of results relates further to this, but concerns relations only *within* the level of formulation. Though NP-coordination is the preferred frame for describing conjunctive movement, we found that latencies for

NP-coordination are systematically ($p < .01$) *longer* than for S-coordination. Figure 6 shows the latencies for the NP- and S-coordinated frames for conjunctive movements (both up or both down), plus the latencies for the S-coordination for disjunctive movements (one up and one down – there being no cases of NP-coordination in this latter case).

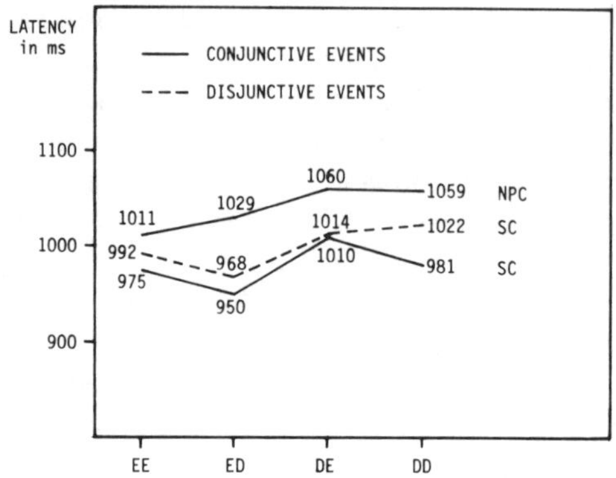

Fig. 6. Mean latencies of Experiment 3. The upper and lower (drawn) curves represent the latencies for descriptions of "conjunctive" events (both figures go up or both down). The upper curve is for descriptions containing noun-phrase coordination; the lower curve for sentence-coordinated descriptions. The middle (dotted) line gives latencies for descriptions of "disjunctive" events (one figure up, the other down); these were all sentence-coordinated. The abscissa partitions the latencies according to the order of "easy" and "difficult" names in the utterance.

The figure shows clearly that in general the latencies for easy-name-first utterances are relatively short. But it is clear that NP-coordination takes more time to initiate than S-coordination, even when both can be considered as appropriate syntactic frames (i.e. for conjunctive and disjunctive movements, respectively). The latencies of S-coordinated descriptions for conjunctive and disjunctive events, on the other hand, are not reliably different (the bottom two curves in the figure).

Why does it take longer to initiate an NP-coordinated frame? This cannot be due to a strategy whereby a speaker initiates speech for NP-coordinates only after both figure names have been retrieved. As was noted earlier, that strategy would predict that the difficulty of the second name mentioned should also affect speech latencies. But as the figure shows, it doesn't: for NP-coordination there is only a small, non-significant difference between EE and ED frames, and no difference between DE and DD frames. So, that strategy cannot have operated. A slightly modified version of this hypothesis could be stated with reference to the Kempen and Hoenkamp (1979) model of speech production. These authors distinguish between retrieval of a lemma and retrieval of the phonetic form of a lexical item. The lemma contains semantic and syntactic properties of a lexeme, but not its sound or articulatory structure. The latter may be retrieved at a later stage, for instance after "positional level" decisions have been taken (See also Garrett, 1980, for a discussion of this "double retrieval" hypothesis).

The lexicalization difficulty in our experiments can be interpreted in this model as a difficulty of retrieving the articulatory form of the item, *given* the lemma. The subject's strategy for NP-coordination would thus be to, first, decide on NP-coordination and to retrieve both lemma's, second, to retrieve the phonetic form of the first name and to initiate speech, and third, i.e. during speech, to retrieve the articulatory form of the second name. In this way the latencies of Figure 6 could be explained, since only for NP-coordination would *both* lemmas be retrieved before sentence initiation. For S-coordination, only *one* lemma would be retrieved beforehand. Then, for both frames just the first lemma would be given articulatory shape *before* the initiation of speech. If retrieving the phonetic form is easy, latency would be relatively short. For both frames retrieving the other phonetic form would occur during speech and therefore not affect speech latency.

This model cannot be completely correct either, however. We were able to make the following important additional observation: DD-cases (where both names given were difficult) tend to give significantly more S-coordinations than EE-cases (68% and 61%, respectively, $p < .05$), and then ED or DE cases (60% and 62%, respectively). There are two ways by which this result might have been obtained. First, the decision between the two syntactic frames might have been taken only *after* the initiation of speech, however, this would result in no latency difference between NP- and S-coordinated constructions, and that is not what we find. Second, the frame-decision might be taken *before* initiation of speech, as was assumed in the above-model, but with the speaker taking into account some estimation of the difficulty of retrieving the articulatory forms of the elements needed; this must be only an estimation of retrieval, not retrieval itself, since, as we have seen, the articulatory form of the second element is apparently retrieved only after the initiation of speech. With this explanation, however, we also run into serious trouble. When it is possible to make an estimation of the retrieval effort for both articulatory forms, then at least both lemmas must be known to the speaker, since what else should he base his estimation on? But if both lemma's are available before the initiation of speech whatever the eventual choice of syntactic frame, we can no longer explain why S-coordinated constructions have systematically shorter latencies than NP-coordinated descriptions.

We propose the following solution. On the one hand, we assume that speakers normally decide on the syntactic frame rather early in the production process (and based on considerations of appropriateness, i.e. NP-coordinated frame for "conjunctive" events and S-coordinated frame for "disjunctive" events). Depending on the frame selected, the speaker then retrieves one or two lemmas before the initiation of speech, one lemma in case of S-coordination, two lemmas in case of NP-coordination. So far, this conforms fully to the model presented above. On the other hand, we make the additional assumption that it is possible for the speaker to revise the frame decision at a later stage. In particular, the speaker may switch from an initial NP-coordinated frame to an S-coordinated frame. This is especially relevant for cases where the retrieval of the articulatory form of the second noun is not completed in time to permit a fluent continuation of speech. The speaker may then decide to articulate the verb, which may have become available in the meantime. Thus, all findings can be explained by assuming a dual relation between syntactic and lexical decisions: each may precede or follow the other. Thus, for the case of conjoint movement and two "easy" names (but also for DE and ED), a subject would go through the following steps (leaving out steps that are irrelevant for the present discussion):

(1) On grounds of appropriateness, select an NP-coordinated frame
(2) Retrieve both lemmas
(3) Retrieve the articulatory form of the first lemma
(4) Initiate speech
(5) While speaking, retrieve the articulatory form of the second lemma
(6) Articulate second noun and formulate VP.

For the case of two difficult names, this procedure would sometimes be hindered by long retrieval times for the second articulatory form, and a different syntactic frame would be adopted to prevent or limit disfluency:

(1)–(5) as above
(6) If no timely result, revise frame and formulate first VP.
(7) Complete retrieval of the articulatory form of the second lemma
(8) Formulate second VP

If, on grounds of appropriateness, an S-coordinated frame is chosen to start with, we assume that only one lemma and articulatory form is retrieved before initiation of speech, which explains the shorter latencies for these frames.

So, in the case of two difficult names, the total time for retrieving the two phonetic forms of the figure names would sometimes exceed the (parallel) retrieval of the verb's phonetic form. In that case a speaker may decide to shift frames from NP- to S-coordination. The mere difficulty of the second name is not, generally, enough for the speaker to decide on a frame shift: it should also be possible to shift, i.e., the verb should be available. This is more likely when both names are difficult than when only the second one is. If this explanation is correct, one would expect that this shift from NP- to S-coordination during the utterance would lead to a *lengthening* of the utterance.

To investigate this in more detail, we decided to analyze the utterance *durations*, i.e. the time spans from speech onset to speech offset. Figure 7 pictures the duration for NP- and S-coordinated utterances, with the latter further partitioned by descriptions of "conjunctive" events (both figures moving in the same direction), and "disjunctive" events (moving in opposite direction). S-coordinated utterances are, not surprisingly, longer than NP-coordinated ones.

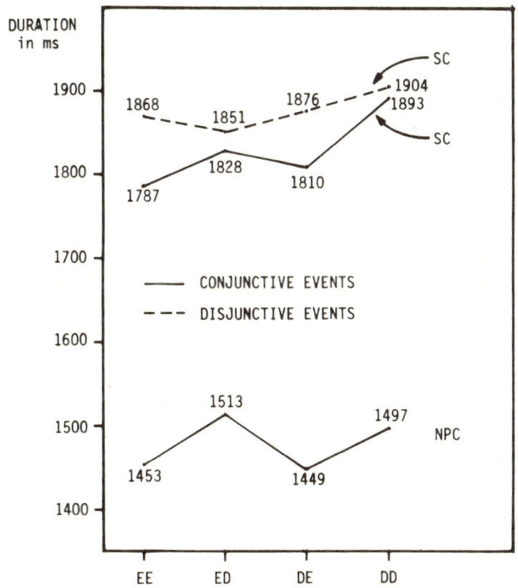

Fig. 7. Durations of utterances of Experiment 3. Drawn lines are for "conjunctive" events; the dotted line is for "disjunctive" events.

Let us first consider the NP-coordinated descriptions (the bottom-curve in the figure). Clearly, utterance durations are longer for ED and DD than for the other two cases. ($F_{1,18} = 20.138$, $p < .001$). In other words, if the second figure noun is hard, the utterance becomes extended in time. So difficulty of the second figure name *does* have an effect on the subject's speech, but only on duration, not latency. This is just the reverse of the effect of the first figure name, which affected the latency as we have seen, but does not affect duration (see Figure 7).

What happens, then, if a conjunctive event is described with an S-coordinated utterance? We argued that, especially for cases where both figure names are difficult (DD-cases) such an S-coordinated frame may be the result of a frame *shift*, i.e. the speaker starting with an NP-coordinated frame in mind, and deciding while speaking to switch to an S-coordinated frame. This shift would require additional time. The middle curve of Figure 7 shows that this is indeed the case. The utterance length for DD-cases is much longer than for the other three cases (EE, ED, and DE – the significance level for the differences is, by t-test, $p < .01$, $p = .06$, and $p < .03$, respectively). If this is indeed due to frame shift, as we argue, then such a difference should not occur when the S-coordinated frame is operative from the very start. This is the case when a disjunctive event is described; here subjects choose S-coordination as the appropriate frame without exception. Durations for such sentences are seen in the topmost curve in Figure 7. Analysis of variance in this case shows no significant effect of first or second name difficulty; DD-sentences do not take significantly more time even than EE ones. DD only differs significantly from ED ($p < .025$, t-test), but this is of no relevance for the present argument.

In summary, it seems that, though speakers select an appropriate syntactic frame early in planning their utterance, they can change to another frame during speech itself. One cause for this can be "lexical trouble", an overtly time consuming process in retrieving a word's phonetic form. The actualization of a word, therefore, can affect how a sentence is generated. This is in agreement with the findings of Bock and Irwin (1980), who found that availability of a lexical item in memory could affect the syntactic frame in which it became used. In other words there seem to be heterarchical feedback and feed-forward relations between the functional and positional linguistic decisions in speech. But at the same time we found that lexical retrieval does not feed back to the level of order of mention decisions. Taken together, we have obtained evidence for a hierarchical organization in speech production, in which perceptual and order of mention decisions (i.e. decisions at the "conceptual level") precede and influence linguistic decisions, but where there is no return influence on the conceptual level. Lexicalization does not affect order of mention. It is hard for words to cross linguistic boundaries.

Max-Planck-Institut für Psycholinguistik, Nijmegen

ACKNOWLEDGEMENT

We are thankful to Robert Jarvella who has greatly contributed to the language and the logic of this chapter, and to Gerard Kempen who was a source of theoretical inspiration and helpful comments.

REFERENCES

Bierwisch, M.: 1979, 'Sprache und Gedächtnis: Ergebnisse und Probleme', in M. Bierwisch (ed.), *Psychologische Effekte sprachlicher Strukturkomponenten*, Berlin: Akademie-Verlag.

Bock, J. K. and Irwin, D. E.: 1980, 'Syntactic effects of information availability in sentence production', *Journal of Verbal Learning and Verbal Behavior* **19**, 467–484.

Bühler, K.: 1908, Tatsachen und Probleme zu einer Psychologie der Denkvorgänge', *Archiv für die gesamte Psychologie* **12**, 1–92.

Bühler, K.: 1934, *Sprachtheorie*, Jena: Fischer (Stuttgart: Fischer, 1965^{II}).

Flores d'Arcais, G. B.: 1975, 'Some perceptual determinants of sentence construction', in G. B. Flores d'Arcais (ed.), *Studies in Perception*, Milano-Firenze: Martello-Giunti.

Garrett, M. F.: 1975, 'The analysis of sentence production', in G. H. Bower (ed.), *The Psychology of Learning and Motivation*, Vol. 9, New York: Academic Press.

Garrett, M. F.: 1980, 'Levels of processing in sentence production', in B. Butterworth (ed.), *Language Production. Vol. 1: Speech and Talk*, New York: Academic Press.

Kempen, G.: 1977, 'Conceptualizing and formulating in sentence production', in S. Rosenberg (ed.), *Sentence Production: Developments in Research and Theory*, Washington: Erlbaum.

Kempen, G. and Hoenkamp, E.: 1979, 'A procedural grammar for sentence production', Internal Report K. U. Nijmegen, Nov. 1979.

Kempen, G. and Huijbers, P.: 1980, 'The lexicalization process in sentence production and naming: indirect election of words', Internal Report K. U. Nijmegan, Oct. 1980.

Levelt, W. J. M.: 1979a, 'Linearization in discourse', memeo, Max-Planck-Institut für Psycholinguistik.

Levelt, W. J. M.: 1979b, 'Describing spatial networks'. To appear in Proceedings of the Sloan Symposium on Formal Semantics and Natural Language Processing. Held at Center for Cognitive Science, University of Texas.

Levelt, W. J. M.: 1981, 'Cognitive styles in the use of spatial direction terms', in R. J. Jarvella and W. Klein (eds.), *Speech, Place and Action. Studies of Language in Context*, Chichester: Wiley.

Levelt, W. J. M. and Kelter, S.: 1981, 'Surface form and memory in question-answering', submitted to *Cognitive Psychology*.

Lindsley, J. R.: 1976, 'Producing simple utterances: Details of the planning process', *Journal of Psycholinguistic Research* **5**, 331–354.

EVE V. CLARK

NEGATIVE VERBS IN CHILDREN'S SPEECH

What principles do young children rely on when they coin new words? What kinds of meanings do they try to express, and what word-forms do they construct to convey those meanings? In the present paper, I will look at one domain of innovative meanings and examine the effect on children's innovations of the productivity of the pertinent adult devices in English, French, and German.

Productivity in a language is the degree to which a particular pattern of word-formation appears as the model for new lexical items (Adams 1973, Aronoff 1976). It is largely, though not entirely, reflected in the relative frequencies of different patterns of word-formation in the well-established lexicon of a language. It is also affected by which words are already part of the well-established or conventional lexicon: the presence of a word-form with the requisite meaning already *in* the language generally prevents the formation of possible but non-occurring new words (Clark & Clark 1979). For example, use of the productive English suffix *-er* to form new agent nouns is pre-empted in the case of the verb *to steal* by the existence of the noun *thief*. Similarly the existence of the German noun *Koch* pre-empts the formation from the verb *kochen* of **Kocher* with just the same meaning.[1]

Productivity, then, is a property of word-formation devices and the patterns they are used in. Some are more productive than others in a language, and some may no longer be productive at all. Productivity is generally tied to frequency – with the more productive device occurring more often – but this relationship may be modified by the properties of the word-bases being used in the construction of new word-forms.[2]

Productivity contrasts with speaker-creativity – the uses to which different word-formation devices are put. Adults freely construct new word-forms to carry new meanings, and in doing so rely on the productive patterns and devices available in their language (e.g. Gleitman & Gleitman 1970, Brekle 1977, Downing 1977, Clark & Clark 1979). Creativity with the lexicon allows speakers great flexibility in conveying their intended meanings to their addressees. They have at their disposal not only the well-established conventional vocabulary but also coinages constructed for the occasion. Adult creativity, then, is a measure of the productivity of particular word-formation devices.

W. Klein and W. Levelt (eds.), Crossing the Boundaries in Linguistics, 253–264.

What effect does productivity have on children's construction of new word-forms for new meanings? I have argued elsewhere (Clark 1980) that productivity is one of several factors children are sensitive to in the acquisition of word-formation rules. I characterized the effects of productivity on word-formation as follows:

The principle of productivity: Those word-formation devices that are the most productive in a language are the ones most likely to be used creatively in adult speech and made the most available to children. Productive devices should therefore be used in preference to unproductive ones in forming new words.

This principle predicts that, *ceteris paribus*, in the process of acquisition, the more productive device or devices of any set, with equivalent or near-equivalent meanings, should be acquired before less productive ones. This seems to be realized, as far as young children are concerned, though reliance on some strategy such as the following:

> "Look for the commonest device that expresses the desired meaning and use that in constructing a new word-form."

Relying on this strategy should lead children to acquire first those word-formation patterns and devices that are productive, or relatively more productive than others, in the language.

This prediction can be examined both *within* and *across* languages by examining sets of word-formation devices and patterns closely related in meaning to see whether the more productive ones are acquired earlier when meaning is held (relatively) constant. I shall focus here on a comparison of devices used across languages, where the meaning in each case is very similar. But first let me spell out the prediction in a little more detail: The more productive a word-formation device, the more likely it should be acquired early and hence turn up in children's spontaneous coinages.[3] One corollary of this prediction is that where a language lacks a productive device to express a particular meaning, (a) one should not expect to find as many coinages expressing that meaning, nor (b) should one expect different children to come up with the same device when they do try to express that meaning. In other words, the principle of productivity I have proposed is two-edged as far as an acquisition model is concerned: it predicts the presence of coinages where there is a productive pattern or device available, *and* the relative absence of coinages (with equivalent meanings) where there is no productive model at hand. With a productive device available, then, there should be consistency from one child to another in expressing the requisite meaning in lexical innovations; lacking a productive device, one can expect much more variability from child to child, and occasion to occasion.

REVERSALS AND MISDEEDS

The domain in which I shall examine the effects of productivity is that of negative verbs, verbs expressing reversals and misdeeds. Reversals are normally expressed either by a derivational prefix added to the verb base or by a particle associated with the verb, and misdeeds – where actions have the wrong outcome – by a derivational prefix on the verb.

English conveys the notion of reversal with the negative prefix *un-*, as in the well-established verbs *undo, unbutton*, or *untangle* (see Marchand 1973). This prefix (unlike *de-*) is highly productive in English and is widely used to form new verbs expressing reversal. At the same time, *un-* is subject to certain constraints in the coining of new verbs. First, some reversal meanings are expressed by separate lexical items that pre-empt the formation of verbs of the same meaning with *un-*, e.g., *go* (come), *lower* (raise), *leave* (arrive). Second, certain actions are by nature irreversible. For instance, one cannot **ungrow* something or **undie* someone.[4] No more can one reverse certain other actions once they have been performed. One cannot therefore **unhit* or **undraw* just as one cannot **unwalk*. One can *stop doing* such actions, but not reverse them.

The prefix *un-* is not the only device available for expressing reversal in English. It can also be conveyed by particles like *off* and *out*, as in *pull off* (put on) or *take out* (take in). Whether reversal in the conventional, well-established lexicon is expressed by *un-* or by a particle like *out* takes children some time to work out (see Bowerman 1979, in press). Both devices should be available to children acquiring English, with productive *un-* the most available for constructing new verbs of reversal.

Misdeeds are also expressed by a prefix in English, the prefix *mis-*, as in the well-established *misfile, misrule*, or *misguide*, with the general meaning of doing something wrongly, or with the wrong outcome. This prefix, however, is not very productive, especially in comparison with *un-*. But since the meanings of *un-* and *mis-* cannot be equated, one cannot make any prediction about which should be the easier of the two for children to acquire. From the standpoint of sheer productivity, however, *un-* would seem to have the advantage.

The second language, *French*, relies on a single device for the expression of reversal – the prefix *dé-* (*dés-* before vowels). As in English, some reversals of action are lexicalized, so the positive verb base cannot simply have *dé-* added to convey reversal. For example, the existence of *éteindre* (= turn off, put out) pre-empts the formation of **délumer* ("un-light"), just as *éloigner* (= go away) pre-empts the formation of **déprocher* ("un-approach"). And French speakers, like English ones, observe the general pragmatic constraints that distinguish potentially reversible actions from irreversible ones. Lastly, French does not offer the option of expressing reversal through verb particles like *off* or *out*, but children nonetheless have to learn where they can use *dé-* in the conventional lexicon and where they must use lexicalized reversal verbs like *sortir* (= go out) or *éteindre* (= turn off). The only productive device for coining new verbs of reversal, though, is the prefix *dé-*.

French, like English, also uses a prefix for indicating that an action has gone stray or produced the wrong result, namely *mé-*, as in the well-established *méfaire* (= do someone ill) or *méjuger* (= misjudge). And, as in English, this prefix is not really productive, especially compared to *dé-*. Since the meanings of the two cannot be equated, of course, one can make no direct prediction about order of acquisition. Productivity alone would favour *dé-*.

German, the third language under consideration, looks more like English. Reversal can be expressed either by means of a negative prefix on verbs, *ent-*, or by means of a negative particle associated with the verb, usually *aus* (= out, off) or *ab* (= down, from). However, the prefix *ent-* is no longer productive for the expression of reversal and appears only on a number of well-established negative verbs (e.g., Marchand 1973). Particles though appear to express reversal quite frequently, as in such conventional pairs as *anziehen* (= put on)/*ausziehen* (= take off) or *ansteigen* (= get on)/*austeigen* (= get off), but the verb base with which the particle goes may change with the change of particle from positive to negative, as in *anzünden* (= turn on)/*ausloschen* (= put out, turn off). There are also other particle combinations to express reversal, as in the pair *festmachen* (= fasten, do up)/*losmachen* (= unfasten, undo). And, as in English and French, reversal is lexicalized in some conventional pairs so there is not necessarily any overt negative morpheme apparent. Compare *kommen* (= come) with *gehen* (= go), *steigen* (= climb, go up) with *fallen* (= fall, drop), *zeigen* (= show) with *verbergen* (= hide), or *finden* (= find) with *verlieren* (= lose). Despite all these ways of expressing the notion of reversal, German currently relies on no single productive device.

For misdeeds, German uses two negative prefixes, *ver-* and *miß-*. Both appear on a number of well-established verbs. The negative meaning of *ver-* may not always be easy for children to discern because the prefix is homophonous with at least two other *ver-* prefixes, one a verbalizer and one an intensifier

(Curme 1952). Negative *ver-* is somewhat productive for adults with the meaning of wrong outcome or of an activity that has lasted too long. *Miß-* is also somewhat productive, with the meanings of failure, error, or oppositeness (e.g., *mißgönnen* versus *gönnen*).

English, French, and German can be ordered by the relative productivity of the different devices they possess for lexical negation in verbs. For reversals of action, the language that would appear simplest from the point of view of acquisition is French, with a single productive device, the prefix *dé-*. English should be somewhat more complex since the productive prefix *un-* is not the only way to express reversal: one can also use negative particles like *off* or *out*. English-speaking children, then, will have to decide between two different devices: the prefix *un-* or a particle like *out*. Finally, German would appear to be the hardest of the three since there is no current productive device for the expression of reversal.

If productivity has a direct influence on acquisition, then children's lexical innovations in the domain of reversal should reflect the order just described. French children should find it easiest to coin new "reversal" verbs when needed; English children should find it somewhat harder, and German children should find it harder still.

For misdeeds, the situation is much less clear. The German prefixes appear to be the only ones, of the three languages, that are at all productive. So they might be acquired before English *mis-* or French *mé-*. However, the situation in German is complicated by the fact that the misdeed *ver-* is homophonous with several other prefixes. Its misdeed meaning, then, may be hard for young children to discern. Both *ver-* and *miß-* are further complicated by general constraints on verb prefixes in German. On the grounds of the relative productivity, the German devices should be mastered before the English or French one.

The different devices available in each language for expressing reversal or misdeed are summarized in Table 1. The more productive devices in each case are shown in italics.

TABLE 1
Making Verbs Negative*

A. Reversals:	English	French	German
	un-	*dé-*	ent-
	out		aus
	off		ab
B. Misdeeds:	mis-	mé-	*ver-, miß-*

* Productive forms are italicized.

The Acquisition Data

For all three languages, I have drawn on data from diary studies of language development, records of vocabulary development, and recent observational studies, as well as some unpublished data from colleagues and my own observations (Clark, in preparation). The data for each language were gathered by extracting from the records of children's coinages all verbs that expressed any form of negation by means of a prefix or particle, together (where possible) with information about the intended meaning in context of each particular coinage. From this corpus, I selected all those verbs that expressed reversal or misdeed (the latter included both actions with the wrong result and actions lasting too long) in order to assess the effects of productivity.[5]

EFFECTS OF PRODUCTIVITY

I examined the effects of productivity in children's coinages in two ways. First, I looked at whether children coined verbs that expressed the meanings of reversal and misdeed in all three languages. The prediction was that productive devices in the language would be more likely to give rise to innovative negative verbs than unproductive ones. This prediction applies both within languages (if there is more than one device available for the requisite meaning) and across languages (where the requisite devices differ in their relative productivity). Second, I looked at how consistently different children chose the same device to express the same meaning. With productivity, they should pick the same device – the more productive one – within any one language. I also looked at how consistently individual children relied on particular devices on different occasions. (The latter comparison was only possible, of course, where children each produced more than one coinage with the pertinent meaning.)

Productivity and innovation. Productivity appears to have a clear effect on children's innovations. Children nearly always relied on appropriate word-formational devices when they coined verbs for reversals and misdeeds, as shown in Table 2, and the devices used most frequently were the more productive ones in the language. Typical examples of these coinages are given in Table 3.

Of the three languages considered here, French is the only one with a single productive device for constructing new reversal verbs. And children acquiring French rely on this device, the negative prefix *dé-*, for coining new

TABLE 2
Devices Used by Children in Coining Negative Verbs

	Frequency	English	French	German
A. Reversals:	frequent	un-	dé-	–
	occasional	out, off	–	aus, ab
B. Misdeeds:	occasional	–	–	ver-
	rare	–	–	aus

TABLE 3
Typical Examples of Children's Innovative Negative Verbs

A. Reversals		Child's form*	Meaning	Adult form**
	English	undisappear (3;5)	(re)appear	(re)appear
		uncapture (3;10)	release, let go	release
		uncrowd (3;11)	make less crowded	------
		unblow (4;3)	let air out	deflate
		unbury (4;4)	dig up	dig up
		unhate (4;7)	like	like
		unbend (5;1)	straighten	straighten
		unshorten (5;1)	lengthen	lengthen
		unhang (7;11)	take down (off wall)	take down
	French	dégrandir (2;6)	get smaller	rétrécir
		désendormir (3;3)	wake up	réveiller
		démonter (3;5)	come/go down	descendre
		déchauffer (3;5)	make less hot	refraîchir
		défroidir (3;6)	make less cold	rechauffer
		défatiguer (3;6)	make less tired	se restaurer, se reposer
		déprocher (3;6)	go away	s'éloigner
		débâtir (3;10)	demolish	démolir
		déprisonner (4;1)	free, let go	libérer
	German	forträdeln (2;1)	wheel away	fortgefahren
		abzangen (2; 3)	remove with tongs	----------
		aussinden (3;4)	turn off	auslöschen
B. Misdeeds				
	German	verknien (3;5)	kneel too long	(sich verknien)
		vergeben (5;1)	give x to the wrong person	irren im Geben
		verlaufen (5; 7)	run too much	(sich verlaufen)
		sich verklingeln (6; 3)	ring the wrong doorbell	(sich verklingeln)

* The child's age, in years and months, follows each example cited.
** Possible but innovative adult forms are given in parentheses.

reversal verbs as young as 2;6. The other negative prefix, *mé-*, for misdeeds, is much less productive in French. And, consistent with the prediction, children produced no innovative verbs with *mé-*. In French, then, children rely early on the productive prefix *dé-* to express reversal of action.

The situation in English and German is less clearcut since there is more than one device available to convey some of the meanings. In English, there are both prefixes, *un-*, and, rarely, *de-*, and particles like *out* or *off*. Of the prefixes, *un-* is far more productive than *de-*, and, as predicted, is the only *prefix* used in coining new reversal verbs. However, English-speaking children also use negative particles with reversal meaning, as in **tuck out* (for *untuck*, the opposite of *tuck in*, of blankets). The presence of two kinds of devices in the language, and the mixed paradigms found in the well-established vocabulary, seems to cause some confusion at times as to whether a verb should be negated with a prefix or with a particle. For good measure, children sometimes use both at once (see further Bowerman 1979). The other negative prefix, *mis-*, for misdeeds, is relatively unproductive, and in fact, like French *mé-*, fails to appear at all in the English corpus. So English-speaking children, like French ones, use only the most productive of the prefixes (*un-*), plus some negative particles in their coinages of reversal verbs.

What of children acquiring German? As indicated in Table 1, there is no productive device for expressing reversal, although, like English, it is possible to use negative particles to convey the requisite meaning. Inspection of an extensive corpus of innovations from German children revealed hardly any reversal verbs at all. For example, Stern and Stern reported only one instance, from Tögel's son at 2;3, namely *abzangen*, and Neugebauer likewise only observed one, constructed with two different negative particles used in succession – *abgeschnabelt* followed immediately by *weggeschnabelt* (R, 2;9,15). The absence of any productive device to express the notion of reversal clearly has a direct effect on the kinds of word-forms children construct to express particular meanings. Unlike both French- and English-speaking children, German children appear not to coin verbs to express reversals of action.[6]

In contrast to reversals, misdeeds are expressed in German by means of two moderately productive prefixes, and one, *ver-*, does appear in children's coinage of verbs for actions that have the wrong result or last too long. These coinages are not particularly common, but they do occur from about age 5;0 on (see Table 3 for examples). The fact that they do occur strongly suggests that their absence from the speech of children acquiring French and English is due not to the conceptual complexity of misdeeds, but to the lack of any productive device for expressing the pertinent meaning.

The predictions derived from the principle of productivity are generally supported for both reversals and misdeeds. Children make use of the most productive devices in their coinages, and where there is no productive device, they simply do not coin new verbs. A few *caveats* are in order, however, about the data used to test these predictions. First, the data were collected from a variety of children by different observers[7] who were not directly concerned with expressions of reversal or misdeed in children's speech. This can be taken as an advantage in that the data may be considered generally representative of the proportions of innovative reversal and misdeed verbs children are likely to produce in each language. But there is also the disadvantage that since the observers were not looking for words or phrases with those meanings as a category, there is no way to assess the actual occurrence of those negative meanings in the children's speech as a whole. Second, and this is more general point, where children construct legitimate but innovative negative verbs, their innovations may go unnoticed. For if they follow adult-like rules, their innovations do not stand out in the same way as when they don't follow the rules of word-formation or happen to construct new words illegitimate in meaning or form because of words already in the language (Clark, in press). As a result, observational data like these may under-estimate children's innovations and hence their knowledge of the requisite word-formation devices. Both shortcomings in the present study should be remediable.

One or many devices? Do children opt for the same device everywhere to convey the same meaning? Of if there is more than one available, are they inconsistent in their uses in innovations? This question is mainly of relevance for the English and German situations. (Children acquiring French have only one choice to express reversal, the productive prefix *dé-*.) Children acquiring English have to decide between the productive prefix *un-* and verb particles like *out* or *off*. Although they tend to favour *un-*, the same children may make use of both devices. In part, this may be the result of "mixed" paradigms in the well-established lexicon. For instance, the adult opposite of *tuck in* is *untuck*, but children frequently coin the form **tuck out*. Their reliance on *out* in such cases is probably influenced by the presence of *in* in the positive verb. The predominance of *un-*, though, is also indicated in another way: children often go through a stage when the over-mark the notion of reversal by adding *un-* to verbs that are already negative in meaning, as in **unerase* for *erase*, **unsplit* for *split*, or **unbreak* for *break* (Bowerman 1979, in press).

These data suggest that where there is a single productive device, children find it easier to grasp the pertinent meaning and then use the device to coin new verbs as needed. French-speaking children, for example, coin reversal verbs early and coin many of them. Where there is more than one device available or where there is no productive device, children have greater difficulty working out what the form-meaning correspondences are (Slobin 1973). They show less consistency in the devices they pick, from child to child, and occasion to occasion, and they coin fewer verbs of the type under consideration.

CONCLUSION

The more productive a device for forming new negative verbs, the more likely children are to coin such verbs in the course of acquisition. Moreover, the presence of a productive device makes for more uniformity across children and across occasions in the construction of new word-forms, as shown in the data from French-speaking children. Where there is more than one device for expressing reversal, there is less consistency, as shown in the English data. And where there is no productive device at all, there is inconsistency combined with very little coinage, as in German children's reversal verbs.

In summary, the diversity of means children rely on in their innovative negative verbs is also an indicator of the difficulty children face in acquiring word formation devices. Productivity plays an important role, but it also interacts with the nature of the form and meaning pairings within each language. Many forms for one meaning will make that meaning and those forms harder for children to acquire. Children acquiring French, then, should find it easier to acquire the word-formation device for talking about reversals of action (a) because it is very productive and (b) because it is the only device used. And they might therefore be expected to coin more negative verbs than children acquiring either English or German. They do. Moreover, because English *un-* is productive (unlike German *ent-*), English-speaking children in turn should coin more negative verbs than German-speaking ones. Again, the data show that they do. Finally, because prefixes for expressing misdeed in German are more productive than the equivalent devices in English and French, it is more likely that German-speaking children would coin some misdeed verbs. And they do. Productivity, then, both within and across languages, is a factor to contend with in constructing a theory and a model of when and why children acquire different word-formation devices in their first languages.

Stanford University

ACKNOWLEDGEMENTS

This paper was begun while I was a Fellow at the Center for Advanced Study in the Behavioral Sciences, supported in part by CASBS and in part by The Spencer Foundation. It was completed with support from the National Science Foundation (BNS 80–07349). I am grateful to Werner Deutsch, Elborg Forster, and Wolfgang Klein for discussion of the German data. A preliminary account of these findings was given at the XXIInd International Congress of Psychology, Leipzig, DDR, July 1980.

NOTES

[1] Provided there is a contrast in meaning, of course, such forms as *stealer* in English or *Kocher* in German would be quite acceptable innovations. Cf. Clark and Clark 1979: 798–800.

[2] For example, although *-ness* is the most productive device, overall, in English for forming nouns from adjectives, all Romance bases form nouns with *-ity* instead. Thus, *-ity* is the more productive for that particular set of adjective forms (cf. Aronoff 1976).

[3] Use of even the most productive devices in conventional, well-established word-forms, of course, is no guarantee of acquisition for *new* word-forms. The child could have picked up the well-established word wholesale and know nothing about the pertinent word-formation rules. Coinages, spontaneous or elicited, are therefore the only real measure of what children know about particular aspects of word-formation *per se*.

[4] Forms preceded by an asterisk are unacceptable to adults with the meanings specified because they are pre-empted either semantically (by other form/meaning composites) or pragmatically.

[5] Since the sources from which I drew my data were not concerned with children's acquisition of the notions of reversal and misdeed, I cannot assess how many lexicalized items children acquire early on with the requisite meanings. Ideally, one should examine every expression of such meanings in the child's repertoire in assessing the effects of productive morphological devices. The nature of the available data makes that impossible.

[6] Presumably they have recourse to other linguistic means to express this notion.

[7] The corpus for each language also differed in how many children were observed, for how long. There were fewer data available for English and French than for German, which makes the absence of innovative reversal verbs all the more striking for German. Ideally, the corpora should be comparable in size, and contain equal amounts of longitudinal and cross-sectional data.

[8] The only exception I found was a child who coined *ausbanken* with the meaning "to sit on a bench for too long."

REFERENCES

Adams, V.: 1973, *An Introduction to Modern English Word-Formation*, London: Longman.

Aronoff, M.: 1976, *Word Formation in Generative Grammar*, (Linguistic Inquiry, Monograph Supplement No. 1), Cambridge, MA: M. I. T. Press.

Bowerman, M.: 1979, 'Explorations in recombinant semantics: The child's acquisition of patterns for lexicalizing the notion of motion', paper presented at the Sloan Workshop on "Words and Concepts," Stanford University, March 30/April 1, 1979.

Bowerman, M.: 1981, 'Reorganizational processes in lexical and syntactic development', in L. R. Gleitman and E. Wanner (eds.), *Language Acquisition: The State of the Art*, Cambridge: Cambridge University Press, in press.

Brekle, H. E.: 1977, 'Reflections on the conditions for the coining, use and understanding of nominal compounds', paper presented at the XIIth. International Congress of Linguists, Vienna, August/September 1977.

Clark, E. V.: 1980, 'Convention and innovation in acquiring the lexicon', Keynote Address, Twelfth Annual Child Language Research Forum, Stanford University, March 1980. (In *Papers and Reports on Child Language Development* [Stanford University] **19**, 1–20).

Clark, E. V.: 1981, 'The young word-maker: A case study of innovation in the child's lexicon', in: L. R. Gleitman and E. Wanner (eds.), *Language Acquisition: The State of the Art*, Cambridge: Cambridge University Press, in press.

Clark, E. V.: *Young Word-Makers: Lexical Innovations in Children's Speech*, in preparation.

Clark, E. V., and Clark, H. H.: 1979, 'When nouns surface as verbs', *Language* **55**, 767–811.

Curme, G. O.: 1952, *A Grammar of the German Language* (3rd. edition), New York: Macmillan.

Downing, P.: 1977, 'On the creation and use of English compound nouns', *Language* **53**, 810–842.

Marchand, H.: 1973, 'Reversative, ablative, and privative verbs in English, French, and German', in B. B. Kachru, R. B. Lees, Y. Malkiel, A. Pietrangeli, and S. Saporta (eds.), *Issues in Linguistics: Papers in Honor of Henry and Renée Kahane*, Urbana IL: University of Illinois Press, pp. 636–643.

Slobin, D. I.: 1973, 'Cognitive prerequisites for the acquisition of grammar', in C. A. Ferguson & D. I. Slobin (eds.), *Studies of Child Language Development*, New York: Holt, Rinehart & Winston, pp. 175–208.

HAJ ROSS

ROBERT FROST'S 'OUT, OUT –'

A way in

Even if we have never read this poem below before:

The buzz-saw snarled and rattled in the yard
And made dust and dropped stove-length sticks of wood,
Sweet-scented stuff when the breeze drew across it.
And from there those that lifted eyes could count
Five mountain ranges one behind the other
Under the sunset far into Vermont.
And the saw snarled and rattled, snarled and rattled,
As it ran light, or had to bear a load.
And nothing happened: day was all but done.
Call it a day, I wish they might have said
To please the boy by giving him the half hour
That a boy counts so much when saved from work.
His sister stood beside them in her apron
To tell them "Supper." At the word, the saw,
As if to prove saws knew what supper meant,
Leaped out at the boy's hand, or seemed to leap –
He must have given the hand. However it was,
Neither refused the meeting. But the hand!
The boy's first outcry was a rueful laugh,
As he swung toward them holding up the hand
Half in appeal, but half as if to keep
The life from spilling. Then the boy saw all –
Since he was old enough to know, big boy
Doing a man's work, though a child at heart –
He saw all spoiled. "Don't let him cut my hand off –
The doctor, when he comes. Don't let him, sister!"
So. But the hand was gone already.
The doctor put him in the dark of ether.
He lay and puffed his lips out with his breath.
And then – the watcher at his pulse took fright.
No one believed. They listened at his heart.

W. Klein and W. Levelt (eds.), Crossing the Boundaries in Linguistics, 265–282.

Little – less – nothing! – and that ended it.
No more to build on there. And they, since they
Were not the one dead, turned to their affairs.

even if we have never read *any* poem of Frost's before, I venture to say that this first reading of the poem will send a chill down the spine, for many of us.

After all, the topic – the transitoriness of life, the thinness of the veil that separates the quick from the dead – is an eternal one. And while the death of anyone touches us, the snuffing out of a child's breath is all the more tragic. So many years that could have been!

And death seems to come so casually to the boy. "No one believed" – we can hardly believe, either. No one seems to get excited – the first thing the boy utters is "a rueful laugh." We are not told of others crying, running for the doctor; or of the doctor rushing to try to save the boy's life. The boy knows that the doctor will come – and then the next that we hear is that the doctor has already administered the anesthetic (*put* in line 28 is in the past tense). It is all so natural.

And yet imagine the difference in the way we would react to a newspaper story describing roughly "the same events" – under the headline,

Boy Dies in Saw Accident

That would leave us no room, nothing to do but accept the finality of the tragedy. But in the poem we are not presented with a *fait accompli*. Frost's art draws us into the event: we see the dreadful instant described lightly as a "meeting" of saw and hand; the boy's laugh and his desire to keep his hand from the doctor, these are what we seize on to reassure ourselves that all will be well, *must* end well, it will only be another brush with death, nothing final.

We are the watcher at his pulse, we take fright. "No one believed" – here the poet leaves out the *it* that we might expect in normal prose, as if saying that *it* would reify death, would give death a chance to get its foot in the door. We too listen at his heart, we hope against hope, our heart sinks as we read the fateful sequence "Little – less – nothing!"

And then we hear the reaction to this tragedy: *and that ended it.* A laconic comment about the years never to be lived through: *no more to build on there.* And the word "dead" does not close the case forever until the last line, where we hear how "they," who served the saw with the boy, accept such a routine fatality as a matter of course. And turn to their affairs – the boy's death has happened and is gone, it is no longer their affair.

Frost's understatement heightens the poem's impact. And so does the setting of the poem: among New England farmers, who are known for the spareness of their speech, who see no need to say anything (the only people who speak in this poem are the children) – this too acts to bottle up our shock.

Frost has purposely given us only a clue as to where the poem's title could come from – probably not until the irrevocability of the boy's death has begun to sink in will we hear Macbeth's famous line about the impermanency of life "Out, out, brief candle!" In this monologue, Macbeth compares life to a poor player on a stage, and says it is a tale told by an idiot, full of sound and fury, signifying nothing. If we catch this allusion, the poem acquires a deeper ring, the boy's death takes on a more somber hue.

There is much more along the lines of the above that could, and should, be said, but I have a different concern in this brief article. I want to show the hidden sinews of this poem – the facts about its structure that make it sing, that give it the power to move us.

Here, too, there is much too much to say. So I would like to focus the discussion around the following question:

Why does this poem have 34 lines?

Could Frost have omitted, say, line 9? Or line 29? Or both? Or could he have added a 35th line?

In other words, I am posing the question of what makes this poem an organism, a gestalt. What hangs it together?

I am aware that these are not simple questions, and that in particular, to the question as to whether a 35-line poem about the boy's death would have been possible, I am sure the answer is yes. But it would be a vastly different poem, I believe, for reasons I will now attempt to sketch.

The poem seems to be in iambic pentameter, but if it rhymes in some regular way, I have thus far not been able to see it. So must we assume that the 34 lines of the poem are merely an accumulation of iambic lines, an aggregate? Or are there "sections" in the poem?

My hypothesis is that though Frost does not indicate this fact typographically, by leaving three lines blank, the poem is in fact "sectioned" into four hidden stanzas, which I will refer to as A, B, C, and D, as shown below:

A:

The buzz-saw snarled and rattled in the yard
And made dust and dropped stove-length sticks of wood,

Sweet-scented stuff when the breeze drew across it.
And from there those that lifted eyes could count
Five mountain ranges one behind the other
Under the sunset far into Vermont.
And the saw snarled and rattled, snarled and rattled,
As it ran light, or had to bear a load.
And nothing happened: day was all but done.

B:

Call it a day, I wish they might have said
To please the boy by giving him the half hour
That a boy counts so much when saved from work.
His sister stood beside them in her apron
To tell them "Supper." At the word, the saw,
As if to prove saws knew what supper meant,
Leaped out at the boy's hand, or seemed to leap –
He must have given the hand. However it was,
Neither refused the meeting. But the hand!

C:

The boy's first outcry was a rueful laugh,
As he swung toward them holding up the hand
Half in appeal, but half as if to keep
The life from spilling. Then the boy saw all –
Since he was old enough to know, big boy
Doing a man's work, though a child at heart –
He saw all spoiled. "Don't let him cut my hand off –
The doctor, when he comes. Don't let him, sister!"

D:

So. But the hand was gone already.
The doctor put him in the dark of ether.
He lay and puffed his lips out with his breath.
And then – the watcher at his pulse took fright.
No one believed. They listened at his heart.
Little – less – nothing! and that ended it.
No more to build on there. And they, since they
Were not the one dead, turned to their affairs.

What evidence can be given for such a four-sectioning? In what follows, I will try to show that if we assume this structure, we will find that the distributions of many types of elements in the poem, which would otherwise appear to be placed at random places in an undifferentiated 34-line aggregate, can be stated in a way that "makes sense." That is, these distributions *draw the partitions* between the four stanzas. They dance to the drum of this sectioning.

1. *Line-final major marks of punctuation*

Note first that the placing of major marks of punctuation – i.e., periods and exclamation points – varies systematically within the proposed quadripartition. In A, all major marks of punctuation are at the ends of lines. In B, we find the first three cases, in lines 14, 17, and 18, of sentences ending in mid-line. B is ended by the short exclamation *But the hand!*, which is the first return to a line-final major punctuation mark since line 12.

In C, we find *only* mid-line major punctuations until line 26, which closes C.

And in D, while we find some mid-line punctuations, in particular, the only mid-line exclamation point (at the "point" of death), we also find that each line, except the penultimate, ends with a punctuation mark. In a way, then, D presents a resolution of the two patterns.

Note that this criterion alone would not yield the proposed 9–9–8–8 sectioning unambiguously. For one might say that the first stanza should include all of the first sentences of the poem that end at the end of lines, which would give A twelve lines, instead of the nine I propose.

We will see, however, that other kinds of evidence can be brought to bear which are explicable only under the original 9–9–8–8 hypothesis.

2. *Thematic content of the four sections*

Note that we can assign a definite topic to each of A–D.

A: The setting: the saw

B: The boy and what happens to him

C: The boy's reaction to the accident

D: The doctor and the boy's death

However, if we had included lines 10–12 in our first stanza, as was considered briefly in § 1, then the characterization of the topic of A would have been more complicated.

The case is a difficult one, in a way, for these lines are thematically almost unique, in that they give the poet's view of the event. They contain the only first person reference to the narrator (*I wish*), and the first taste of the tragedy – the foreshadowing of *might have said*. The only other fairly clear instance of the narrator's voice is the shortest sentence of the poem – the *So*. that opens D. Thus under the quadripartitioning I would advocate, the even-numbered stanzas would share the feature of opening with the narrator's voice.

A last point about the thematic functions of the four stanzas: when we recall the placing of major punctuations discussed in § 1 above, we can see a chilling iconicity: in A, the sentences run smoothly, reaching their natural ends at the ends of lines. In B, which takes us through a terrible cutting, we find the first sentence that "cuts" a line. The cutting is synchronized, probably not by accident, with the uttering of the first word "Supper."

3. *The boy*

Let us now look at the way Frost places references to the main figure of the poem. In A, we find almost no direct references to any people. A is dominated by the noise of the saw: *snarled and rattled* we hear three times. With hindsight, we hear the blind killing beast lurking in the first of these verbs, but the first time we read it, it may strike us only as an apt simile for the sound.

And then there is an oblique reference to those who can smell: *sweet-scented*. But not until the phrase *those that lifted eyes* do we find a reference to an animate entity (presumably a human one, since it is said of the owners of these eyes that they could count). But all in all, A is phrased in a way to suggest a world of nature, and a world in which those mentioned are so engrossed in their work that they do not even see the beauties of the mountains above them. They are prosaic folk.

And then in B, we find the boy referred to: six times.

l. 11: To please the boy
l. 11: by giving *him* the half hour
l. 12: That a boy counts so much
l. 13: *his* sister
l. 16: the boy's hand
l. 17: *He* must have given the hand

I have cited them with pronominal references in italics and aligned under full mentions of *boy* to highlight an important fact: there is an alternation between full and pronominal reference to the boy.

This pattern continues in C, with another six references.

l. 19: The boy's first outcry
l. 20: As *he* swung toward them
l. 22: Then the boy saw all
l. 23: Since *he* was old enough to know
l. 23-4: big boy/Doing a man's work
l. 25: *He* saw all spoiled.

And in D, we find another six references, though this time all are pronouns:

l. 28: The doctor put *him* in the dark of ether
l. 29: *He* lay
l. 29: and puffed *his* lips out
l. 29: with *his* breath
l. 30: the watcher at *his* pulse took fright.
l. 31: They listened at *his* heart.

I take it not to be by coincidence that there are exactly six references to the boy in the last three stanzas. This type of hidden harmony – *the repetition of the number of times an element recurs in a section of a poem* – is a type of poetic device that I have called *a balancing*. It is a device that I have found used in poems in a number of languages, written over quite a span of years. One could view it as a kind of rhyme, though not a rhyme in sound, but in number. We will have occasion to observe quite a few uses of this type of rhymes in the present poem – it is one of the principal "materials" out of which Frost crafts the sinews of the poem.

In the 18 references to the boy, we see a further pattern. The boy comes into the poem as the object of *please* and the indirect object of *give* – two positions that typically require human nouns. Then in line 12, we find *a boy* as the subject of a verb of activity, for the first time, and again in line 17, as the subject of *must have given*. The change from object to subject is a change towards life. We will see the opposite change take place later in the poem.

In C, the boy is the (nominalized) subject of the activity verb *cry out*, which is nominalized into *outcry*. And *he swung* in line 20 shows the boy as another subject, acting volitionally, being alive. But in lines 22 and 25 we find him the subject of a verb which suggests less activity: *saw*. We conceptualize *watch* or *look at* as a volitional, agentive act, and view seeing as more passive, or receptive. Thus these lines show a diminution of the boy's control, life, volitionality. And the intervening reference to him, in line 23, has him clearly as a subject of two stative predicates: the adjective *old* and the verb *know*.

Thus we see the boy's "life" to have peaked, syntactically, in line 17, where he was the subject (though in a curious way, because of the epistemic qualification imposed by *must have*) of *give*. After this peak, he slides down in agentivity through C, and in D, he has become an object again, but this time the object of *put*, a verb which views its objects as things, as opposed to *please*, which happens to people.

And we see the boy as a subject one last time: *he lay*. But the activity is drained out of him, just as his life is draining away.

I have not mentioned the possessives yet, of which there are also six:

B:
l. 13: his sister
l. 16: the boy's hand

D:
l. 29: his lips
l. 29: his breath
l. 30: his pulse
l. 31: his heart

In D, it is particularly clear: the possessed nouns go from outward, perceptible entities, to his core, where life holds on the longest. But even in B, the same *diminution of connectedness* can be felt: he is first related to another human noun – *his sister* – and then only to a part of himself – *the boy's hand*. So in a way, this sequence is a small version of the slide towards passivity that we see with especial clarity in D.

And now I think we have a basis to explain the choice of full nouns, as opposed to pronouns, in the 18 references to the boy. Again, it has to do with the thematic content of the stanzas. In D, which tells of the boy's death, we find only pronouns. So pronouns, which are after all, a *phonetically diminished* variant of the full [NB] nouns, are symbols for death. And the alternation between full form and pronoun that we see in B and C is symbolic of the thematic content there: the boy's life hangs in the balance. An alternating sequence is a particularly apt way to "show" the process of balancing.

4. *Negation*

We find exactly 8 occurrences of words containing the negative prefix n-:

l. 9: In the last line of A: And *n*othing happened:
l. 18: In the last line of B: *N*either refused the meeting.
l. 25–26: In the last two lines of C: Do*n*'t let him cut my hand off –
Do*n*'t let him, sister!

l. 31–34: In the last four lines of D: *N*o one believed.
Little – less – *n*othing!
*N*o more to build on there.
Were *n*ot the one dead,

Thus we see a monotonic increasing of negativity, the symbol *par excellence* of death. Note that here we have a balancing, but of a different kind: the four negatives of D are set off against, "rhyme with" the four negatives in the rest of the whole poem. We could write this distribution formulaically as follows, where the '/' shows the "fulcrum" of the balancing:

$$\text{Negation [8]:}\quad \underset{1}{\text{A}}\text{–}\underset{1}{\text{B}}\text{–}\underset{2}{\text{C}}\overset{=}{/}\underset{4}{\text{D}}$$

Thus we see that the distribution of negation plays a number of roles simultaneously: as the stanzas move closer to the boy's death, the number of negatives increases to keep pace. And balancing four on each side of the hidden boundary between lines 26 and 27 helps support one part of the quadripartition: the setting off of D from the first three stanzas. Finally, the positioning of all negatives only at the ends of A–D supports the quadripartitioning in another way – by providing a flag at each stanza division.

There is, however, another point to make in connection with this "flagging" – after all, the flagging itself could have been done just as well if Frost had *started* each stanza with one or more negatives. So why has he chosen instead to end them with negatives?

The answer lies in what I have called *hologramming.* The poem as a whole moves from life to death – from positive to negative. The coherence of such a structure will be increased if each section also exhibits *the same transition.* Then the part will mirror the whole, as it does in a hologram. Thus Frost's use of section-*final* negations to flag with is a case of hologramming – section-initial negative flags would not exhibit this extra type of connectedness.

5. *The hand*

There are six occurrences of this noun:

B:
l. 16: Leaped out at the boy's hand,
l. 17: He must have given the hand.
l. 18: But the hand!

C:
l. 20: holding up the hand
l. 25: Don't let him cut my hand off –

D:
l. 27: But the hand was gone already.

Here we see a monotonic decrease, and the balancing involved sets off B, the section primarily connected with the hand, against the other three stanzas of the poem. Formulaically,

$$\textit{hand}\ [6]:\ \begin{array}{cccc} B\overset{=}{/} & A- & C- & D \\ 3 & 0 & 2 & 1 \end{array}$$

One more subpattern to note here is the graphic separation of the referent of *boy* from the occurrence of *hand* in the first three cases: in *the boy's hand*, the two nouns are contiguous. In *He must have given the hand, He* has been moved away from hand, though they are at least in the same sentence. However, in *But the hand!*, the boy is gone – the separation is complete.

6. *The saw*

There are four occurrences of this noun, two each in A and B.

$$\textit{saw}\ [4]:\ \begin{array}{cccc} A\overset{=}{/} & B- & C- & D \\ 2 & 2 & 0 & 0 \end{array}$$

This type of distribution actually exemplifies a further type of abstract "rhyme," one which I refer to as *splitting*. In this case, all occurrences of *saw* are in the first two stanzas. Thus this all-or-none distribution helps draw the boundary between AB and CD, and the balancing draws the boundary between A and B. We therefore have another case of the distribution of one element playing multiple roles. If we use the symbol '±' to indicate the all/none division which constitutes a splitting, we might formulaically indicate the functions described above as shown below:

$$\textit{saw}\ [4]:\ \begin{array}{cccc} A\overset{=}{/} & B\overset{\pm}{//} & C- & D \\ 2 & 2 & 0 & 0 \end{array}$$

There is a funny additional fact about *saw*: this same syllable occurs two times more, in C – but as a *verb* – in lines 22 and 25. I am almost inclined to regard this as a coincidence – I would let it go as that, if the pattern of two *saw's* per stanza had not been established in A and B, and if it were not the case that both of the verbs in C have the same word following them (*all*). Even more suspiciously, their subjects are the same – both refer to the boy.

However, there is a subtle difference. I will place the two occurrences above one another, to facilitate comparison:

l. 22: Then the boy saw all – [Since he was old enough to know, big boy/
Doing a man's work, though a child at heart]
l. 25: He saw all spoiled

In § 3 above, I have linked pronominal reference to *boy* with death – and here in l. 25, concurring with a changed subject pronoun, we also find a change in the object, from *all*, to *all spoiled*. It seems to me that Frost is showing us, while apparently "repeating" a phrase, how all has changed for the boy – how the boy has in that instant felt his death touch him. To be sure, he does not acknowledge it in what he says to his sister: he speaks of keeping his hand. But I wonder if he could really have believed that such a future, or any future, was possible. For in the next line after his words, the poet says that the hand was gone already.

I think that for now, we must leave the question somewhat open as to whether we are to "equate" the noun *saw* with the verb *saw*. It is a question I would like to think more about.

7. *Conjunctions: independent versus dependent clauses*

Conjunctions are the small words which introduce clauses or parts of clauses in English, and show how the clauses or their parts are related to each other. There are three coordinating conjunctions in the poem (namely, *and, or,* and *but*), and a number of subordinating ones. The former three seem to articulate the four-part structure in one way or another, and we shall return to examine subordination shortly.

The simplest pattern for a coordinating conjunction is that of *or*, which splits the poem in the same way that *saw* does.

or [2]: A–B$\overset{\pm}{/}$C–D (lines 8, 16)
1 1 0 0

We find a balancing of the four *but*'s: one to each stanza.

but [4]: $A \overset{=}{/} B \overset{=}{/} C \overset{=}{/} D$ (lines 9, 18, 21, 27)
1 1 1 1

When we turn to the prototypical coordinating conjunction, *and* we find it performing a splitting, though of a kind that we have not seen previously:

and [12]: $A \overset{\pm}{/} B - C \overset{\pm}{/} D$ (lines 1, 2, 2, 4, 7, 7, 7, 9; 29, 30, 32, 33)
8 0 0 4

That is, *and* splits the outside of the poem off from the inside, the peripheral stanzas (A, D) off from the central ones (B, C). In a way, it says that *and*, whose basic meaning is that of giving a list or a sequence, *is a property of the world before the accident and after it, but not during the events.*

To say it in slightly different terms, *and* signifies "business as usual." This matter-of-fact meaning is most in evidence, for me, at the beginning of lines 7 and 9, and maybe also in line 32 – after the shock of "nothing!", to continue with '– and that ended it." (as opposed to "that ended it.") feels to me a bit forced. Too much as if the death had to be trivalized, quickly forgotten, so that life could go on, in the usual groove.

Let us follow this line of thought a bit further. If it is correct to see coordinate conjunction with *and* as denoting business as usual, then subordinating conjunction should be a symbol of a perturbation of the usual, as something out of the ordinary. And given that we know that the thematic materials in B and C, which describe the accident and the boy's reaction, are the locus of the extraordinary, we expect to find subordination there, iconically.

And that is what we find, massively. In A, we find only three subordinate clauses: *when the breeze drew across it*, the relative clause *that lifted eyes*, and the second time adverbial: *As it ran light, or had to bear a load.* The first four verbs of A are all coordinate, and do not even have the standard interpretation of temporal sequence – these four activities of the saw are merely given in a list. We do not encounter a subordinate clause in A until its third line.

But what happens in B? Semantically, the independent statement seems to be *I wish*, with *they might have said* subordinate to *wish*, and *call it a day* subordinate to *said*. And *to please* is a subordinate adverb modifying *said*, with *by giving* modifying *to please*, and the relative clause *that a boy counts so much* modifying *the half hour,* with, finally, the *when*-clause of line 12 modifying *counts*. Thus of (at least) 8 verbal forms that appear in the first 3 lines of B, only *wish* is an independent clause, with the other 7 forming a tightly nested subordinating group. By my count, as B continues, there is an overwhelming preponderance of subordinated verbs (at least 12 in all), compared with only 6 independent verbs (${}_{10}$*wish*, ${}_{13}$*stood*, ${}_{16}$*leaped*, ${}_{16}$*seemed*, ${}_{17}$*must (have given)*, ${}_{18}$*refused*).

However, when we reach D, there is a dramatic reversal, and return to the pattern of A. D has *only one* clear subordinate clause (the *since*-clause of lines 33–34) – I am not sure whether to regard *to build on* in line 33 as subordinate or not.

To recapitulate these patterns, I represent them as fractions below, with the numerator counting independent verbs, and the denominator dependent ones.

$$\text{A: } \frac{11}{5} \qquad \text{B: } \frac{6}{12\text{–}15} \qquad \text{C: } \frac{5}{9} \qquad \text{D: } \frac{9}{1\text{–}2}$$

It seems clear that the syntactic contrast between independent and dependent clauses is bound up with the thematic functions of the four sections.

8. *Verbal forms*

In close connection with the meaning of subordinations that I have just discussed, we find that the forms of verbs also articulate the boundary between peripheral and central stanzas. I have suggested the phrase "business as usual" as a rough meaning for the *and*'s of the periphery, and we find that the form of the verb that correlates with this routine is the simple past tense.

Thus in A, we find 14 past tense verbs, and a past tense modal (${}_{4}$*could*). The only other verb forms that we find in A are the bare stem ${}_{4}$*count* in construction with this modal, and the infinitive ${}_{8}$*to bear* that follows the semi-auxiliary verb ${}_{8}$*had*. And in D, we find only one non-simple-past-tense verb: ${}_{33}$*to build*, as opposed to 10 past tense forms.

When we turn to the central stanzas, we find the action. There we see the poem's only three present tense verbs (${}_{10}$*wish*, ${}_{12}$*counts*; ${}_{26}$*comes*), the only four present participles (${}_{11}$*giving*; ${}_{20}$*holding*, ${}_{22}$*spilling*, ${}_{24}$*Doing*), and the only two past participles (${}_{10}$*have said*, ${}_{17}$*have given*). The 12 infinitive verb forms, and the four bare stem verbs (namely ${}_{10}$*call*; ${}_{25}$*let*, ${}_{25}$*cut*, ${}_{26}$*let*) not following one of the three modal verbs (${}_{4}$*could*, ${}_{10}$*might*, ${}_{17}$*must*) are positioned in the central stanzas, except for ${}_{8}$*to bear* in the penultimate line of A, and *to build*, in the corresponding line of D. The resulting structure is a balancing around of the central boundary of the poem:

$$\text{Infinitive(-like) forms [12]:} \quad \underset{1}{\text{A}}\text{–}\underset{5}{\text{B}}\overset{=}{/}\underset{5}{\text{C}}\text{–}\underset{1}{\text{D}}$$

Finally, it should be mentioned that it is only in the central stanzas that we hear any of that type of activity which sets us humans off from the rest of the world: speech. The boy's sister says "Supper.", the boy laughs ruefully (l. 19), and begs his sister to help him keep his hand (lines 25–26). Other than that, the people in the poem are silent.

I will somewhat arbitrarily start to sum up here, though it is probably quite clear that this poem would repay an ever-finer hunt for principles of poetic harmony – what I have called "sinews" – that it manifests.

Let us return to the question with which I opened the exploration of the poem's structure: why does the poem have 34 lines?

If my arguments for the various structures I have discussed above are convincing, I have given a roundabout answer to this difficult question. I have attempted to show:

A: That the 34 lines have a hidden quadripartite structure, of 9, 9, 8, and 8 lines.

B: That an important organizing principle of these 4 hidden stanzas is *outside* versus *inside*. Formulaically, we might write

9 (9–8) 8

C: That the structures of the periphery are largely concerned to convey a feeling of matter-of-factness, of status quo, of a routine that deadens humans against voicing their feelings. The periphery is inanimate and without voice, mute.

We might still ask why Frost put the bigger stanzas first? He could, after all, have supported equally well a structure like 8 (8–9) 9.

The answer I would suggest is that a shortening of stanzas is more congruent to the meaning of the poem, which describes the *loss* of part of a boy, and then the loss of part of the human race.

But even if this is accepted, there are still several other possible ways of breaking up 34 lines so as to keep both the outside/inside structure and the diminishing stanza size. Two possibilities will suffice:

10 (10–7) 7, or 13 (13–4) 4.

Here I feel myself on shakier ground, but what I would like to suggest is that the choice of 9–8 as opposed to the two alternatives mentioned above is again motivated: if A, which sets the stage, has 9 lines, and D, which is the result, or end-state the system after the boy's death, has 8 lines, we feel that symbolically, the initial and final stages are close – that A is almost the same as D. In D, business does go on, *almost* as usual. If the change had been from

10 to 7 lines, or from 13 to 4, the *numerical* difference would have been congruent with a large *human* difference.

But we have seen, and felt, that the poem's impact derives from the understatement of death – from making it casual. A boy loses a hand, bleeds to death – so what? Big deal.

And yet if we return to the part of the structure with which we started this investigation – namely, the distribution of major marks of punctuation – we see that while A has none, and B and C three apiece, D also has three periods and an exclamation point. This would also suggest that there has been a change from A to D. As the change from 9 to 8 lines suggests, as the increase in negations suggests. Things will not be quite the same anymore.

Let us examine one final question about the structure of this poem. All of the evidence I have mustered above was in support of the four-stanza hypothesis. Well, one might ask, if the poem "really" has four stanzas, why not indicate this typographically, with blank lines separating the stanzas?

The buzz-saw snarled and rattled in the yard
And made dust and dropped stove-length sticks of wood,
Sweet-scented stuff when the breeze drew across it.
And from there those that lifted eyes could count
Five mountain ranges one behind the other
Under the sunset far into Vermont.
And the saw snarled and rattled, snarled and rattled,
And it ran light, or had to bear a load.
And nothing happened: day was all but done.

Call it a day, I wish they might have said
To please the boy by giving him the half hour
That a boy counts so much when saved from work.
His sister stood beside them in her apron
To tell them "Supper." At the word, the saw,
As if to prove saws knew what supper meant,
Leaped out at the boy's hand, or seemed to leap –
He must have given the hand. However it was,
Neither refused the meeting. But the hand!

The boy's first outcry was a rueful laugh,
As he swung toward them holding up the hand
Half in appeal, but half as if to keep

The life from spilling. Then the boy saw all –
Since he was old enough to know, big boy
Doing a man's work, though a child at heart –
He saw all spoiled. "Don't let him cut my hand off –
The doctor, when he comes. Don't let him, sister!"

So. But the hand was gone already.
The doctor put him in the dark of ether.
He lay and puffed his lips out with his breath.
And then – the watcher at his pulse took fright.
No one believed. They listened at his heart.
Little – less – nothing! – and that ended it.
No more to build on there. And they, since they
Were not the one dead, turned to their affairs.

I think it is a subtly, or maybe not so subtly, different poem. The visual presentation plays a great role in our understanding of a poem.

If we call the spaces between stanzas "seams," what is the difference between this version of the poem, with seams, and Frost's seamless one? That is, what is the meaning of seamlessness?

I am not sure whether this answer is true in general, but we might suggest that Frost closes up the seams for this poem in service of its continuity, its humdrum, business as usual (almost), nature, which is, as we have seen, reinforced by other elements of the poem's structure.

Possibly one way to explain the poem's structure is to give a graphic representation of it, as I have done below.

This graph begins and ends with horizontal portions: this flatness in the graph indicates business as usual, the coordinate, unremarkable, humdrum sequence of everyday life. Then the graph climbs to a cusp in the middle which represents the events surrounding the boy's death. But just as quickly as this singularity begins, it fades out again, and life goes back to normal.

At this point, I would like to bring up a question that occurs to almost everyone who follows an exposition like the one I have just given. Indeed, when I was shown a similar wealth of "sinews" in a short Blake poem by my teacher, Roman Jakobson, I had to object. I don't remember my exact words, or his, but we may imagine the dialogue in roughly these terms:

"I grant you that one can find many patterns in a poem, but how can we be sure that the poet put them there? How could he be conscious of the number of periods, and present tenses, and negations, and on and on? Why aren't we just reading these into the poem?"

"Poets need not be conscious of the pattern with which poems are structured. But they know, either by a great inborn talent, or by a period of apprenticeship, *what sounds good*. They may start out with a structure of some kind, and listen to it, play with it, improving it bit by bit, in ways they might not be able to describe. And at some point, they lay down their pen, satisfied with the sound of the poem, or with the *feel* of the way its form and meaning reflect off of each other.

In a way, this unconscious ability, though mysterious and poorly understood at present, is quite parallel to our unconscious ability to use more prosaic language. We may have some desire to communicate something, and we produce sentences and paragraphs, which intensive study reveals to be of staggering complexity. And yet we are able to do this without any conscious knowledge of the laws which govern these linguistic structures."

I do not know to what extent Frost was conscious of the structures I have pointed out above. Possibly he was aware of some of them, but I do not think that we should limit the scope of our vision by refusing to notice regularities that we know from what the poet said that he did not intend. I think that poetry is a mysterious gift – recall how the ancient Greeks attributed their creativity to being visited by god-like beings called the Muses. And I think we should allow for the possibility that a poet can structure a poem far beyond conscious intent or knowledge. What guides the poet is a possibly unverbalizable feeling for what sounds right.

I believe, however, that it may be possible for others, who might never be able to create a poem as the poet has, to help us come to a better understanding of this mysterious gift of the Muses. And that studying a poem in depth to try to see its sinews can enrich our appreciation of the wonder that this poem is.

I am only at the beginning of my apprenticeship as an anatomist of poems, and I must therefore try to stay cognizant of the possibility that the above remarks are completely off the mark. However, I will keep working on more poems, trying to remain as open to them as I can. And if I am extremely lucky, the poems that choose me to work on them will move through this openness to show me the secrets of their life.

I will close with a quote from Frost himself. In an article on poetry called 'The Figure a Poem Makes,' he says the following, which feels to me not far from my own present understanding of the relationship between creation and intention:

Just as the first mystery was how a poem could have a tune in such a straightness as metre, so the second mystery is how a poem can have wildness and at the same time a subject that shall be fulfilled.

It should be of the pleasure of a poem itself to tell how it can. The figure a poem makes. It begins in delight and ends in wisdom. The figure is the same as for love. No one can really hold that the ecstasy should be static and stand still in one place. It begins in delight, it inclines to the impulse, it assumes direction with the first line laid down, it runs a course of lucky events, and ends in a clarification of life – not necessarily a great clarification, such as sects and cults are founded on, but in a momentary stay against confusion. It has denouement. It has an outcome that though unforeseen was predestined from the first image of the original mood – and indeed from the very mood. It is but a trick poem and no poem at all if the best of it was thought of first and saved for the last. It finds its own name as it goes and discovers the best waiting for it in some final phrase at once wise and sad – the happy-sad blend of the drinking song.

MIT

ACKNOWLEDGEMENTS

The poem 'Out, Out –' is from *The Poetry of Robert Frost* edited by Edward Connery Lathem. Copyright 1916, ©1969 by Holt, Rinehart, and Winston. Copyright 1944 by Robert Frost. Reprinted by permission of Holt, Rinehart and Winston, Publishers and Jonathan Cape Ltd. The quotation on this page from 'The Figure a Poem Makes' is from the Preface to Robert Frost's *Collected Poems* (1949). Acknowledgements are made to the Estate of Robert Frost, Holt, Rinehart, and Winston, New York, Publishers and Jonathan Cape Ltd., London.

BIBLIOGRAPHY OF MANFRED BIERWISCH'S PUBLICATIONS

1. ARTICLES AND MONOGRAPHS

1960 Zur Morphologie des deutschen Verbalsystems. Diss. Leipzig.

1961 Ein Modell für die syntaktische Struktur deutscher Nominalgruppen. In: *Zeitschrift für Phonetik, Sprachwissenschaft und Kommunikationsforschung* **14**, 244–278.

1962 Über den theoretischen Status des Morphems. In: *Studia grammatica* **1**, 51–89. Berlin/DDR: Akademie-Verl.

1963 Grammatik des deutschen Verbs = *Studia grammatica* **2**. Berlin/DDR: Akademie-Verl.

1965 Über die Rolle der Semantik in grammatischen Beschreibungen. In: A. V. Isacenko, ed., *Beiträge zur Sprachwissenschaft, Volkskunde und Literaturforschung*, Wolfgang Steinitz zum 60. Geburtstag, 44–60. Berlin/DDR: Akademie-Verl.

1965 Eine Hierarchie syntaktisch-semantischer Merkmale. In: *Syntaktische Studien* = *Studia grammatica* 5, 29–86. Berlin/DDR: Akademie-Verl.

1965 Poetik und Linguistik. In: Kreuzer, H., & R. Gunzenhäuser, eds., *Mathematik und Dichtung*, 49–66. München: Nymphenburger Verl.-Hdlg.

1966 Aufgaben und Form der Grammatik. In: 2. Internationales Symposium *'Zeichen und System der Sprache'*, 28–69. Berlin/DDR: Akademie-Verl. Repr. in: Steger, H., ed., *Vorschläge für eine strukturale Grammatik des Deutschen*, 1–51. Darmstadt: Wiss. Buchges.

1966 Regeln für die Intonation deutscher Sätze. In: *Studia grammatica* 7, 99–201. Berlin/DDR: Akademie-Verl.
Repr. in: Kiefer, F., ed., *Phonologie und generative Grammatik* **1**, 53–95. Frankfurt/M.: Athenäum.

1966 Strukturalismus. Geschichte, Methoden, Probleme. In: *Kursbuch* **5**, 77–152. Frankfurt/M.: Suhrkamp.
(In Spanish: El Estructuralismo. Historia, problemas, métodos, transl. by Gabriel Ferrater, Barcelona: Tusquets 1971;
In English: Modern Linguistics. The Hague: Mouton 1971, and New York: Humanities 1971.)

1966 On the Relation between Natural and Artificial Languages, Preprints for the Second International Conference on Semiotics, Warszawa.

1967 Some Semantic Universals in German Adjectivals. In: *Foundations of Language* **3**, 1–36.
(German ed. in: Steger, H., ed., *Vorschläge für eine strukturale Grammatik des Deutschen*, 269–318. Darmstadt: Wiss. Buchges.)

1967 Syntactic Features in Morphology. General Problems of So-called Pronominal Inflection in German. In: *To Honor Roman Jakobson*, 239–270. The Hague: Mouton.

W. Klein and W. Levelt (eds.), Crossing the Boundaries in Linguistics, 283–286.

(In German: Syntaktische Merkmale in der Morphologie. In: Kiefer, F., ed., *Morphologie und generative Grammatik*, 1–55. Frankfurt/M.: Athenäum 1975.)

1967 Skizze der generativen Phonologie. In: *Studia grammatica* **6**, 7–33. Berlin/DDR: Akademie-Verl.

1968 Two Critical Problems in Accent Rules. In: *Journal of Linguistics* **4**, 173–178. (In German: Zwei kritische Probleme der Akzentregeln. In: Kiefer, F., ed., *Phonologie und generative Grammatik* **1**, 1–10. Frankfurt/M.: Athenäum 1975.)

1969 Strukturelle Semantik. In: *Deutsch als Fremdsprache* **2**, 66–74.

1969 On Certain Problems of Semantic Representations. In: *Foundations of Language* **5**, 153–184.
(In German: Über einige Probleme semantischer Darstellungen. In: Kiefer, F., ed., *Semantik und generative Grammatik* **1**, 33–67. Frankfurt/M.: Athenäum 1972.)

1969 Stand und Probleme der Generativen Grammatik. In: *Wissenschaftliche Zeitschrift der Humboldt-Universität zu Berlin*, Ges.–sprachwiss. Reihe **18**, 255–261.

1970 On Classifying Semantic Features. In: Bierwisch, M. & K. E. Heidolph, eds., *Progress in Linguistics*, 27–50. The Hague: Mouton.
(Augm. in: Steinberg, D. A., & L. A. Jakobovits, eds., *Semantics, an Interdisciplinary Reader*, 410–435. London: Cambridge Univ. Pr. 1971.
In German: Zur Klassifikation semantischer Merkmale. In: Kiefer, F., ed., *Semantik und Generative Grammatik*, 69–99. Frankfurt/M.: Athenäum 1972.
In Spanish: Sobre la clasificación de los rasgos semanticos. In: *Semántica y sintaxis* **2**, 105–39. Madrid: Alianza 1976. Transl. also into Czech and Portuguese.)

1970 Semantics. In: Lyons, J., ed., *New Horizons in Linguistics*, 166–184. Harmondsworth: Penguin.
(German transl. in: Lyons, J., ed., *Neue Perspektiven der Linguistik.* Reinbek: Rowohlt 1975.)

1970 Selektionsbeschränkungen und Voraussetzungen. In: *Linguistische Arbeitsberichte* **3**, 8–22. Leipzig,

1970 Fehler-Linguistik. In: *Linguistic Inquiry* **1**, 397–414.

1970 with Egon Weigl: Neuropsychology and Linguistics. Topics of Common Research. In: *Foundations of Language* **6**, 1–21.
(In German: Neuropsychologie und Linguistik. In: *Probleme und Ergebnisse der Psychologie* **43**, 1972, 5.
In French: Neuropsychologie et Neurolinguistique. In: *Languages* **44**, 1976, 4–19.)

1970 with Ferenc Kiefer: Remarks on Definitions in Natural Language. In: Kiefer, F., ed., *Studies in Syntax and Semantics*, 55–79. Dordrecht: D. Reidel.

1971 Generative Grammar and European Linguistics. In: Sebeok, T. A., ed., *Current Trends in Linguistics* **9**, 313-342. The Hague: Mouton. (Augm. in: Kiefer, F. & N. Ruwet, eds., *Generative Grammar in Europe.* Dordrecht: D. Reidel 1973.)

1972 Schriftstruktur und Phonologie. In: *Probleme und Ergebnisse der Psychologie* **43**, 21–44.
Repr. in: Kiefer, F., ed., *Phonologie und Generative Grammatik* **1**, 11–51. Frankfurt/M.: Athenäum 1975.

1974 Strukturelle Aspekte der Bildung natürlicher Begriffe. In: Klix, F., ed., *Organismische Informationsverarbeitung*, 297–312. Berlin/DDR: Akademie-Verl.

1975 Psycholinguistik. Interdependenz kognitiver Prozesse und linguistischer Strukturen. In: *Zeitschrift für Psychologie* **183**, 1–52.

1975 Sprache und Gedächtnis. Ergebnisse und Probleme. In: *Linguistische Studien*, A. Berlin/DDR; ZISW.
Repr. in: Klix, F., & H. Sydow, eds., *Zur Psychologie des Gedächtnisses*, 117–149. Bern: Huber 1977.
Augm. in: Bierwisch, M., ed., *Psychologische Effekte sprachlicher Strukturkomponenten*, 29–130. Berlin/DDR: Akademie-Verl. 1979.

1976 Social Differentiation of Language Structure. In: Kasher, A., ed., *Language in Focus*, 407–456. Dordrecht: D. Reidel.
Also in: Bever, Katz, Langendorn, eds., *An Integrated Theory of Linguistic Ability*, 271–312. New York: Cromwell 1976.

1978 Struktur und Funktion von Varianten im Sprachsystem. In: Motsch, W., ed., *Kontexte der Grammatiktheorie = Studia Grammatica* 17, 81–130. Berlin/DDR: Akademie-Verl.

1979 Eine tote Sprache und lebendige Linguisten. In: *Meroitica* **3**, 95–112.

1979 Strukturen und Prozesse im Sprachverhalten. In: Bierwisch, M., ed., *Psychologische Effekte sprachlicher Strukturkomponenten*, 1–28. Berlin/DDR: Akademie-Verl.

1979 Three Psychological Aspects of Meaning. In: *Zeitschrift für Psychologie* **187**, 295–309.

1979 Musik und Sprache. Überlegungen zu ihrer Struktur und Funktionsweise. In: *Jahrbuch der Musikbibliothek Peters*, 9–102. Leipzig.

1979 Wörtliche Bedeutung - eine pragmatische Gretchenfrage. In: *Linguistische Studien des ZISW*
also in: Rosengren, ed., *Sprache und Pragmatik*, 63–85. Lund: Läromedel.
also in: Grewendorf, G., ed., *Sprechakttheorie und Semantik*, 119–148. Frankfurt/M.: Suhrkamp.

1980 Utterance Meaning and Mental States. In: Klix, F., & J. Hoffmann, eds., *Cognition and Memory*. Berlin: Akademie-Verl.

1980 Semantic Structure and Illocutionary Force. In: Kiefer, F., J. Searle and M. Bierwisch, eds., *Speech Act Theory and Pragmatics*, 1–35. Dordrecht: D. Reidel.

Article about Sprache, Psycholinguistik etc in *Wörterbuch der Psychologie*. Leipzig: Bibliographisches Inst. 1976.

Article Grammatik, Sprache etc. in: *Wörterbuch der Kybernetik*. Berlin/DDR: Dietz 1976.

Articles in: Kleine Enzyklopädie: *Die deutsche Sprache*. Leipzig: Bibliographisches Institut 1970.

2. REVIEWS

1965 Harris, Zellig S., Discourse Analysis Reprints, in: *Linguistics* **13**, 61–73.

1968 Greenberg, Joseph H., Language Universals, in: *Current Anthropology* **9**, 134–136.

1968 Weinreich, Uriel, Explorations in Semantic Theory, in: *Current Anthropology* **9**, 160–161.

1970 Glinz, H., Grundbegriffe und Methoden inhaltsbezogener Text- und Sprachanalyse, in: *Foundations of Language* **6**, 284–296.

1973 Hörmann, H., Psycholinguistics, in: *Zeitschrift für Psychologie* **181**, 92–96.
1973 Smaby, R. M., Paraphrase Grammars, in: *Zeitschrift für Angewandte Mathematik und Mechanik* **53**.
1974 Veith, W. H.: Intersystemare Phonologie, in: *Deutsche Literaturzeitung* **94**.
Short reviews in: Sprachwissenschaftliche Informationen, Referatedienst des ZISW und Germanistik.

3. EDITORSHIP

1962 *Studia grammatica*, **1–10**. Berlin/DDR: Akademie-Verl. 1962–1969.
1970 with Karl-Erich Heidolph: *Progress in Linguistics*. The Hague: Mouton 1970.
1979 *Psychologische Effekte sprachlicher Strukturkomponenten*. Berlin/DDR: Akademie-Verl. 1979 and München: Fink 1980.
English edition Dordrecht: D. Reidel forthcoming.
1980 with Ferenc Kiefer and John R. Searle: *Speech Act Theory and Pragmatics*. Dordrecht: D. Reidel 1980.

INDEX OF NAMES

INDEX OF SUBJECTS

SYNTHESE LANGUAGE LIBRARY

Texts and Studies in Linguistics and Philosophy

1. Henry Hiż (ed.), *Questions*. 1978.
2. William S. Cooper, *Foundations of Logico-Linguistics. A Unified Theory of Information, Language, and Logic*. 1978.
3. Avishai Margalit (ed.), *Meaning and Use*. 1979.
4. F. Guenthner and S. J. Schmidt (eds.), *Formal Semantics and Pragmatics for Natural Languages*. 1978.
5. Esa Saarinen (ed.), *Game-Theoretical Semantics*. 1978.
6. F. J. Pelletier (ed.), *Mass Terms: Some Philosophical Problems*. 1979.
7. David R. Dowty, *Word Meaning and Montague Grammar. The Semantics of Verbs and Times in Generative Semantics and in Montague's PTQ*. 1979.
8. Alice F. Freed, *The Semantics of English Aspectual Complementation*. 1979.
9. James McCloskey, *Transformational Syntax and Model Theoretic Semantics: A Case Study in Modern Irish*. 1979.
10. John R. Searle, Ferenc Kiefer, and Manfred Bierwisch (eds.), *Speech Act Theory and Pragmatics*. 1980.
11. David R. Dowty, Robert E. Wall, and Stanley Peters, *Introduction to Montague Semantics*. 1981.
12. Frank Heny (ed.), *Ambiguities in Intensional Contexts*. 1981.
13. Wolfgang Klein and Willem Levelt (eds.), *Crossing the Boundaries in Linguistics: Studies Presented to Manfred Bierwisch*. 1981.
14. Zellig S. Harris, *Papers on Syntax*, edited by Henry Hiż. 1981. (Forthcoming).
15. Pauline Jacobson and Geoffrey K. Pullum (eds.), *The Nature of Syntactic Representation*. 1981. (Forthcoming).